AN IMPLEMENTATION GUIDE TO COMPILER WRITING

AN IMPLEMENTATION GUIDE TO COMPILER WRITING

Jean-Paul Tremblay
Paul G. Sorenson

Department of Computational Science
University of Saskatchewan, Saskatoon
Canada

McGRAW-HILL BOOK COMPANY

New York St. Louis San Francisco Auckland Bogotá
Hamburg Johannesburg London Madrid Mexico Montreal New Delhi
Panama Paris São Paulo Singapore Sydney Tokyo Toronto

The editor was James E. Vastyan;
the production supervisor was Dennis J. Conroy.
The cover was designed by Anne Canevari Green.
The Whitlock Press, Inc., was printer and binder.

An Implementation Guide to Compiler Writing

2 3 4 5 6 7 8 9 0 W H W H 8 9 8 7 6 5 4

ISBN 0-07-065166-3

Library of Congress Cataloging in Publication Data

Tremblay, Jean-Paul, date
   An implementation guide to compiler writing.

   Bibliography: p.
   Includes index.
   1. Compiling (Electronic computers) I. Sorenson,
P. G. II. Title.
QA76.6.T728   001.64'25   82-7119
ISBN 0-07-065166-3   AACR2

CONTENTS

CHAPTER 3 THE RUN-TIME ENVIRONMENT

APPENDIX DESCRIPTION OF THE OBJECT-MACHINE LANGUAGE

INDEX

PREFACE

An important aspect of teaching a course in compiler writing is to illustrate the key theoretical concepts normally taught in such a course. A frequently used strategy for achieving this goal is to have a student design a simple programming language and implement a compiler for this language. Many texts in compiler writing do not, because of size considerations and level of presentation, adequately present details that illustrate the implementation of a compiler. This book presents, in a case study manner, the development of a small compiler typical of those developed in a first compiler course. Instructors can use this book as a guide to illustrate difficulties that commonly arise when implementing a compiler. They can also use the guide as an example document that is similar to what students should produce for their own compilers. It is necessary for instructors that teach a course in compiler writing to set up their own "toy" compiler as a vehicle for illustrating techniques for implementing a compiler. Also, many of the problems that are encountered in writing a compiler for a newly designed language must be illustrated. This guide is an attempt to fulfill this role.

Although this book has been written to accompany our main text entitled "The Theory and Practice of Compiler Writing", it can also be used with any other book that contains the key theoretical concepts of compiler writing. In particular, this guide requires a basic knowledge of scanners, LL(1) parsing, attributed grammar translation, error detection and repair, symbol-table methods, run-time storage management, code generation and interpreters.

This book begins with a documented description of a simple programming language, GAUSS, which serves as an example for the student. GAUSS is a block-structured language whose design was influenced by ALGOL, PASCAL, PL/I and FORTRAN. It also contains string-manipulation facilities capable of manipulating variable-length strings.

Chapter 2 illustrates the topics of scanner generation, LL(1) parsing, symbol table construction, code generation, semantic analysis, error detection and repair for the GAUSS language.

Chapter 3 describes an interpreter for the code generated by the GAUSS compiler and discusses the run-time environment in which the machine code is executed. The code generated by the compiler executes on a hypothetical machine which is stack-oriented. The compiler and interpreter are programmed in PL/I.

We owe a debt of thanks to the many people who assisted in the preparation of this manuscript and the implementation of the GAUSS compiler and hypothetical-machine interpreter. Doug Bulbeck and Darwin Peachey assisted in the design of GAUSS and the implementation of the scanner, parser and the error handler. Joe Wald contributed to the code generation phase, attribute translation and the design of the hypothetical machine. Lyle Opseth assisted throughout the preparation of the manuscript and, in particular, wrote the interpreter for the hypothetical machine. Beth Protsko assisted in the preparation of the index. We are also grateful for the comments of our students in the Department of Computational Science at the University of Saskatchewan, who have class-tested preliminary versions of the book over the last five years.

Jean-Paul Tremblay

Paul G. Sorenson

Chapter 1

The Design and Description of the Programming Language GAUSS

1-1 INTRODUCTION

This chapter describes a small, reasonably well-structured programming language named GAUSS. GAUSS incorporates many of the features one would hope to find in a small programming language whose data types are integers, strings, and logical values, and arrays of these types. Programming languages in the family of ALGOL-derived languages require integers for counting and indexing arrays and strings, and require logical values to facilitate their flow of control, so GAUSS without its string data type could be looked upon as a sort of minimum ALGOL-like language. Thus, if we look for the area of application to which GAUSS is tailored, string manipulation is our only candidate.

GAUSS is advanced beyond PL/I in string manipulation because GAUSS contains strings which may vary freely in length from zero to some implementation-defined upper bound. GAUSS also contains a few operators which exist in PL/I only as built-in functions; this tends to make the GAUSS formulation of string-manipulation tasks easier and more readable than the PL/I formulation. It cannot be said, however, that GAUSS is oriented toward string manipulation to the extent that SNOBOL4 is. In fact, the present form of GAUSS is primarily due to the desire to design a programming language whose overall shape is similar to the typical ALGOL-like language. Thus the problems posed in the task of constructing a compiler for GAUSS are a reasonable subset of those encountered in constructing a compiler for the most commonly implemented programming languages.

As one might expect from the preceding discussion, specific features found in GAUSS are derived from several of the more common programming languages. The overall format of the language is influenced by ALGOL-W (Sites [1972]) and C (Ritchie [1974]). Some details of the operators, expressions, and syntax are derived from PL/I (IBM), PASCAL (Jensen and Wirth [1975]), EULER (Wirth and Weber [1966]), and others.

The design of a programming language is usually motivated by an intended area of application. The only application area intended for GAUSS is its implementation by computer science students. The choice of language constructs was made primarily on the basis of their implementation difficulty. The syntax of some constructs was modified so that it would be consistent throughout the language. Some constructs were omitted because they were considered detrimental to structured programming techniques (e.g., the GOTO construct).

The metalanguage used to describe the syntax of the GAUSS language is an extended BNF form. For a complete description of this metalanguage, see Sec. 2-4.4 of the text "The Theory and Practice of Compiler Writing." (Tremblay and Sorenson [1982]).

1-2 PROGRAM

Programs in GAUSS have the following form:

<program> ::= {<declaration>;} <procedure>; {<procedure>;}

A program is defined as any number of declarations followed by one or more procedures. The global declarations are discussed in Sec. 1-3 and the procedures are described in Sec. 1-4. The program is initiated by a call to the procedure called MAIN. This procedure must occur in the source text, and it must be parameterless.

Note that separate compilation is not available in GAUSS. This means that all procedures of a program must be present in the source file.

The following is an example of a GAUSS program:

```
$$ THIS PROGRAM READS INTEGERS AND
$$ PRINTS THEIR FACTORIAL VALUE

INTEGER PROC FACTORIAL (INTEGER PARM) FORWARD;
PROC MAIN
     INTEGER I;

     LOOP
     WHILE NOT END_OF_FILE;

        READ I;

        IF I < 0
```

```
        THEN
                WRITE "ILLEGAL VALUE READ IN:", I
                    USING "S, X2, I, N";
            ELSE
                WRITE FACTORIAL (I) USING "I10, N";
            ENDIF;
        ENDLOOP;
ENDPROC;


$$ 'FACTORIAL' RETURNS THE FACTORIAL VALUE OF ITS ARGUMENT.

INTEGER PROC FACTORIAL (INTEGER I)
        INTEGER I_MINUS_ONE;

        IF I > 1
        THEN
                I_MINUS_ONE := I - 1;
                RETURN I * FACTORIAL (I_MINUS_ONE);
        ELSE
                RETURN 1;
        ENDIF;
ENDPROC;
```

This program computes the factorial of the given integers. The MAIN procedure of the program begins by reading in an integer. If the integer read in is greater than or equal to zero, the factorial value is computed by calling the FACTORIAL procedure. This value is then printed. If the integer read in is less than zero, the program prints an error message. This process is then repeated. When the input stream is exhausted (when END_OF_FILE becomes TRUE), the program stops. The factorial of the integer read in is computed by the recursive FACTORIAL procedure.

1-3 DECLARATIONS

This section describes the syntax for declaring variable identifiers and constant identifiers in GAUSS. These declarations are used to associate a specific type with an identifier. The three basic types are INTEGER, LOGICAL and STRING. Values of integer type have the precision allowed by the machine on which the compiler runs (e.g., -32768 to 32767 on a PDP11/40). The logical type has either TRUE or FALSE as a value. String-type values are character strings of arbitrary dynamically varying length. The only aggregate data type is the ARRAY type. Arrays are multi-dimensional and consist of simple elements.

In order to discuss the scope of identifiers, it is necessary to define "global" and "local" identifiers. Global identifiers are those that are declared at the beginning of the program, before any procedures are defined. These identifiers are available to every procedure in the program. The local identifiers are those declared at the beginning of a procedure, and they are known only within the procedure (see Sec. 1-4.1 on procedure definitions).

To define the scope of identifiers in GAUSS we introduce the notion of an entity. An entity is a procedure name, a global identifier, a local identifier, or a parameter. The scope of a global identifier or a procedure name extends from the point at which it is declared to the end of the program. The scope of a local identifier or a parameter extends from the point at which it is declared to the end of the procedure in which it is declared. At any point in the program no two entities may be named by the same identifier.

Consider the following program example:

```
INTEGER COUNT;

PROC MAIN
      INTEGER I;
      ...

ENDPROC;

PROC ALPHA (LOGICAL PARM)
      STRING I;
      ...

ENDPROC;
```

The scope of the global variable COUNT declared in the first line of the program extends from the point where it is declared to the end of the program. Thus it would be illegal to have an identifier COUNT within either of the two procedures, or to have a procedure called COUNT. The scope of the identifier I declared in the MAIN procedure extends only to the end of that procedure. Therefore, the second declaration of the identifier I in the ALPHA procedure is perfectly valid. The parameter PARM extends from its declaration in the parameter list of the ALPHA procedure to the end of that procedure. Note that the ALPHA procedure is not declared until after the MAIN procedure. Therefore, the scope of the ALPHA procedure does not include the MAIN procedure. It follows that MAIN cannot have a call to ALPHA.

All identifiers which are used must be previously declared. There are no default declarations.

Declarations in GAUSS are defined as follows:

<declaration> ::= <type specifier> <identifier list>
                | <type specifier> CONST <const list>
    <const list> ::= <identifier> = <constant>
                {, <identifier> = <constant>}
<type specifier> ::= <simple type> | <array>
    <simple type> ::= INTEGER | STRING | LOGICAL
        <array> ::= ARRAY (<bound pair> {,<bound pair>})
                OF <simple type>
    <bound pair> ::= [<integer expression> :] <integer expression>
    <constant> ::= <simple constant> | <array constant>
<simple constant> ::= [–]<number> | <literal> | TRUE | FALSE
<array constant>::= (<simple constant> {, simple constant>})
<identifier list> ::= <identifier> {, <identifier>}

Some examples of declarations as they might appear in a program follow. They are discussed in the subsequent paragraphs.

```
INTEGER I;
STRING ALPHA, BETA, GAMMA;
LOGICAL CONST TEST = TRUE, FAIL = FALSE;
ARRAY (5, 10, –12 : 33) OF LOGICAL HOSPITAL_DRUG_RECORD;
ARRAY (2, 3) OF INTEGER CONST CARDS = (1, 3, 6, 9, 12, 15);
```

The first example declares the identifier I to be an integer type variable. The next example declares ALPHA, BETA, and GAMMA to be string variables. The third example declares TEST and FAIL to be logical constant identifiers, with the values of TRUE and FALSE respectively. The next line gives a declaration of a three-dimensional array whose name is HOSPITAL_DRUG_RECORD. Each of the 2,300 elements can contain one logical value. The next array declaration declares a constant array CARDS with the given integer values.

As can be seen, a list of identifiers can be associated with one type specification. This eliminates the need to repeat the specifications for every identifier when several identifiers are of the same type.

There are two basic kinds of declarations in GAUSS. The first kind, the variable declaration, is used to associate an identifier with a storage location whose contents may vary over its lifetime. The <type specifier> indicates the data type of the storage location, that is, the set of values it may contain. The possible data types are INTEGER, STRING, LOGICAL, or an ARRAY of type INTEGER, STRING, or LOGICAL.

The second kind, the constant declaration, is used to specify constant identifiers. The CONST keyword indicates that each identifier in the list is associated with the specified value and retains that association throughout its lifetime. The constants assigned to the identifiers in the list must be of the same type as the <simple type> specified at the beginning of the declaration. Constants for arrays must be all of the same type, and are listed in row-major order. These constants are enclosed in parentheses and separated by commas.

The <bound pair> for an array specifies the lower and upper bounds of one particular dimension of the array. The number of such <bound pairs> is the number of dimensions in the array. The upper bound must be greater than or equal to the lower bound. If the lower bound is missing, it is assumed to be 1.

Note that the integer expressions which specify the bounds of global arrays or constant arrays must be defined at compile time. Therefore, these expressions must be constants or constant identifiers. The bounds of local arrays can be defined at run time; specifically, at the time the procedure is called. Therefore, these expressions can be arbitrarily complex.

The referencing of array elements is done by including the subscript list. An example of declaring an array and referencing one of its elements follows:

```
ARRAY (31, 12, 1925 : 1979) OF STRING HISTORY;
HISTORY (1, 1, 1930) := "THE THIRTIES BEGIN.";
```

The declaration sets up a 31-by-12-by-55 array of strings, where the dimensions in this case are used to represent the day, month, and year, respectively, for the years from 1925 to 1979 inclusive. The second statement then assigns a string to one of these positions, which corresponds to 1 January 1930.

1-4 PROCEDURES

The main vehicle which permits the writing of modular programs in GAUSS is the procedure. Descriptions of how procedures are defined and subsequently invoked are given in this section. The specification of return of control from a procedure is also presented.

1-4.1 Procedure Definition

This section defines a procedure, which is the basic unit of a GAUSS program. GAUSS supports nonrecursive and recursive procedures, both of which are defined in the same way. The procedure definition is:

<procedure> ::= [<simple type>] PROC <identifier>
                        <procedure tail>
<procedure tail> ::= FORWARD | <procedure body>
<procedure body> ::= { <declaration> ; } <statement>;
                        {<statement>;} ENDPROC
::= [(<parameter>, {<parameter>})]
::= <parameter type> <identifier>
::= <simple type>
            | ARRAY ({,}) OF <simple type>

In the following discussion some examples of procedure declarations are presented.

INTEGER PROC ALPHA (ARRAY (,,) OF STRING CHARS, LOGICAL TEST)
...

ENDPROC;

This first example defines a procedure called ALPHA which returns an integer value to the calling routine. It has two parameters, the first of which is a three-dimensional array of strings called CHARS. Note that the bounds on the dimensions of the array are obtained from the calling procedure. The second parameter is a logical variable called TEST.

The next example shows the declaration of a procedure that does not return a value to the calling procedure, and has no parameters.

PROC CHECK FORWARD;

The following discussion examines the procedure declaration in a more detailed manner.

A <procedure> consists of a "procedure head" followed by a <procedure tail>. The <procedure tail> can be the keyword FORWARD, indicating that the procedure is defined later. A FORWARD declaration is required only when a procedure call is encountered before its definition appears during compilation. This is necessary to allow one-pass compilation of the GAUSS programs.

A <procedure tail> can also be a <procedure body>, that is, a group of declarations and statements defining a unit of execution to be performed when the procedure is called at run time. The <procedure body> consists of any number of <declaration>s, followed by at least one <statement>. The <procedure body> must be ended with the ENDPROC keyword.

The <simple type> specification in the procedure head refers to the type of the value to be returned by the procedure. This must be present for a procedure that acts as a function, where a returned value is needed. For a procedure which does not return a value, the <simple type> must be omitted. Note that procedures with a <simple type> specifier must always return a value.

After the optional <simple type> comes the keyword PROC which specifies the beginning of the procedure. The identifier following the keyword PROC is the name of the procedure, which must not be defined previous to this point in the program, except if a FORWARD declaration has been used.

The <parameter list>, if present, is a list of <parameter>s enclosed in parentheses. If there are no <parameter>s, then there is no <parameter list> in the procedure definition. Argument-parameter correspondence between the procedure call and the parameter list of the procedure is determined by relative order (i.e., the ith argument is associated with the ith parameter).

Parameters consist of a <parameter type> followed by an identifier. The appearance of the identifier in the parameter list constitutes its declaration. Corresponding parameters and arguments must, of course, have the same type and dimension. Parameters of type ARRAY are specified without explicit bounds. The number of commas between the parentheses indicates the number of dimensions of the array parameter (i.e., the number of commas plus one). The bounds for each dimension of the parameter are copied from the bounds of the argument at run time.

1-4.2 Procedure Calls

A procedure call can be used like a statement, or like an expression. The difference depends on whether or not the optional <simple type> specification is present before the PROC keyword in the procedure declaration. The procedure call is a statement when the <simple type> specifier has been omitted. The procedure call can be used as an expression if and only if the <simple type> specifier is present. The procedure call is defined as:

```
<procedure call> ::= <identifier> <argument list>
<argument list> ::= [(<argument> {, <argument>})]
    <argument> ::= <identifier> [ <sublist > ]
```

Pass-by-reference is the standard parameter passing convention used by GAUSS. This means that whenever a variable has its value changed in the called procedure, it is changed in the calling procedure as well. Therefore, all arguments in the argument list must be variable identifiers (as opposed to constant identifiers or expressions). Pass-by-value can be easily simulated by a GAUSS programmer. A dummy variable in the calling procedure is assigned the desired value and then used in the procedure call.

Some examples of procedure calls are as follows:

```
MOVE (SOURCE, DESTINATION, COUNT);
X = PI;
```

The first call is to a procedure called MOVE which takes three arguments. This call is used as a statement and, therefore, the called procedure cannot return a value. The second procedure call is to a procedure called PI which does not take any arguments. This call is used as an expression, and therefore the called procedure must return a value.

The identifier in the procedure call is the name of the procedure. It is illegal to call a procedure which has not been previously declared. The <argument list> is a possibly empty list of <argument>s. An argument must be a variable identifier whose type and dimension are consistent with the corresponding parameter. Also, the number of arguments and parameters must be the same.

The optional <sublist>, which is used to select a single array element, is of the form:

$$\text{<sublist>} ::= (\text{<integer expression>} \{, \text{<integer expression>} \})$$

The number of <integer expression>s in the <sublist> must be equal to the number of <bound pair>s in the declaration for the array named by the identifier. Furthermore, the value of each expression must fall between the bounds specified by the corresponding <bound pair> in the declaration. The identifier must be associated by a prior declaration with a variable of array type. The optional <sublist> is used to pass one element of an array to a procedure. If the optional <sublist> is not used with an array identifier, the entire array is passed to the procedure. The <sublist> is valid only if it is used with an array identifier.

1-4.3   Procedure Returns

The return statement is used to stop execution of the procedure and return to the calling procedure, or to the run-time support system, in the case of a return from the MAIN procedure. The return statement can also return a value to the point of call in the calling procedure. The return statement must return a value if the procedure is declared to return a value (see Sec. 1-4.1). The value of the expression returned must be of the same <simple type> as that specified in the procedure head. If the procedure is not declared to return a value, then no value can be returned.

The return statement is specified as follows:

$$\text{<return stmt>} ::= \text{RETURN } [\text{<expression>}]$$

If a procedure executes its last statement and tries to proceed beyond the ENDPROC delimiter, an automatic return takes place. If the procedure has been declared to return a value, it must execute an explicit return statement, which contains the value of an expression of the appropriate type.

1-5   STATEMENTS

The following is a definition of the executable statements of the GAUSS language. The syntax of each statement is defined in subsequent sections, except for the <procedure call> and the <return stmt> which have already been described.

$$<statement> ::= <procedure\ call>$$
$$| <return\ stmt>$$
$$| <if\ stmt>$$
$$| <while\ stmt>$$
$$| <stop\ stmt>$$
$$| <assignment\ stmt>$$
$$| <read\ stmt>$$
$$| <write\ stmt>$$

The <procedure call> must be to a procedure which does not return a value.

1-6 CONTROL STRUCTURES

GAUSS provides three major control structures which can be used in a procedure. These structures allow choice, repetition and termination in the flow of control of a program.

1-6.1 Choice

The choice control structure is the IF-THEN-ELSE-ENDIF construct whose syntax is as follows:

$$<if\ stmt> ::= IF\ <logical\ expression>\ <then\ clause>$$
$$[<else\ clause>]\ ENDIF$$
$$<then\ clause> ::= THEN\ <statement>\ ;\ \{\ <statement>\ ;\ \}$$
$$<else\ clause> ::= ELSE\ <statement>\ ;\ \{\ <statement>\ ;\ \}$$

The <logical expression> is evaluated at execution time and, if it is true, the group of statements following the THEN is executed. If the <logical expression> evaluates to false, then the group of statements following the ELSE is executed. If the optional <else clause> is not present, and the <logical expression> evaluates to false, then no statements are executed, and execution continues with the statement following the ENDIF keyword. An example of the IF construct is as follows:

```
IF A < B
THEN
        K := A;
        A := B;
ELSE
        K := B;
        B := A;
ENDIF
```

This construct has the result of making A and B equal to the larger of the values of A and B, and setting K to the smaller of the values of A and B.

1-6.2   Repetition

The control construct for affecting repetition is the LOOP-WHILE construct whose syntax is as follows:

```
<while stmt> ::= LOOP {<statement> ;}
                 WHILE <logical expression> ;
                 {<statement> ;}
                 ENDLOOP
```

This loop construct is executed at run time in the following manner. First, the statements before the WHILE portion of the loop are executed. The logical expression is then evaluated. If it is true, then execution continues with the statements between the WHILE part of the loop and the ENDLOOP delimiter. When the ENDLOOP delimiter is encountered, execution continues from the beginning of the loop construct, and the process is repeated. If the <logical expression> evaluates to false, then the loop is terminated, and the next statement executed is the one following the ENDLOOP delimiter.

The following illustration is an example of a WHILE statement which reads in a student number and uses the student number as an array index. This is done for each iteration of the loop. When the student number is the dummy value 9999, the loop terminates.

```
LOOP
    READ STUDENT_NO;
WHILE STUDENT_NO <> 9999;
    WRITE CLASS (STUDENT_NO) USING "S, N";
ENDLOOP;
```

1-6.3   Procedure and Program Termination

The STOP control construct is provided to allow the programmer to end execution immediately. This is useful when a deeply nested procedure activation determines that the program should terminate. The only way such a construct may be avoided is by means of an elaborate use of returned flags which indicate the status of procedures upon their return. Such complexity is well worth avoiding, especially since the STOP statement provides no real challenge for the compiler. The syntax of the STOP statement is as follows:

```
<stop stmt> ::= STOP
```

As described in the previous section on procedures, GAUSS contains a RETURN statement which causes the termination of a procedure, with or without a returned value.

1-7   ASSIGNMENT STATEMENT

The GAUSS assignment statement has the form

```
<assignment stmt> ::= <target> := <expression>
```

The value of the <expression> is copied into the <target> which has the following form:

<target> ::= <identifier> [<sublist>] [<substring>]

The identifier in the <target> must be a variable identifier. The optional <sublist> is given if and only if the identifier designates an array variable. The <sublist> has been discussed previously, but note that in this case, the <sublist> must be present if the identifier is an array variable (see Sec. 1-4.2). The optional <substring> may be given only if the identifier is type string or array of string.

The optional <substring> has the form

<substring> ::= (<start> '|' [<length>])
<start> ::= <integer expression>
<length> ::= <integer expression>

The <substring> specifies the start and length of a portion of the contents of a string variable. The integer expressions given by <start> and <length> and enclosed in parentheses, denote the starting position and length of the substring. The position of the first symbol in the string is designated by the integer 1. The <length> expression is optional. If it is missing the substring extends from the <start> position to the end of the string. It is illegal to specify a substring which does not lie entirely within the current bounds of the string. A <string expression> of arbitrary length may be assigned to a <target> with the optional <substring> specification. The resulting value of the string (of which the substring is a part) is the original value with the substring replaced by the value of the right-hand side of the assignment statement. For example, the assignment, ZAP(5 | 0) := "THINGS";, will insert the string "THINGS" between the fourth and fifth characters of the string called ZAP.

Note that in all cases of assignment, the expression must be of the same type as the target.

The following illustration demonstrates some simple assignment statements. It has been assumed that X and Y have been declared INTEGER, A has been declared STRING, and FOREVER has been declared to have LOGICAL type.

    X := 37 * Y + 3;
    A := "HELLO WORLD";
    FOREVER := FALSE;

The next example shows assignments to array elements. It is assumed that the identifiers have had the proper declarations, and that the indices into an array are within the bounds for each dimension of the array.

    TABLE (3, 4) := TABLE (3, 1) / TABLE (1, 4);
    FLAGS (M – N + 1) := L AND S OR (FLAGS (M) AND FLAGS (N));

The next examples show how an assignment to a substring is made. Again, it is assumed all identifiers have been declared with the appropriate types.

    SA (4 | 2) := "THIS";
    STR_ARRAY (2, 2) (4 | 0) := "REALLY ";

If SA originally had the value

    "OF IT"

after the assignment, it would have the value

    "OF THIS"

This could also have been accomplished using the assignment

    SA (4 |) := "THIS";

If STR_ARRAY (2, 2) originally had the value

    "IT IS"

then after the assignment, this element will have the value

    "IT REALLY IS"

1-8 EXPRESSIONS

The expression is an important construct in GAUSS because it is the structural unit which may occupy the right-hand side of an assignment statement. Since an assignment is the most commonly used operation in the ALGOL family of languages (ALGOL–60, ALGOL–W, ALGOL–68, PL/I, ...) the importance of the expression is obvious.

    <expression> ::= <integer expression>
                  | <logical expression>
                  | <string expression>

1-8.1 Integer Expressions

The following description defines the syntax of the <integer expression> as well as the precedence and associativity of the allowed operators.

    <integer expression> ::= <integer expression> + <term>
                        | <integer expression> – <term>
                        | <term>
            <term> ::= <term> * <factor>
                    | <term> / <factor>
                    | <term> % <factor>
                    | <factor>

The binary operators just presented have the following meanings:

+ Signed integer addition
– Signed integer subtraction
* Signed integer multiplication
/ Signed integer division (the result is truncated)
% Mod or remainder function

The following statements demonstrate the evaluation of the mod function.

$-10 \% 3 = 2,$ $10 \% -3 = -2$
$10 \% 3 = 1,$ $-10 \% -3 = -1$
$-(a \% b) = -a \% -b$
$-a \% b = b - (a \% b)$
$a \% -b = (a \% b) - b$

The sole unary operation on integer values is the unary minus '–' which has the effect of multiplying its operand by –1. Its syntax is as follows:

<factor> ::= [–] <integer primary>
<integer primary> ::= (<integer expression>)
                    | <identifier> [<sublist>]
                    | <number>
                    | <procedure call>
                    | <string expression> @ <string expression>
                    | # <string expression>

Some of the possible <integer primary>s require further qualification. The identifier must be associated by a prior declaration with an object of integer type. The optional <sublist> is to be used if and only if the identifier is used to designate an array of integer type. Note that constant array elements are allowed as integer primaries.

The <procedure call> must be to a procedure which has been declared to have an integer value, i.e., a procedure of the form

INTEGER PROC whatever ...

The <integer primary> '<string expression> @ <string expression>' which provides some pattern matching capabilities is illustrated below.

STRING_1 @ STRING_2

This expression gives the number of the position in STRING_1 where the first occurrence of STRING_2 in STRING_1 begins. If STRING_2 does not occur in STRING_1 then the value of the expression is 0. The @ operator behaves exactly like the built-in INDEX function of PL/I.

The final possible <integer primary> is of the form

STRING

and it yields the current length of the string.

1-8.2   String Expressions

The syntax of a string expression is as follows:

<string expression> ::= <string expression> & <string primary>
       | <string primary>

The operator & specifies the concatenation of the <string primary> onto the end of the <string expression>.

<string primary> ::= (<string expression>)
       | <literal>
       | <identifier> [<sublist>] [<substring>]
       | <procedure call>

Some examples of <string expressions> and assignments are:

DATE := MONTH & DAY & YEAR;
STR_ARRAY (2, 3) (1 | 4) := "GOOD-BYE CRUEL WORLD" &
       NOTE (1 | # NOTE / 2);

The first expression concatenates the values of the three string variables, MONTH, DAY and YEAR together, and assigns the resulting string to DATE. The second example concatenates the given literal, plus the first half of the string value of NOTE, and assigns the resulting string to a substring of an array element.

The identifier must be associated by a prior declaration with an object of type string. The optional <sublist> is used if and only if the identifier is an array identifier. The optional substring selection has been described in Sec. 1-7. A <procedure call> may be a <string primary> if the procedure is defined to return a string value.

1-8.3   Logical Expressions

The syntax of the logical expression is as follows:

<logical expression> ::=
       <logical part> <relation> <logical part>
       | <integer expression> <relation> <integer expression>
       | <string expression> <relation> <string expression>
       | <logical part>
<logical part> ::= <logical part> OR <logical term>
       | <logical term>
<logical term> ::= <logical term> AND <logical factor>
       | <logical factor>
<logical factor> ::= NOT <logical primary>
       | <logical primary>

This description defines the construction of <logical expression>s from

\<logical primary\>s using the three logical operators OR, AND, and NOT. The precedences of the operators are specified by the syntax as NOT \> AND \> OR. The NOT operator inverts the truth value of its operand. The OR and AND operators differ from those of symbolic logic in the following manner. If the left operand of the OR is true, or the left operand of the AND is false, the operators yield the values TRUE and FALSE respectively, without evaluating their right operands. This means that a compiler for GAUSS must generate code for logical expressions such that the left operand of an AND or OR is always evaluated before the right operand; no optimization can be done which involves reversing the order of evaluation. (In fact, operands in all expressions are always evaluated in left-to-right order in the absence of parentheses or precedence differences.)

The \<relation\> between the expressions found in \<logical primary\> is defined as

$$\<relation\> ::= '='$$
$$| '\<'$$
$$| '\>'$$
$$| '\<='$$
$$| '\>='$$
$$| '\<\>'$$

The relations have their usual meanings, with '\<\>' indicating the test for inequality. All of the relations can be used on string operands as well as on integers. For logical operands, the only relations that can be tested are equality ('=') and inequality ('\<\>'). All other relations are invalid for logical operands.

For string operands, the "less than" and "greater than" comparisons are based on the collating sequence of the machine. A string value X is less than a string value Y if and only if one of the following conditions hold.

1. If X is a leading substring of Y, such as when
      X = "STR"
        and
      Y = "STRING"
   then X is less than Y.

2. Otherwise, if the two strings are equal up to the ith position for some i and the two strings differ in the ith position then X is less than Y if the ith character of X is less than the ith character of Y with respect to the collating sequence.
   For example, when X and Y have the values

      X = "ABCD"
      Y = "ABCR"

the two strings are equal up to, but not including, the fourth character. Assuming that D is less than R in the collating sequence, then X is less than Y.

The logical primary is defined as follows:

$$\<logical primary\> ::= TRUE$$
$$| FALSE$$
$$| (\<logical expression\>)$$

> | <identifier> [<sublist>]
> | <procedure call>

The identifier must be associated by a prior declaration with an object of type logical. The optional <sublist> is used if and only if the identifier is an array identifier. A <procedure call> can be a <logical primary> if the procedure called is defined to return a logical value.

1-9   INPUT AND OUTPUT

GAUSS input/output primitives are designed to be as simple as possible while still allowing easy performance of the usual input/output operations which occur in small programs.

The input primitive is the READ statement whose syntax is as follows:

>   <read stmt> ::= READ <input goal list>
>   <input goal list> ::= <input goal> {, <input goal> }
>   <input goal> ::= <identifier> [<sublist>]

The identifier in the <input goal> can be any variable identifier. The optional <sublist> is to be used if and only if the identifier is an array identifier. Thus only one element of an array can be read at a time; it is impossible to read an entire array with the single execution of one READ statement. The <sublist> has been defined in Sec. 1-4.2.

The READ statement examines the input stream for <simple constants> as defined in Sec. 1-3. Briefly, a <simple constant> can be one of the following.

>   [–] <number>
>   <literal>
>   TRUE
>   FALSE

All characters which are not part of the simple constants are ignored (with a warning). The ith <input goal> in the <input goal list> is assigned the value of the ith <simple constant> in the input stream. If the type of the identifier and the constant differ, an error message is printed, and the value of the <input goal> is unchanged. No constant can run over the end of a line or card in the input stream. This restriction guards against unbounded strings "gobbling up" the entire input stream, and other such holocausts. Logical values and strings which try to run over the end of an input line are not interpreted as valid <simple constant>s, and thus are ignored (with a warning).

The question of how to handle synchronous interrupts (which arise in a repeatable way from the execution of particular statements) in programming languages has not been clearly solved. PL/I has ON-units; other languages provide various flags and predicates to detect overflows, end-of-file, and so on. GAUSS provides no facilities for detecting or recovering from overflows, divisions by zero, and so on, within executing programs. However, an input end-of-file clearly cannot be handled in this lazy manner. ON-units are better avoided because they do not allow someone reading a program to understand easily the operation of the program at a particular point, since an ON-unit (which may be located in a distant piece of code) may be invoked at that point. Furthermore, ON-units have the flavor, and some of the basic problems, of the undisciplined GOTO statement. To handle the end-of-file condition, GAUSS provides a logical procedure called END_OF_FILE which, when called, returns TRUE if the input stream is exhausted, and returns FALSE otherwise. It is important to note that the input system scans ahead, enabling END_OF_FILE to return TRUE as soon as the last valid constant has been read. It is not necessary to attempt to read past the end of file before the procedure returns true. The following example would typically be placed before some READ statement in the program:

```
IF END_OF_FILE
THEN
        WRITE "NOT ENOUGH DATA CARDS" USING "S, N";
        STOP;
ENDIF;
READ whatever ...
```

The output primitive (as seen in the current example) is the WRITE statement, which has the following syntax:

$$<\text{write stmt}> ::= \text{WRITE} [<\text{expression list}>] \text{USING} <\text{format list}>$$
$$<\text{expression list}> ::= <\text{expression}> \{, <\text{expression}>\}$$

The <format list> must have a particular structure defined by the following BNF:

$$<\text{format list}> ::= \text{''} <\text{format item}> \{, <\text{format item}> \} \text{ ''}$$
$$<\text{format item}> ::= \quad S [<\text{number}>]$$
$$\qquad\qquad | \quad I [<\text{number}>]$$
$$\qquad\qquad | \quad L$$
$$\qquad\qquad | \quad X <\text{number}>$$
$$\qquad\qquad | \quad T <\text{number}>$$
$$\qquad\qquad | \quad N$$

The WRITE statement is designed to allow formatted output. If the <expression list> is empty, then the purpose of the write statement is to space, tab, or advance to the next line. For every element of the <expression list>, there must be a corresponding <format item>. The <format item> dictates the type of the variable that is being printed and the field width of the printed item.

The S format is for printing strings. If the optional field width <number> is left out, then the field width is assumed to be the length of the string. If the field width is present, the string is padded with blanks or chopped on the right, as required.

The I format is used to print out integers. Again, if the field width is omitted, then the number of digits in the integer is taken to be the field width. If the field width is included, then integers are padded on the left with blanks, as required. If the integer is longer than the given field width, the entire integer will still be printed out with an accompanying warning message. Printing the number carries more information than filling the field with question marks or some other symbol which indicates an error.

The L format is used to print out logical values. The output is either TRUE or FALSE and is printed in a field that is five characters wide.

The X format produces n spaces, where n is the number following the X.

The T format causes the next output to begin at the nth column, where n is the number that follows the T. If n is less than the current column position, a tab to the nth column of the next line occurs.

The N format item is used to advance to the next line.

Note that in all cases, the number following any of the format items must be positive. A field width of zero is considered to be a programmer error.

The following illustrations give a few examples of GAUSS input and output statements:

```
READ ALPHA, BETA, GAMMA;
READ NUMBER (I, J);
WRITE "THE VALUE OF X IS:", X USING "T 16, S, X 2, I 5, N";
WRITE 3 + FACTORIAL (I) * 27 USING "I";
```

The first READ statement reads values for the identifiers ALPHA, BETA and GAMMA. The second READ statement reads the (I, J) element for the array NUMBER. The first WRITE statement prints out the given literal followed by the value of the identifier X. The format causes the string to be printed out starting in column 16, followed by two spaces, then the value of X is printed in a field of width five, and finally, a "new line" is "printed" so that the next WRITE statement prints on the next line of output. If no N was used in the format list, the next write statement would continue on the same line. The second write statement prints out the value of the integer expression in a field of the width required to hold the value.

1-10 LEXICAL STRUCTURE

This section describes the lexical structure of GAUSS, i.e., the symbols which form the basic units of the language.

$$<\text{identifier}> ::= <\text{letter}> \{<\text{letter}> | <\text{digit}>\}$$
$$<\text{letter}> ::= A | B | ... | Y | Z | \_$$
$$<\text{number}> ::= <\text{digit}> \{<\text{digit}>\}$$
$$<\text{digit}> ::= 0 | 1 | 2 | 3 | 4 | 5 | 6 | 7 | 8 | 9$$
$$<\text{literal}> ::= "\{<\text{symbol}>\}"$$
$$<\text{symbol}> ::= <\text{character}> | ""$$
$$<\text{character}> ::= < \text{any character on the machine except } "">$$

Identifiers are of arbitrary length; however, only the first sixteen characters are significant. Keywords in GAUSS are reserved words; thus no identifier may be the same as any keyword. Identifiers, numbers, or literals cannot be split across input line boundaries. Also note that imbedded blanks are not allowed in identifiers or in numbers. An imbedded blank causes the identifier or number to be regarded as two separate identifiers or numbers.

Numbers are a series of digits interpreted in base 10 notation. The value of the number must not exceed the capacity of the machine. Real or floating point numbers are not allowed.

Literals (string constants) are enclosed in double quotes, and if it is necessary to place a double quote within the string, it is encoded as "". Thus a literal consisting of a double quote mark is encoded as """".

Comments begin with $$. They can begin anywhere in a line and extend to the end of the line.

1-11 CONTROL COMMANDS AND COMPILER AIDS

There are three control commands that can be used with the GAUSS language to allow batching of programs, and to specify options to the compiler. These are the ?PROGRAM command, the ?OPTION command, and the ?DATA command.

The ?PROGRAM command must be in the first line of any program. This is to allow batching of GAUSS programs, so that the compiler needs to be invoked only once to compile several programs. The ?PROGRAM keyword must begin in column 1 of the input line. If there is any other information on the line, it is ignored.

The ?OPTION command is used to specify which options the user would like with the compilation of the program. This command can appear anywhere within a GAUSS source program, thus allowing options to be turned on and off for certain pieces of code. The ?OPTION keyword must begin in the first column of an input line. The options to be changed are specified on the rest of the line. The options, which are listed below, may begin with either a + or a –. If the option begins with the + sign, or if neither the + or – are specified, then this option is enabled. The – indicates that the option is to be disabled. The options in each ?OPTION command must be separated by one or more blanks. The possible options are as follows:

LIST   When this option is enabled, the source listing of the GAUSS program being compiled is given. If the option is disabled, only the error messages (if any) are printed out. Initially, this option is enabled by the compiler.

XREF   When this option is enabled, a cross reference listing of the GAUSS program being compiled is given. A separate table is generated for local identifiers of each procedure and another table for global identifiers. Each table is in alphabetical order and contains the following domains about identifiers: name, type, use, dimension, and line numbers at which they were referenced. The use of an identifier is either as a simple identifier, simple constant identifier, array identifier, array constant identifier, or procedure identifier. The first line number in the reference list of an identifier specifies its first declaration. The only irregularity to this regards the names of the MAIN procedure and procedures which are not declared by the GAUSS programmer (i.e., END_OF_FILE). In such a case a dummy declaration line number of zero is used. Initially this option is disabled by the compiler.

Note that the following options are intended for the use of the systems programmer only, since they produce information that is relevant only to someone who is responsible for maintaining the GAUSS compiler.

SCANNER_DEBUG   This option is designed to help debug the scanner. Each time that the scanner is called, the value of the token, and the type of token that is found are printed out.

LL1_DEBUG   This option is used for debugging the LL(1) parser. When enabled, it causes the stack contents, the input token, and the parse action for every parse operation (i.e., a grammar expansion, a pop, an error, accept or call OP) to be printed out.

REPAIR_DEBUG   This option is used to debug the error recovery portion of the compiler. Each time an error recovery is required, the current stack contents, the input symbol, stack insertions and deletions, and the final stack contents and input symbol are printed out.

CODE_DEBUG   This option can be used to help debug the code generator of the compiler. When it is enabled, the generated code is printed out. As an aid to understanding the code, the GLOBAL area and PROCINFO area are also output. For truly effective debugging of the code the SYM_DEBUG flag should be enabled also.

SYM_DEBUG   This option is used to obtain a listing of the symbol table entries generated by the compiler. A separate table is generated for local identifiers of each procedure and another table for global identifiers. The tables are ordered by hash location and contain the following domains about identifiers: name, hash location, link, and address. The hash location and link field illustrate the structure of the symbol table. They are useful for debugging the symbol table routines or fine-tuning the hashing function. The address field requires further qualification because of its many purposes. If the identifier is a procedure, the address field contains an index into the PROCINFO area (discussed in Sec. 2-5.3). If the identifier is a simple constant identifier, the address field contains the value of the constant. All other information about the identifier can be displayed with the XREF option.

```
$$ THIS PROGRAM READS IN A SERIES OF WORDS, EACH OF WHICH
$$ HAS AN ASSOCIATED PAGE NUMBER. THE WORDS ARE THEN
$$ SORTED SO THAT THEY CAN BE PRINTED IN ALPHABETICAL
$$ ORDER, EACH WITH A LIST OF PAGE NUMBERS ASSOCIATED WITH IT.
$$ EACH WORD IS PRINTED ONLY ONCE, BUT ALL PAGE NUMBERS
$$ ASSOCIATED WITH EACH OCCURRENCE OF THE WORD WILL BE
$$ PRINTED DUPLICATE PAGE NUMBERS IN THE INPUT WILL APPEAR
$$ DUPLICATED IN THE OUTPUT AS WELL.

PROC SORT(INTEGER N)
     FORWARD;

PROC MAIN
     INTEGER N;

     READ N;     $$ THE NUMBER OF WORDS IS KNOWN BEFOREHAND.
     SORT(N);
ENDPROC;
```

Fig. 1-1   Simple sort program

```
$$ THIS SORT ROUTINE DOES ALL THE WORK, IN THAT IT READS, SORTS,
$$ AND PRINTS THE WORDS.
$$ A SIMPLE SELECTION SORT IS USED, AND NAMES ARE PRINTED AS
$$ THEY ARE SORTED.

PROC SORT(INTEGER N)
     ARRAY(N) OF STRING NAME;
     ARRAY(N) OF STRING PAGE;
     STRING FIRST, PAGELIST;
     INTEGER I, J;
     STRING CONST LARGE = "ZZ", VERY_LARGE = "ZZZ";

     I := 1;
     LOOP WHILE I <= N;
          READ NAME (I), PAGE (I);
          I := I + 1;
     ENDLOOP;

$$ NOW DO THE SORT AND PRINT:
     LOOP
          FIRST := LARGE;
          I := 1;
          J := 0;
          LOOP
          WHILE I <= N;
               IF NAME (I) < FIRST
               THEN
                    IF J <> 0
                    THEN
                         NAME (J) := FIRST;
                         PAGE (J) := PAGELIST;
                    ENDIF;

                    J := I;
                    FIRST := NAME (I);
                    NAME (I) := VERY_LARGE;
                    PAGELIST := PAGE (I);
               ELSE
                    IF NAME (I) = FIRST
                    THEN
                         NAME (I) := VERY_LARGE;
                         PAGELIST := PAGELIST & "," & PAGE (I);
                    ENDIF;
               ENDIF;
               I := I + 1;
          ENDLOOP;
     WHILE FIRST <> LARGE;
          WRITE FIRST, PAGELIST USING "S20,X3,S40,N";
     ENDLOOP;
ENDPROC;
```

Fig. 1-1 Simple sort program (cont'd.)

The ?DATA command indicates the beginning of the data for a GAUSS program. The command and the data following this command must come immediately after the end of the program. If there is no data for the program, this command may be omitted. The keyword ?DATA must begin in column one.

1-12   SAMPLE PROGRAMS

This section gives two sample GAUSS programs. With each program is a short explanation of what the program does.

The program given in Fig. 1-1 works as follows. The main procedure reads in the number of words and associated page numbers that the program has to sort. Then the SORT routine is called. The SORT routine begins by reading in the words and the page numbers into the string arrays NAME and PAGE respectively. The rest of the procedure consists of two nested WHILE loops.

The outer loop is repeated once for each word to be printed. Each iteration prints the next word according to the alphabetical ordering. The inner loop goes through all of the words finding the next one to be printed and collecting the page numbers. It works in the following way.

If the name being looked at is less than any encountered so far, then the name being looked at is the one that should be printed. The current name and its

```
$$
$$ THIS PROGRAM GENERATES ALL PERMUTATIONS OF
$$ THE LETTERS OF AN N-LETTER WORD (STRING) BY MEANS OF
$$ ADJACENT TRANSPOSITIONS. THE TRANSPOSITIONS ARE
$$ PERFORMED SIMULTANEOUSLY ON THE FIRST N POSITIVE INTEGERS
$$ AND ON THE SYMBOLS OF THE STRING.

STRING SUBJECT; $$ GLOBAL VARIABLE CONTAINING THE STRING TO BE
        $$ PERMUTED.
INTEGER PROC LARGEST_MOBILE (ARRAY () OF INTEGER PERM,
            ARRAY () OF LOGICAL DIRECTION, INTEGER N)
            FORWARD;
PROC PERMUTE (INTEGER N) FORWARD;

$$ THE MAIN PROCEDURE READS IN THE STRING TO BE PERMUTED,
$$ AND INVOKES THE PERMUTE PROCEDURE

PROC MAIN
        INTEGER N;
        READ SUBJECT;
        N := # SUBJECT;
        WRITE SUBJECT USING "S,N";
        N := #SUBJECT;
        PERMUTE(N);
ENDPROC;
```

Fig. 1-2   Permutation program

page list are put back in the array at the first occurrence of the current name. This position is kept in the variable J. Then the name being looked at and its page number become the new current name and page list. As each name becomes the new current name, it is replaced by a special token so that it will not be used again. This special token is the string "ZZ". Thus the program assumes that no name will begin with "ZZ". When the name being looked at is the same as the current name, then it is also replaced by a special token, and its page number is added to the page list of the current name.

When the inner loop is done, the current name in FIRST and its associated page list are then printed.

The program given in Fig. 1-2 is designed to generate all permutations of the letters of a given string by means of adjacent transpositions. This program is based on Algorithm 1.1 of Even [1973]. It is assumed that the reader is familiar with this method of generating such permutations.

```
$$ PERMUTE PERFORMS THE ACTUAL TRANSPOSITIONS, AND PRINTS
$$ ALL OF THE PERMUTATIONS.

PROC PERMUTE (INTEGER N)
     INTEGER CONST INFINITY = 32767;

     $$ LOCAL VARIABLES:

     ARRAY (-1:N+1) OF INTEGER PERM; $$ A PERMUTATION OF THE
          $$ FIRST N POSITIVE INTEGERS, WITH GUARD
          $$ VALUES IN 0, -1, N+1, TO
          $$ ELIMINATE SOME CHECKS.
     ARRAY(N) OF LOGICAL DIRECTION; $$ DIRECTION OF MOVEMENT
          $$ OF THE CORRESPONDING NUMBER IN PERM.
     INTEGER ILM;    $$ INDEX OF THE LARGEST MOBILE ELEMENT IN
                     $$ PERM.
     INTEGER I;
     STRING S;

     $$ INITIALIZE PERM AND DIRECTION.
     $$ DIRECTION (I) = FALSE MEANS THAT PERM (I) IS TENDING
     $$ TO MOVE LEFTWARD.

     I := 1;
     LOOP WHILE I <= N;
          PERM (I) := I;
          DIRECTION (I) := FALSE;
          I := I + 1;
     ENDLOOP;

     $$ SET UP GUARD VALUES:
```

Fig. 1-2   Permutation program (cont'd.)

```
PERM (−1) := 0;
PERM (0) := INFINITY;
PERM (N + 1) := INFINITY;

LOOP
WHILE TRUE;
      $$LOCATE THE LARGEST MOBILE INTEGER IN PERM.

      ILM := LARGEST_MOBILE (PERM, DIRECTION, N);
      IF ILM = −1 $$ NO MOBILE ELEMENT
      THEN
            RETURN;
      ENDIF;

      $$ PERFORM TRANSPOSITION ON PERM AND SUBJECT

      I := PERM (ILM);
      S := SUBJECT (ILM | 1);

      IF DIRECTION (ILM)
      THEN
            PERM (ILM) := PERM (ILM + 1);
            SUBJECT (ILM | 1) := SUBJECT (ILM + 1 | 1);
            PERM (ILM + 1) := I;
            SUBJECT (ILM + 1 | 1) := S;
      ELSE
            PERM (ILM) := PERM (ILM − 1);
            SUBJECT (ILM | 1) := SUBJECT (ILM − 1 | 1);
            PERM (ILM − 1) := I;
            SUBJECT (ILM − 1 | 1) := S;
      ENDIF;

      ILM := I; $$ VALUE OF LARGEST MOBILE INTEGER

      I := 1;

      LOOP
      WHILE I <= N;
            IF PERM (I) > ILM
            THEN
                  DIRECTION (I) := NOT DIRECTION (I);
            ENDIF;
            I := I + 1;
      ENDLOOP;
      WRITE SUBJECT USING "S,N";
ENDLOOP;
ENDPROC;
```

Fig. 1-2 Permutation program (cont'd.)

```
$$ LARGEST_MOBILE (PERM, DIRECTON, N) LOCATES THE LARGEST
$$ MOBILE ELEMENT IN PERM, AND RETURNS THE INDEX OF IT.

INTEGER PROC LARGEST_MOBILE (ARRAY () OF INTEGER PERM,
            ARRAY () OF LOGICAL DIRECTION, INTEGER N)

    INTEGER I, ILM;

    ILM := -1;
    I := 1;

    LOOP
    WHILE I <= N;
         IF DIRECTION (I)
         THEN
              IF PERM (I) > PERM (I + 1)
              THEN
                   IF PERM (I) > PERM (ILM)
                   THEN
                        ILM := I;
                   ENDIF;
              ENDIF;
         ELSE
              IF PERM (I) > PERM (I - 1)
              THEN
                   IF PERM (I) > PERM (ILM)
                   THEN
                        ILM := I;
                   ENDIF;
              ENDIF;
         ENDIF;
         I := I + 1;
    ENDLOOP;
    RETURN ILM;
ENDPROC;
```

Fig. 1-2   Permutation program (cont'd.)

The MAIN procedure reads the subject string and calls the PERMUTE procedure to obtain the permutations. Note that the permutations are actually performed on an array of integers, called PERM. The permutations on the string are obtained by moving the same elements in the string as those moved in PERM.

The PERMUTE procedure first initializes the PERM and DIRECTION arrays. The DIRECTION array is used to determine which direction (left or right) the corresponding element of the PERM array is moving. After initialization, the PERMUTE procedure goes into a loop which first transposes the correct two elements (specified by ILM — index of the largest mobile element and the corresponding entry in DIRECTION), and then reverses the direction of the elements in PERM (as indicated by DIRECTION) that are greater than the element at PERM (ILM)). The new permutation is then printed out and the loop repeats until there is no longer a mobile element, indicated by ILM = –1. When this happens, all permutations have been computed and the program terminates.

ILM is calculated by the LARGEST_MOBILE procedure, which simply looks for the largest element k of PERM such that there is an integer smaller than k adjacent to k on the side that is in the same direction as k is moving. The index of the element k in PERM is then returned, with –1 being returned if such a k does not exist.

BIBLIOGRAPHY

EVEN, S., "Algorithmic Combinatorics," The Macmillan Company, New York, 1973.

IBM, "System/360 Operating System PL/I (F) Language Reference Manual," Form GC28-8201-3.

JENSEN, K., and N. WIRTH, "PASCAL User Manual and Report," 2d ed., Springer-Verlag, New York, 1975.

RITCHIE, D. M., "C Reference Manual," in "Documents for Use with the UNIX Time-sharing System," Bell Laboratories, Murray Hill, N. J., 1974.

SITES, R. L., "ALGOL W Reference Manual," Technical Report STAN-CS-71-230, Computer Science Department, Stanford University, Feb. 1972.

TREMBLAY, J.P., and P.G. SORENSON, "The Theory and Practice of Compiler Writing," McGraw-Hill Book Company, New York, 1982.

WIRTH, N., and H. WEBER, "EULER: A Generalization of Algol and its Formal Definition, Parts I and II," Communications of the ACM, Vol. 9, No. 12 , Jan. - Feb. 1966, pp. 13 - 35, 89 - 99.

Chapter 2

The Implementation of A Compiler For GAUSS

2-1 INTRODUCTION

Implementing a compiler presents many problems, especially to the novice compiler writer. Since a guide of this type can not hope to answer all of the questions related to compiler writing for different languages and different types of implementations, perhaps the best strategy is to give one example of a compiler, and hope that in this way some of the questions a student may have about writing his or her own compiler can be answered. This chapter illustrates one particular implementation of a compiler for the GAUSS language. More specifically, the compiler developed is a single pass compiler that produces high-level, stack-oriented intermediate language instructions.

In each section of the chapter, an attempt is made to explore some basic problems involved in writing a certain portion of the compiler as well as to present the solution to these problems. First, the goal of the particular part of the compiler is determined. Then, the method and data structures used to implement this section of the compiler are explored. Finally, each section presents the PL/I source code which implements the function that has been discussed. This allows the reader to examine the programming techniques that were used to put the algorithms and data structures together in a workable fashion.

In Fig. 2-1 a breakdown of the compiler into four basic submodules is presented. These are the scanner, the parser, the table handler, and the code generator. The scanner reads the GAUSS program as input, and returns a token representation of the input to the parsing module. The parser performs the syntactic analysis of the GAUSS program being compiled. The routines of the table handler look after the insertion, look-up and deletion of symbols from the symbol table. The code generator must analyze the semantics of the program and generate appropriate code which will perform the required operations in order to execute the GAUSS program being compiled. Figure 2-1 illustrates how the procedures can invoke each other. The parser invokes the scanner and the code generation routines. The scanner and code generation routines both invoke the table handler.

This chapter follows the basic order outlined in the preceding paragraph. Section 2-2 describes the scanner. Section 2-3 presents the parser, and Sec. 2-4 presents the table handler, which maintains the symbol table. In Sec. 2-5, the code generator and the semantic analysis necessary to ensure the appropriate generation of code are presented. Section 2-6 provides a centralized description of compilation errors in the scanner, table handler, parser, and code generation routines.

2-2 SCANNER

The scanner is invoked by the parser to read the next lexical unit of source text and return an input token representing this lexical unit to the parser. This section describes the implementation of a scanner for the GAUSS language. In Sec. 2-2.1, some of the goals of a scanner are introduced. In Sec. 2-2.2, a finite state machine representation of the scanner is described, and in Sec. 2-2.3, a top-level

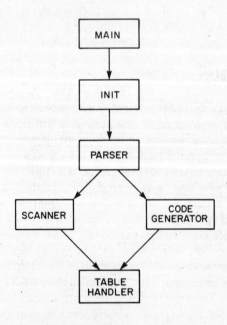

Fig. 2-1   Structure chart of a GAUSS compiler

breakdown of the routines in the scanner is given. Section 2-2.4 describes the nature of the information that must be handled and stored by the scanner and Sec. 2-2.5 deals with the implementation of the scanner. Finally, the PL/I source code for the scanner is given in Sec. 2-2.6.

2-2.1 Introduction

The purpose of the scanner is to return the next input token to the parse module. Tokens consist of all keywords, identifiers, and symbols found in a program. To be able to return a token, the scanner must isolate the next sequence of characters in the input stream which designate a valid token. Thus, the basic task of the scanner is that of editing the source program so as to remove information that is not important to the parsing and code generating phases of the compiler, and passing on to the parser an intermediate representation of the source program. This means that the scanner must be able to ignore such things as blanks and comments. Also, the scanner is responsible for differentiating between an identifier and a keyword of the language. The scanner should not only find a token, but should make sure that it has found the complete token. For example, ZAP 3 in the input stream should cause the tokens for an identifier and a number to be returned. On the other hand, ZAP3 should cause a single token for an identifier to be returned. Also, 3ZAP and 3 ZAP should both cause a token for a number and an identifier to be returned since identifiers cannot begin with a digit in GAUSS.

Having introduced the notion of a scanner, let us formalize a method which will perform the required lexical analysis.

2-2.2 The Scanner as a Finite-State Machine

Since the scanner's output is a function of the input, and there are only a finite number of actions which the scanner can take for any input, the scanner can be easily described by a finite-state machine.

The scanner is initially in the start state whenever it is invoked. The transition from its start state depends on the next character of the input stream. The operation of a scanner for GAUSS is shown in the state transition diagram in Fig. 2-2. Most of the arcs of this diagram are labelled with the input symbol which causes the transition. Arcs that are not labelled indicate the transition to be made whenever the input symbol is not one of those marked on the other arcs leaving a particular state. A set of symbols listed on an arc indicates that any member of the set causes the transition. If the input symbol is such that it corresponds to no arc leaving the state, the symbol is invalid and the scanner prints an error message.

The arcs are labelled with the actions to be performed when a transition is made. The following two types of actions occur

1. RETURN (*token*) signifies that *token* should be returned to the parser as the input token.
2. READ means that the next character from the input stream should be read. This action is discussed in more detail in Sec. 2-2.5.

Given this basic design for the operation of the scanner, a procedure can be implemented which will emulate the actions of the finite state machine given in Fig. 2-2. First, however, a breakdown of the scanner into its major components and their purpose is given.

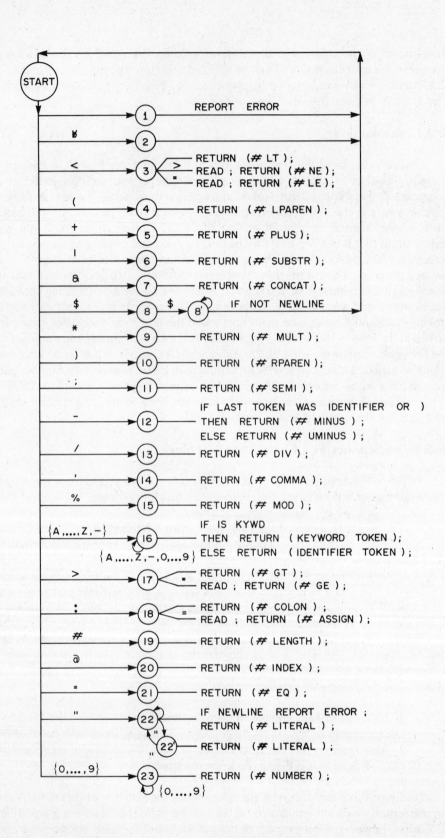

Fig. 2-2 Finite-state diagram of a scanner for GAUSS

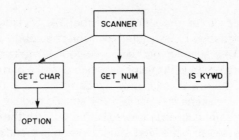

Fig. 2-3   Structure chart of the GAUSS scanner

2-2.3 Top-down Description of Scanner

The scanner is designed to be an interface between the input stream and the parser for the compiler. The scanner may call three subordinate procedures, namely, *get_char*, *get_num*, and *is_kywd*. The purpose of these procedures is now introduced and they will be discussed fully in Sec. 2-2.5.

The *get_char* routine is used to read in the source program and return characters from the input, one at a time. Adjacent blanks are merged. It is also responsible for processing the ?PROGRAM and ?OPTION commands which were discussed in Chap. 1. These commands are processed by the *option* routine.

The *get_num* routine is used to read in the character representation of a number from the input stream and convert it to its corresponding numeric representation.

The *is_kywd* procedure takes a given identifier and determines whether it is actually a keyword, or an identifier.

Figure 2-3 demonstrates the calling sequences of the scanner and its subordinate procedures. In the diagram, a procedure invokes those procedures at a lower level with which it is connected. For example, the scanner invokes the *get_char* procedure, and the *get_char* procedure invokes the *option* procedure.

2-2.4 Structural Representation of Data

Before examining the scanner and each of its submodules in more detail, it is necessary to describe how the necessary data can be structured. The first data structure to be discussed is the representation of the tokens.

Although the tokens are not represented by a complex data structure, their use is so important that they are discussed here. When a token is encountered, some representation of that token must be returned to the parser. The easiest and simplest way to do this is to have a unique number for each token. Unfortunately, this representation makes the code for the compiler difficult to understand, since the numerical representation for each token must be remembered. To overcome this difficulty, our implementation uses a macro facility to define a literal text replacement for each token. Thus for a keyword such as ARRAY, there is a corresponding macro token called *#array* which is defined to be a certain integer value, say 2. When the keyword ARRAY is encountered in the input stream by the scanner, the scanner's action is to return the macro token *#array* (i.e., RETURN (*#array*);) which is equivalent, in this case, to returning a value of 2 (i.e., RETURN (2);).

There are macros for the symbols of the GAUSS language as well. For example, the macro #*assign* is associated with the := symbol. The use of macros not only enhances the readability of the source code for the compiler, but it also makes it much easier to change the value associated with a particular token, if this should be required. Such a change only needs to be done once in the macro definition instead of each time it is used in the source code.

The next important data structure to be discussed is the *char_class* vector. When the scanner is entered, the next state decision is made on the basis of the next input character as indicated by the state diagram given earlier. To perform the state transitions, a mapping from the set of possible input characters to the set of possible states is required. This is realized through the *char_class* vector. This vector contains 256 entries, one for each of the possible members of the EBCDIC character set. The EBCDIC value of the input character gives the index into this vector for the corresponding entry of the given character. Each entry in this vector contains the next state number for the given input symbol.

For example, if a > symbol is the next character, it is converted into its EBCDIC encoded value (i.e., decimal 110) by the PL/I function UNSPEC. *char_class (110)* then yields a result of 17. Thus the initial state transition with > as the input, is to state 17.

The state for each character can be determined by inspection from the state transition diagram. For example, since any uppercase letter of the alphabet, or the underscore, causes a transition to state 16, the corresponding entries for each of these characters in the *char_class* table is 16.

It is important to note that the *char_class* vector is used only to determine the initial state transition when the scanner is entered, and plays no role in determining subsequent state transitions.

The label array *state* is associated with the *char_class* vector. It contains the addresses of the code which is to be executed for that particular state. For example, *state (17)* gives the address of the code which processes the input for state 17.

In order to determine when a keyword has been read, it is necessary to compare the given string with the possible keywords. In order to do this, a list of the keywords is required for comparison. This list is found in the initial segment of the *token_str* vector. This vector contains the string representation for all keywords, special symbols, and nonterminal symbol names. For example, the entry for a keyword such as ARRAY is 'ARRAY'. For a special symbol, such as the assignment operator, the entry is := and for a nonterminal symbol name, such as <program>, the entry is 'PROGRAM'.

The only use of this vector in the scanner is for identifying keywords. In the parser (Sec. 2-3) this vector is also used for debugging and error recovery.

When the scanner encounters a string which may be a keyword, the part of the *token_str* vector which contains the keywords is searched. If there is a match with the input string, then the input token is a keyword; otherwise, it is some other type of token. The tokens have been chosen such that if the matching keyword is the *i*th one in this vector, then the value of the token for this keyword is *i*.

2-2.5 Implementation of the Scanner

The scanner may invoke any one of three subordinate procedures. These are the *get_char*, *get_num*, and *is_kywd* procedures.

The *get_char* procedure is used to return the next character of the input stream to the scanner. Adjacent blanks are merged. This is done by reading one input line at a time into the global string variable *line_buf*. Because a token is not allowed to be split across lines, a blank, which acts as a delimiter between tokens, is appended to *line_buf*. The global variable *line_ptr* is used as an index into *line_buf*. Therefore, when this procedure is called, *line_ptr* is incremented and the character in *line_buf* pointed to by *line_ptr* is returned.

If the *get_char* routine is called when *line_ptr* points to the last blank character of *line_buf*, then the *new_line* flag is set to *true* and a blank is returned. The next time the *get_char* routine is called with the *new_line* flag set to *true*, the error messages associated with the previous line are printed, a new line is read into *line_buf*, and the *new_line* flag is set to *false*.

If the new line is a ?PROGRAM command (i.e., the start of a new GAUSS program) or a ?DATA command (i.e., the data for a just compiled program), then a logical end-of-file condition is indicated by setting the global flag *eof* to *true* and returning a blank. A physical end-of-file condition is indicated by setting the global variables *real_eof* and *eof* to *true* and returning a blank. If the line is a ?OPTION command, then the *option* procedure is called to set the appropriate option flags. The line is then printed providing the *list_flag* is on, and the next character is returned.

The *get_num* procedure simply reads in the digits of a number from the input stream, and converts them from their string representation into numerical form. Checking is also done to ensure that the number is not too large for the machine for which the compiler generates code.

When an identifier is read by the scanner, it must be determined whether it is a GAUSS keyword or a user identifier. This is done by the *is_kywd* procedure. This procedure takes the given string and compares it with the keyword elements of the vector *token_str* using a binary search (see Tremblay and Sorenson [1976]). If the given string matches an element in *token_str*, then it is a keyword, and the index of the string in *token_str* is returned, since this is the same as the value of the token for the given keyword. If the given string is not an element of *token_str*, then a 0 is returned, which indicates to the scanner that the token is an identifier.

Before the scanner is called for the first time, a line is read into *line_buf*, *line_ptr* is set to 0, and *next_char* is initialized to a blank. *next_char*, a global character variable, contains the next character to be processed by the scanner.

The scanner procedure works in the following manner. *next_char* is converted into its binary representation by the UNSPEC function. This number is then used as an index into the *char_class* vector, which contains the number of the state to which the scanner should transfer.

The states are entered by means of a GOTO and the *state* label array by the statement

GO TO *state* (x)

where *x* represents the value returned from the *char_class* vector. Although the use of a GOTO statement is considered a bad programming practice, it can be very useful when it is used to simulate a construct, such as a CASE statement, which is not available in the programming language being used. The use of a GOTO statement in this case makes the program clearer and easier to read than if some other construct, such as multiple IF statements, had been used.

Once in the appropriate state, the scanner proceeds to process as much input as necessary in order to obtain the next token. The processing of the input for most of the states is fairly simple and will not be discussed here. Two exceptions, however, require further explanation.

When a minus sign is read, it must be determined whether it is a binary or unary minus sign. This can be done by looking at the token returned previously, since the set of items that can precede a unary minus is disjoint from the set of items that can precede a binary minus. The parser stores the tokens returned by the scanner in the global variable *next_token*. Thus, if *next_token* is one of *#rparen*, *#simpident*, *#simpconident*, or *#procident*, then the token to be returned is a binary minus sign. Otherwise, the token is a unary minus sign.

If the input token is an identifier, then the scanner must determine what type of identifier is to be returned. This is done by calling the *look_up* routine which finds the symbol table entry of the given identifier and returns its address in the symbol table. The scanner then determines what token is to be returned by examining the use information of the symbol table entry. The possible tokens that can be returned for identifiers, along with their meanings are

#newident	a new identifier
#simpident	a simple identifier
#simpconident	a simple constant identifier
#arrayident	an array identifier
#arrayconident	an array constant identifier
#procident	a procedure identifier

Note that after the initial state transition, which is based on the particular input character, there are no further explicit state transitions. The state is imbedded into the code. For example, when state 17 is entered with the input symbol '>', the code basically reads as follows:

```
next_char = get_char;
IF next_char = '='
THEN next_char = get_char;
        RETURN (#ge);
ELSE RETURN (#gt);
```

The state entered is still decided by the next input character, but the transition is determined by the THEN and ELSE clauses of the IF statement.

Note that in this example, when the token returned is the token for '>', the next input character has already been read into *next_char*. However, when the token returned is the token for '>=', the next input character is unknown and hence it must be read into *next_char* before returning. This corresponds to the READ operation shown in the state transition diagram.

In three cases the scanner must also provide some additional information besides returning a token. This occurs whenever the token is an identifier, an integer constant, or a string constant. For identifiers, the symbol table entry location is placed in the global variable *idptr*. For integer constants, the value is placed in the global variable *value*. The value of the integer constant is obtained by the *get_num* procedure. The value of a string constant is its reference pointer. The calculation of the reference pointer is postponed until later in the code generation phase (*see* Sec. 2-5.2). Instead, the string constant is stored by the scanner in the global string variable *strbuf*.

To allow debugging of the scanner, all states converge to the point labelled *out* before returning the token to the parser. At this point, if the *scanner_debug* flag is on, the token value and its corresponding string representation are printed.

The following section gives the source code for the scanner.

2-2.6 Scanner Source Code

Figure 2-4 contains the source code for the scanner.

```
/***************************************/
/*                                     */
/*          SCANNER                    */
/*                                     */
/***************************************/
```

```
/* The scanner is used to return the tokens to the parser.
Every time that it is called, it will return the next token.
The scanner works by using the first character read to
find out what class the next token will be.  This is done
by using the table as described below.  Then the scanner
processes the rest of the token, according to its class.
The predefined token is then returned (actually a number)
to the calling routine.  */
```

```
scanner:  PROCEDURE RETURNS (FIXED BIN (15));

        DECLARE
                get_char ENTRY RETURNS (CHARACTER (1)),
                get_num ENTRY RETURNS (FIXED BIN (15)),
                is_kywd ENTRY (CHARACTER (*) VARYING) RETURNS
                        (FIXED BIN (15));

        DECLARE
                class FIXED BIN (15),    /* class of the char */
                state (1 : 23) LABEL,    /* 23 state labels  */
                idbuf CHAR (idlen) VAR,  /* holds identifiers */
                char_int FIXED BIN (15), /* int. rep. of char */
                (i,z) FIXED BIN (15),    /* temporaries      */
                token FIXED BIN (15);    /* token returned   */

        /* The following table is used to map the characters
        returned by the get_char routine into their
        various classes.  i.e., if the character returned
```

Fig. 2-4   Source code for the scanner

is a comma, its integer value (107 or 6B hex) is
used as an index into this table. The integer
that is found at this location (14 in this case)
represents the state that the scanner should go
into with this character as the first character of
the token being scanned. 0 entries indicate an
illegal character. */

```
DECLARE char_class (0 : 255) FIXED BIN (15) STATIC INITIAL
        ((64) 1, 2, (11) 1, 3, 4, 5, 6, 7, (9) 1, 1,
        8, 9, 10, 11, 1, 12, 13, (9) 1, 14, 15, 16, 17,
        1, (10) 1, 18, 19, 20, 1, 21, 22, (65) 1, (9) 16,
        (7) 1, (9) 16, (8) 1, (8) 16, (6) 1, (10) 23,
        (6) 1);

case:
IF (eof)
THEN DO;
        token = #eof;
        GO TO out;
END;

UNSPEC (char_int) = '00000000'B || UNSPEC (next_char);
class = char_class (char_int);
begin_tok = line_ptr;

/* The following go to, along with the state label */
/* array is used to simulate a case statement.  */

GO TO state (class);

state(1):       /* unknown character */
        CALL error (1, 0, 0, 0);
        next_char = get_char;
        GO TO case;

state(2):       /* a blank character */
        next_char = get_char;
        GO TO case;

state(3):       /* a less than sign (<) */
        next_char = get_char;
        IF (next_char = '>')
        THEN DO;
                token = #ne;
                next_char = get_char;
        END;
        ELSE
```

Fig. 2-4   Source code for the scanner (cont'd.)

```
            IF (next_char = '=')
            THEN DO;
                    token = #le;
                    next_char = get_char;
            END;
            ELSE token = #lt;
            GO TO out;

state(4):        /* a left parenthesis */
        token = #lparen;
        next_char = get_char;
        GO TO out;

state(5):        /* a plus sign */
        token = #plus;
        next_char = get_char;
        GO TO out;

state(6):        /* substring operator (|) */
        token = #substr;
        next_char = get_char;
        GO TO out;

state(7):        /* a concatenation operator (&) */
        token = #concat;
        next_char = get_char;
        GO TO out;

state(8):        /* a comment delimiter */
        next_char = get_char;
        IF (next_char ¬= '$')
        THEN CALL error (2, 0, 0, 0);
        DO WHILE (¬new_line);  /* end of line */
                next_char = get_char;
        END;
        next_char = get_char;
        GO TO case;

state(9):        /* multiplication operator */
        token = #mult;
        next_char = get_char;
        GO TO out;

state(10):       /* right parenthesis */
        token = #rparen;
        next_char = get_char;
        GO TO out;
```

Fig. 2-4 Source code for the scanner (cont'd.)

```
state(11):      /* a semi colon */
     token = #semi;
     next_char = get_char;
     GO TO out;

state(12):      /* a minus sign */
     /* check previous token */
     IF (next_token = #rparen | next_token = #simpconident
      | next_token = #simpident | next_token = #procident)
     THEN token = #minus;
     ELSE token = #uminus;
     next_char = get_char;
     GO TO out;

state(13):      /* a division sign */
     token = #div;
     next_char = get_char;
     GO TO out;

state(14):      /* a comma */
     token = #comma;
     next_char = get_char;
     GO TO out;

state(15):      /* a mod operator (%) */
     token = #mod;
     next_char = get_char;
     GO TO out;

state(16):      /* an alphabetic character */
     idbuf = '';
     DO WHILE(class = 16 | class = 23);
          IF (length (idbuf) < idlen)
          THEN
               idbuf = idbuf || next_char;
          next_char = get_char;
          UNSPEC (char_int) = '00000000'b ||
                    UNSPEC (next_char);
          class = char_class (char_int);

     END;
     token = is_kywd (idbuf);
     IF (token = 0)
     THEN DO;
          idptr = lookup(idbuf);
          token = symtab(idptr).use;
     END;
     GO TO out;
```

Fig. 2-4   Source code for the scanner (cont'd.)

```
state(17):      /* a greater than sign */
      next_char = get_char;
      IF (next_char = '=')
      THEN DO;
            token = #ge;
            next_char = get_char;
      END;
      ELSE token = #gt;
      GO TO out;

state(18):      /* a colon */
      next_char = get_char;
      IF (next_char = '=')
      THEN DO;
            token = #assign;
            next_char = get_char;
      END;
      ELSE token = #colon;
      GO TO out;

state(19):      /* a string length operator (#) */
      token = #length;
      next_char = get_char;
      GO TO out;

state(20):      /* a string index operator (@) */
      token = #index;
      next_char = get_char;
      GO TO out;

state(21):      /* an equals sign */
      token = #eq;
      next_char = get_char;
      GO TO out;

state(22):      /* a double quote mark */
      strbuf = '';
      z = 0;
      next_char = get_char;
      strloop:
      DO WHILE (next_char ¬= ' ' & ¬new_line);
            IF (z < strlen)
            THEN strbuf = strbuf || next_char;
            z = z + 1;
            next_char = get_char;
      END;

      IF (new_line)
```

Fig. 2-4   Source code for the scanner (cont'd.)

```
                    THEN CALL error (4, 0, 0, 0);
                    ELSE DO;
                            next_char = get_char;
                            IF (next_char = ' ')
                            THEN DO;
                                    IF (z < strlen)
                                    THEN strbuf = strbuf || ' ';
                                    z = z + 1;
                                    next_char = get_char;
                                    GO TO strloop;
                            END;
                    END;

                    IF (z > strlen)
                    THEN CALL error (3, 0, 0, 0);
                    token = #literal;
                    GO TO out;

        state(23):       /* a number */
                value = get_num;
                token = #number;


        out:    /* print token for debugging */
        IF (scanner_debug)
        THEN DO;
                PUT EDIT ('token <', token, ', ', token_str (token),
                        '>')(X(5), A, F(3), A, A, A);
                IF (token = #number)
                THEN PUT EDIT (value)(F(7));
                IF (token = #literal)
                THEN PUT EDIT (strbuf)(A);
                IF (token = #newident | token = #simpident |
                        token = #simpconident | token = #arrayident |
                        token = #arrayconident | token = #procident)
                THEN PUT EDIT (idbuf)(A);
                PUT EDIT ('        ')(A);
        END;
        RETURN (token);


                /*********************************************/
                /*                                           */
                /*          get_char                         */
                /*                                           */
                /*********************************************/
```

/* The get_char routine will return the next character in the
input stream. The input is read in 80 character lines at

Fig. 2-4 Source code for the scanner (cont'd.)

a time. Before each line is read, the error messages (if
any) from the previous statement are printed out. The
next line of 80 characters is then read in, and also
printed out in the listing if the list_flag is true.
If the line read is a '?OPTION' line, then the option
routine is called to pick off the options from the
line and set appropriate flags. If a '?PROGRAM' line is
read, then a fake end of file is returned to indicate
the end of the previous program. When all the programs
have been read, then 'real_eof' is set to true, and
the end of file marker is returned. Since the '?' is
used as an end of file to be passed to the scanner, but
'?' is an invalid character as far as GAUSS is concerned
each input character must be checked against '?'. */

```
get_char:  PROCEDURE RETURNS (CHARACTER (1));
        DECLARE

                cha CHARACTER (1), /* character to be returned */
                i FIXED BIN (15);      /* index into line_buf    */

        ON ENDFILE (SYSIN) BEGIN;
                real_eof = '1'B;
                line_buf = '?PROGRAM';
        END;

        IF (new_line)
        THEN DO;
                IF (line_errors > 0)
                THEN CALL list_err;
                get_line;
        END;

        IF (line_ptr = 0)
        THEN DO;

                DO WHILE (SUBSTR (line_buf, 1, 7) = '?OPTION');
                        CALL option;
                END;

                IF (SUBSTR (line_buf, 1, 8) = '?PROGRAM' |
                    SUBSTR (line_buf, 1, 5) = '?DATA')
                THEN DO;
                        eof = '1'B;
                        RETURN (' ');
                END;
        END;
```

Fig. 2-4 Source code for the scanner (cont'd.)

```
i = VERIFY (SUBSTR (line_buf,line_ptr + 1), ' ');
IF (i = 1)
THEN DO;
        line_ptr = line_ptr + 1;
        cha = SUBSTR (line_buf,line_ptr,1);
        RETURN (cha);
END;

IF (i = 0)
THEN DO;
        new_line = '1'B;
        RETURN (' ');
END;

line_ptr = line_ptr + i - 1;
RETURN (' ');


/******************************************/
/*                                        */
/*               option                   */
/*                                        */
/******************************************/
```

/* The option routine will pick off the options from the '?OPTION'
line and set the appropriate flags. */

```
option: PROCEDURE;
    DECLARE
            flag CHARACTER (1), /* the '+' or '-' sign */
            enable BIT (1),              /* turn opt. on or off */
            name CHAR (15) VARYING; /* option name */

    line_buf = SUBSTR (line_buf, 8);
    line_ptr = VERIFY (line_buf, ' ');

    DO WHILE (line_ptr ¬= 0);

            /* isolate the flag, if present */

            line_buf = SUBSTR (line_buf, line_ptr);
            flag = SUBSTR (line_buf, 1, 1);
            IF (flag = '+')
            THEN DO;
                    enable = '1'B;
                    line_buf = SUBSTR (line_buf, 2);
            END;
            ELSE
```

Fig. 2-4   Source code for the scanner (cont'd.)

```
                    IF (flag = '-')
                    THEN DO;
                            enable = '0'B;
                            line_buf = SUBSTR (line_buf, 2);
                    END;
                    ELSE
                            enable = '1'B;

            /* isolate the option to be set */

            line_ptr = INDEX (line_buf, ' ');
            begin_tok = 80 - LENGTH (line_buf) + 1;
            IF (line_ptr = 0)
            THEN DO;
                    CALL error (9, 0, 0, 0);
                    name = '';
            END;
            ELSE DO;
                    name = SUBSTR (line_buf, 1, line_ptr - 1);
                    line_buf = SUBSTR (line_buf, line_ptr);
            END;

            /* now set the appropriate flag */

                IF (name = 'list')
                THEN list_flag = enable;
            ELSE IF (name = 'xref')
                THEN xref_flag = enable;
            ELSE IF (name = 'scanner_debug')
                THEN scanner_debug = enable;
            ELSE IF (name = 'll1_debug')
                THEN ll1_debug = enable;
            ELSE IF (name = 'code_debug')
                THEN code_debug = enable;
            ELSE IF (name = 'sym_debug')
                THEN sym_debug = enable;
            ELSE IF (name = 'int_debug')
                THEN int_debug = enable;
            ELSE CALL error (10, 0, 0, 0);

            line_ptr = VERIFY (line_buf, ' ');
        END;
        IF (line_errors > 0)
        THEN
                CALL list_err;
        get_line;
END option;
END get_char;
```

Fig. 2-4   Source code for the scanner (cont'd.)

```
/******************************************/
/*                                        */
/*              get_num                   */
/*                                        */
/******************************************/
```

/* The get_num procedure reads a number and converts it from
character format to integer format. If the number is too
big to convert, an error message is printed, and the
largest possible number is used. */

get_num: PROCEDURE RETURNS (FIXED BIN (15));

```
        DECLARE
                number FIXED BIN (15), /* number to be returned */
                digit FIXED BIN (15);  /* converted digit       */

        number = 0;

        ON FIXEDOVERFLOW BEGIN;
                CALL error (5, 0, 0, 0);
                DO WHILE (next_char >= '0' & next_char <= '9' );
                        next_char = get_char;
                END;
                number = 32767;
                GO TO done;
        END;

        DO WHILE (next_char >= '0' & next_char <= '9');
                GET STRING (next_char) EDIT (digit) (f(1));
                number = number * 10 + digit;
                next_char = get_char;
        END;

        done:
        RETURN (number);
END get_num;
```

```
/******************************************/
/*                                        */
/*              is_kywd                    */
/*                                        */
/******************************************/
```

/* This procedure is designed to take the given string
and decide whether or not it is a keyword. This is
done by using a binary search on a list of the keywords

Fig. 2-4   Source code for the scanner (cont'd.)

from token_str to find the match.
If the string is a keyword, the token value
of the keyword is simply its index in the vector.
This value is then returned as the value of the keyword.
If the string is not a keyword, then 0 is returned. */

```
is_kywd:  PROCEDURE (string) RETURNS (FIXED BIN (15));

        DECLARE
                string CHARACTER (*) VARYING,  /* given string    */
                first FIXED BIN (15),  /* first record in search */
                last FIXED BIN (15),   /* last record in search  */
                i FIXED BIN (15);       /* used for indexing      */

        first = 1;
        last = #_of_keywords;

        DO WHILE (first <= last);
                i = FLOOR ((first + last) / 2.0);
                IF (string < token_str (i))
                THEN
                        last = i - 1;
                ELSE
                        IF (string > token_str (i))
                        THEN
                                first = i + 1;
                        ELSE
                                RETURN (i);
        END;

        RETURN (0);
END is_kywd;
END scanner;
```

Fig. 2-4   Source code for the scanner (cont'd.)

2-3   PARSER

The parser's task is to analyze the syntax of the GAUSS program being compiled. This section describes the parser used in this implementation of a GAUSS compiler. In Sec. 2-3.1, the basic concepts of a parser, and the type of parser that is used for this implementation are introduced. Section 2-3.2 describes the formalization of LL(1) grammars, the class of grammars for which the parser is constructed. Also given in this section is the LL(1) grammar for the GAUSS language. This section includes a discussion of how the FIRST and FOLLOW sets are constructed. Section 2-3.3 presents the parsing function which contains the basic information required to parse a GAUSS program. A top-down description of the parser is given in Sec. 2-3.4. In Sec. 2-3.5 the implementation of the parser is described, and in Sec. 2-3.6 the method used to recover from parsing errors is outlined. Finally, Sec. 2-3.7 presents the PL/I source code used in the implementation of the parser as described in this section.

2-3.1 Introduction

The purpose of the parser is to decide whether or not the given GAUSS program follows the syntax rules for the GAUSS language as described in Chap. 1. This process of validating the syntactic correctness of a program is accomplished by reading the input stream and deciding whether the next input symbol can legally follow what has already been read.

The parser obtains tokens from the input stream by calling the scanner. For certain tokens, it will also expect additional information to be available in a global variable provided for this purpose. This happens whenever the input token is a number, a literal, or an identifier as was discussed in the description of the scanner (see Sec. 2-2.5). As the parser analyses the GAUSS program, it must at certain times call appropriate semantic routines to generate code for the program being parsed. After a semantic routine has completed its processing, the parser continues parsing the program.

For this implementation of a compiler for GAUSS, it was decided to perform a top-down parse with no back-up. The information required during such a parse can be characterized in terms of an LL(1) grammar. LL(1) grammars have been used for defining actual programming languages for several years, and the parsing algorithm for this class of grammars is efficient. Thus, a parser of this type should provide an efficient and practical example of a parsing technique. The LL(1) grammar for the GAUSS language is described in the next subsection.

2-3.2 LL(1) Grammar

An LL(1) grammar allows us to determine the production to be applied given that it is known which nonterminal is being expanded and what the next input symbol is. This is the problem that arises when a top-down parse with no back-up is attempted.

Consider the following LL(1) example grammar:

0.	S′ ::= A#	4.	S ::= [eC]
1.	A ::= iB ← e	5.	S ::= .i
2.	B ::= SB	6.	C ::= eC
3.	B ::= ϵ	7.	C ::= ϵ

To illustrate the notions of a top-down parse using an LL(1) grammar, a derivation for the input string i[e]←e# is given. The sentential forms obtained during this parse are illustrated as follows.

1.	S′ ⇒	A#
2.	⇒	iB ← e#
3.	⇒	iSB ← e#
4.	⇒	i[eC]B ← e#
5.	⇒	i[e]B ← e#
6.	⇒	i[e] ← e#

In the first two expansions of this parse, the choice of which production to expand is trivial, since both S' and A have only one right-hand side. When the third expansion is about to be made, a decision must be made as to whether B should be expanded to SB or to ε. The next input symbol to be matched by the expansion of B is a [. By examining the grammar, it can be seen that the expansion that should be made is given by rule number 2. Now S is the first symbol to be expanded and the decision of what expansion to make must again be made. The input symbol that must be matched is still a [. By examining the grammar, it can be seen that production 4 must be applied if the input symbol is to be matched. When the nonterminal C is to be expanded in step 4 of the parse given previously, the input symbol that is to be matched is a]. By examining the grammar, it can be seen that if production 6 was applied, the symbol e would be generated instead of a]. Thus production 7 must be the one to be applied. Finally, the second B must be expanded. Since the input symbol to be matched is now ←, rule 3 of the grammar is used to expand B. Once this is done, all nonterminals have been expanded, and the parse is finished.

Now that an informal strategy for parsing an LL(1) grammar has been introduced, there are several questions that must be answered. For example, how do you tell if a grammar is LL(1)? How can the parsing algorithm conveniently determine from the grammar which production to apply next? What is the actual parsing algorithm for this type of grammar? These questions are answered in the subsections that follow. First, however, we will present the LL(1) grammar for GAUSS.

The grammar given in Chap. 1 to define the GAUSS language was designed to be easily understood. Unfortunately, this grammar is not LL(1). Thus the grammar had to be changed so that it would be LL(1), but still equivalent to the grammar which defines the GAUSS language. When the attempt was made to change the grammar to an LL(1) grammar, it was found that this could not be done easily. In order to simplify matters, the grammar is changed to allow a slightly larger language than that specified by the original grammar, and then to restrict these expanded areas in the semantic portion of the compiler. The compiler as a whole, however, accepts only the language specified by the original grammar.

The two expanded areas affected by these changes involve the parsing of the type of the first procedure encountered, and the parsing of expressions. Because global variables are declared before procedures, the new grammar will allow the first procedure to have an ARRAY type. This is invalid, and is checked for in the semantic portion of the compiler. The grammar for the expressions allows the operands of an operator to be of any type. For example,

X = (3 + "ABC") < TRUE;

will parse correctly, since the only thing wrong with this expression is that the types of the operands do not match the types required by the operators. The type checking of operands is done in the semantic portion of the compiler.

The revised grammar is given here for a reference.

```
1       <program> ::= <global> #eof
2       <global> ::= <procedure>; <procedure list>
3             | <type specifier> <core>
4       <core> ::= <procedure>; <procedure list>
5             | <entity list>; <global>
```

```
6    <declaration list> ::= <declaration>; <declaration list>
7       | ε
8    <procedure list> ::= <procedure>; <procedure list>
9       | <simple type> <procedure>; <procedure list>
10      | ε
11   <declaration> ::= <type specifier> <entity list>
12   <entity list> ::= CONST <newident> = <constant> <const list>
13      | <newident> <ident list>
14   <const list> ::= , <newident> = <constant> <const list>
15      | ε
16   <type specifier> ::= <simple type>
17      | <array>
18   <simple type> ::= INTEGER
19      | STRING
20      | LOGICAL
21   <array> ::= ARRAY ( <bound pair> <bound pair list> ) OF <simple type>
22   <bound pair list> ::= , <bound pair> <bound pair list>
23      | ε
24   <bound pair> ::= <expression> <second bound>
25   <second bound> ::= : <expression>
26      | ε
27   <constant> ::= <simple constant>
28      | <array constant>
29   <simple constant> ::= θ <number>
30      | <number>
31      | <literal>
32      | TRUE
33      | FALSE
34   <array constant> ::= ( <simple constant> <simple constant list> )
35   <simple constant list> ::= , <simple constant> <simple constant list>
36      | ε
37   <ident list> ::= , <newident> <ident list>
38      | ε
39   <procedure> ::= PROC <procname> <parameter list> <procedure tail>
40   <procedure tail> ::= FORWARD
41      | <procedure body>
42   <procedure body> ::= <declaration list> <statement>; <statement list> ENDPROC
43   <statement list> ::= <statement>; <statement list>
44      | ε
45   <parameter list> ::= ( <parameter> <parameters> )
46      | ε
47   <parameters> ::= , <parameter> <parameters>
48      | ε
49   <parameter> ::= <parameter type> <newident>
50   <parameter type> ::= <simple type>
51      | ARRAY ( <comma list> ) OF <simple type>
52   <comma list> ::= , <comma list>
53      | ε
54   <statement> ::= <procedure call>
55      | <return stmt>
56      | <if stmt>
57      | <while stmt>
58      | <stop stmt>
59      | <assignment stmt>
60      | <read stmt>
61      | <write stmt>
62   <procedure call> ::= <procident> <argument list>
63   <argument list> ::= ( <argument> <arguments> )
64      | ε
65   <arguments> ::= , <argument> <arguments>
66      | ε
```

```
67       <argument> ::= <simpident>
68           | <arrayident> <sublist>
69       <sublist> ::= ( <expression> <expressions> )
70           | ε
71       <expressions> ::= , <expression> <expressions>
72           | ε
73       <return stmt> ::= RETURN <ret expression>
74       <ret expression> ::= <expression>
75           | ε
76       <if stmt> ::= IF <expression> <then clause> <else clause> ENDIF
77       <then clause> ::= THEN <statement>; <statement list>
78       <else clause> ::= ELSE <statement>; <statement list>
79           | ε
80       <while stmt> ::= LOOP <statement list> WHILE <expression>;
                 <statement list> ENDLOOP
81       <stop stmt> ::= STOP
82       <assignment stmt> ::= <simpident> <substring> := <expression>
83           | <arrayident> ( <expression> <expressions> ) <substring> := <expression>
84       <substring> ::= ( <start> '|' <length> )
85           | ε
86       <start> ::= <expression>
87       <length> ::= <expression>
88           | ε
89       <read stmt> ::= READ <input goal list>
90       <input goal list> ::= <input goal> <input goals>
91       <input goals> ::= , <input goal> <input goals>
92           | ε
93       <input goal> ::= <simpident>
94           | <arrayident> ( <expression expressions> )
95       <write stmt> ::= WRITE <expression list> USING <literal>
96       <expression list> ::= <expression> <expressions>
97           | ε
98       <expression> ::= <part> <etail>
99       <etail> ::= > <part>
100          | < <part>
101          | = <part>
102          | >= <part>
103          | <= <part>
104          | <> <part>
105          | ε
106      <part> ::= <term> <ptail>
107      <ptail> ::= + <term> <ptail>
108          | – <term> <ptail>
109          | OR <term> <ptail>
110          | ε
111      <term> ::= <factor> <ttail>
112      <ttail> ::= * <factor> <ttail>
113          | / <factor> <ttail>
114          | % <factor> <ttail>
115          | AND <factor> <ttail>
116          | ε
117      <factor> ::= NOT <index>
118          | θ <index>
119          | <index>
120      <index> ::= # <catena>
121          | <catena> <itail>
122      <itail> ::= @ <catena>
123          | ε
124      <catena> ::= <primary> <ctail>
125      <ctail> ::= & <primary> <ctail>
```

```
126         | ε
127    <primary> ::= ( <expression> )
128         | <procident>
129         | <simpident> <substring>
130         | <simpconident> <substring>
131         | <arrayident> ( <expression> <expressions> ) <substring>
132         | <arrayconident> ( <expression> <expressions> ) <substring>
133         | <number>
134         | <literal>
135         | TRUE
136         | FALSE
137    <procname> ::= <newident>
138         | <procident>
```

Note that each production is numbered. These numbers are used in the parser to refer to their associated productions. Note, also, that in the grammar the special symbol θ is used to represent the unary minus operator. Although the unary and binary minus symbols are the same, the scanner is able to determine whether a unary or binary minus sign is being read. Therefore, the parser can be constructed as if these two symbols were different (see Sec. 2-2.5). An empty right-hand side of a production is represented by ϵ.

A formal definition of an LL(1) grammar is presented as follows. A grammar G is LL(1) if and only if

for all rules $A \rightarrow \alpha_1 \mid \alpha_2 \mid ... \mid \alpha_n$,
1. FIRST $(\alpha_i) \cap$ FIRST $(\alpha_j) = \phi$ for all $i \neq j$
and, furthermore, if $\alpha_i \overset{*}{\Rightarrow} \epsilon$, then
2. FIRST $(\alpha_j) \cap$ FOLLOW $(A) = \phi$ for all j.

The FIRST and FOLLOW sets used in this definition can be defined as follows. Given some string $\alpha \in V^*$, the set of terminal symbols given by FIRST (α) represent the leftmost derivable symbols of α and this set is given by the equation

FIRST $(\alpha) = \{w \mid \alpha \overset{*}{\Rightarrow} w... $ and $w \in V \}$

The FOLLOW sets are defined for a nullable nonterminal A (one which can produce the empty string). The definition for the FOLLOW sets is given by

FOLLOW $(A) = \{w \in V \mid S' \overset{*}{\Rightarrow} \alpha A \gamma\}$ where $w \in$ FIRST (γ) and S is the start symbol of the grammar.

The purpose of the FIRST and FOLLOW sets should be intuitive, once the reader has an understanding of the LL(1) parsing algorithm. Recall that when the input stream is being parsed according to an LL(1) grammar, the parsing strategy depends on the leftmost symbol to be expanded and the next input symbol to be matched. The parser must decide on which of the several possible right-hand sides the nonterminal should be expanded. The FIRST set of each right-hand side tells us which input symbols can be matched by that production, if the nonterminal is expanded to that right-hand side. To help illustrate this process, the FIRST sets for the example grammar given earlier in this section are as follows:

FIRST (A#) = {i}   FIRST ([eC]) = {[}
FIRST (iB ← e) = {i}   FIRST (.i) = {.}
FIRST (SB) = {[, .}   FIRST (eC) = {e}

FIRST $(\epsilon) = \{\epsilon\}$ FIRST $(\epsilon) = \{\epsilon\}$

Now consider the situation when S is the nonterminal to be expanded, and the input symbol that is to be matched is [. There are two first sets corresponding to the possible right-hand sides of S. These are {[} and {.}. Since [is an element of the first FIRST set, S is expanded to the right-hand side which has this FIRST set. Therefore, in this situation, S should be expanded using the production S ::= [eC]. As can be seen, if two FIRST sets of one nonterminal contained a common element, then the parser does not know which production to choose when expanding the given nonterminal with the common element as the input symbol. This is the reason why all FIRST sets for one nonterminal must be disjoint in the definition of an LL(1) grammar.

The FIRST sets for the LL(1) grammar of the GAUSS language are given below. The reader is encouraged to check several of these sets in order to gain confidence with the technique that is used to generate them. For simplicity, all FIRST sets are represented as FIRST (x), where x is an integer representing the production number according to the grammar given earlier. The nonterminal associated with each production is also given, so that the reader can verify that the FIRST sets for any nonterminal are mutually disjoint.

\<program\>
        FIRST (1) = {PROC, INTEGER, STRING, LOGICAL, ARRAY}
\<global\>
        FIRST (2) = {PROC}
        FIRST (3) = {INTEGER, STRING, LOGICAL, ARRAY}
\<core\>
        FIRST (4) = {PROC}
        FIRST (5) = {CONST, \<newident\>}
\<declaration list\>
        FIRST (6) = {INTEGER, STRING, LOGICAL, ARRAY}
        FIRST (7) = ϵ
\<procedure list\>
        FIRST (8) = {PROC}
        FIRST (9) = {INTEGER, STRING, LOGICAL}
        FIRST (10) = ϵ
\<declaration\>
        FIRST (11) = {INTEGER, STRING, LOGICAL, ARRAY}
\<entity list\>
        FIRST (12) = {CONST}
        FIRST (13) = {\<newident\>}
\<const list\>
        FIRST (14) = {,}
        FIRST (15) = ϵ
\<type specifier\>
        FIRST (16) = {INTEGER, STRING, LOGICAL}
        FIRST (17) = {ARRAY}
\<simple type\>
        FIRST (18) = {INTEGER}
        FIRST (19) = {STRING}
        FIRST (20) = {LOGICAL}

<array>
      FIRST (21) = {ARRAY}
<bound pair list>
      FIRST (22) = {,}
      FIRST (23) = ϵ
<bound pair>
      FIRST (24) = {NOT, TRUE, FALSE, θ, #, (, <literal>, <number>,
            <simpident>, <arrayident>, <simpconident>,
            <arrayconident>, <procident>}
<second bound>
      FIRST (25) = {:}
      FIRST (26) = ϵ
<constant>
      FIRST (27) = {θ, TRUE, FALSE, <number>, <literal>}
      FIRST (28) = {(}
<simple constant>
      FIRST (29) = {θ}
      FIRST (30) = {<number>}
      FIRST (31) = {<literal>}
      FIRST (32) = {TRUE}
      FIRST (33) = {FALSE}
<array constant>
      FIRST (34) = {(}
<simple constant list>
      FIRST (35) = {,}
      FIRST (36) = ϵ
<ident list>
      FIRST (37) = {,}
      FIRST (38) = ϵ
<procedure>
      FIRST (39) = {PROC}
<procedure tail>
      FIRST (40) = {FORWARD}
      FIRST (41) = {INTEGER, STRING, LOGICAL, ARRAY, <simpident>,
            <arrayident>, <procident>, RETURN, IF, LOOP, STOP,
            READ, WRITE}
<procedure body>
      FIRST (42) = {INTEGER, STRING, LOGICAL, ARRAY, <simpident>,
            <arrayident>, <procident>, RETURN, IF, LOOP, STOP,
            READ, WRITE}
<statement list>
      FIRST (43) = {<simpident>, <arrayident>, <procident>, RETURN, IF,
            LOOP, STOP, READ, WRITE}
      FIRST (44) = ϵ
      FIRST (45) = {(}
      FIRST (46) = ϵ
<parameters>
      FIRST (47) = {,}
      FIRST (48) = ϵ

      FIRST (49) = {INTEGER, STRING, LOGICAL, ARRAY}
      FIRST (50) = {INTEGER, STRING, LOGICAL}
      FIRST (51) = {ARRAY}
<comma list>
      FIRST (52) = {,}
      FIRST (53) = ϵ
<statement>
      FIRST (54) = {<procident>}
      FIRST (55) = {RETURN}
      FIRST (56) = {IF}
      FIRST (57) = {LOOP}
      FIRST (58) = {STOP}
      FIRST (59) = {<simpident>, <arrayident>}
      FIRST (60) = {READ}
      FIRST (61) = {WRITE}
<procedure call>
      FIRST (62) = {<procident>}
<argument list>
      FIRST (63) = {(}
      FIRST (64) = ϵ
<arguments>
      FIRST (65) = {,}
      FIRST (66) = ϵ
<argument>
      FIRST (67) = {<simpident>}
      FIRST (68) = {<arrayident>}
<sublist>
      FIRST (69) = {(}
      FIRST (70) = ϵ
<expressions>
      FIRST (71) = {,}
      FIRST (72) = ϵ
<return stmt>
      FIRST (73) = {RETURN}
<ret expression>
      FIRST (74) = {NOT, θ, #, (, TRUE, FALSE, <literal>, <number>,
             <simpident>, <simpconident>, <arrayident>, <arrayconident>,
             <procident>}
      FIRST (75) = ϵ
<if stmt>
      FIRST (76) = {IF}
<then clause>
      FIRST (77) = {THEN}
<else clause>
      FIRST (78) = {ELSE}
      FIRST (79) = ϵ
<while stmt>
      FIRST (80) = {LOOP}

<stop stmt>
      FIRST (81) = {STOP}
<assignment stmt>
      FIRST (82) = {<simpident>}
      FIRST (83) = {<arrayident>}
<substring>
      FIRST (84) = {(}
      FIRST (85) = ϵ
<start>
      FIRST (86) = {NOT, θ, #, (, TRUE, FALSE, <literal>, <number>,
            <simpident>, <simpconident>, <arrayident>,
            <arrayconident>, <procident>}
<length>
      FIRST (87) = {NOT, θ, #, (, TRUE, FALSE, <literal>, <number>,
            <simpident>, <simpconident>, <arrayident>,
            <arrayconident>, <procident>
      FIRST (88) = ϵ
<read stmt>
      FIRST (89) = {READ}
<input goal list>
      FIRST (90) = {<simpident>, <arrayident>}
<input goals>
      FIRST (91) = {,}
      FIRST (92) = ϵ
<input goal>
      FIRST (93) = {<simpident>}
      FIRST (94) = {<arrayident>}
      FIRST (95) = {WRITE}
<expression list>
      FIRST (96) = {NOT, θ, #, (, TRUE, FALSE, <literal>, <number>,
            <simpident>, <simpconident>, <arrayident>,
            <arrayconident>, <procident>}
      FIRST (97) = θ

<expression>
      FIRST (98) = {NOT, θ, #, (, TRUE, FALSE, <literal>, <number>,
            <simpident>, <simpconident>, <arrayident>,
            <arrayconident>, <procident>}
<etail>
      FIRST (99) = {>}
      FIRST (100) = {<}
      FIRST (101) = {=}
      FIRST (102) = {>=}
      FIRST (103) = {<=}
      FIRST (104) = {<>}
      FIRST (105) = ϵ
<part>
      FIRST (106) = {NOT, θ, #, (, TRUE, FALSE, <literal>, <number>,
            <simpident>, <simpconident>, <arrayident>,
            <arrayconident>, <procident>}

<ptail>
      FIRST (107) = {+}
      FIRST (108) = {−}
      FIRST (109) = {OR}
      FIRST (110) = ϵ
<term>
      FIRST (111) = {NOT, θ, #, (, TRUE, FALSE, <literal>, <number>,
            <simpident>, <simpconident>, <arrayident>,
            <arrayconident>, <procident>}
<ttail>
      FIRST (112) = {*}
      FIRST (113) = {/}
      FIRST (114) = {%}
      FIRST (115) = {AND}
      FIRST (116) = ϵ
<factor{
      FIRST (117) = {NOT}
      FIRST (118) = {θ}
      FIRST (119) = {#, (, TRUE, FALSE, <literal>, <number>, <simpident>,
            <simpconident>, <arrayident>, <arrayconident>,
            <procident>}
<index>
      FIRST (120) = {#}
      FIRST (121) = {(, TRUE, FALSE, <literal>, <number>, <simpident>,
            <simpconident>, <arrayident>, <arrayconident>,
            <procident>}
<itail>
      FIRST (122) = {@}
      FIRST (123) = ϵ
<catena>
      FIRST (124) = {(, <simpident>, <simpconident>, <arrayident>,
            <arrayconident>, <procident>, TRUE, FALSE, <literal>,
            <number>}
<ctail>
      FIRST (125) = {&}
      FIRST (126) = ϵ
<primary>
      FIRST (127) = {(}
      FIRST (128) = {<procident>}
      FIRST (129) = {<simpident>}
      FIRST (130) = {<simpconident>}
      FIRST (131) = {<arrayident>}
      FIRST (132) = {<arrayconident>}
      FIRST (133) = {<number>}
      FIRST (134) = {<literal>}
      FIRST (135) = {TRUE}
      FIRST (136) = {FALSE}
      FIRST (137) = {<newident>}
      FIRST (138) = {<procident>}

The FOLLOW sets are similar to the FIRST sets, but they need to be defined only for those nonterminals which can produce the empty string. The FOLLOW set for a nonterminal A, is defined such that, if there exists a right-hand side of the form AB, and A can be expanded to the empty string, then FOLLOW (A) gives the leftmost derivable symbols that can be generated from B.

As an example, we give the FOLLOW sets for our example grammar given earlier.

FOLLOW (B) = {←}
FOLLOW (C) = {]}

Consider now, the case where an attempt is made to expand the nonterminal symbol C to match the input symbol]. The FIRST sets of C are {e} and {ε}. Since the input symbol is not an element of either of these sets, the FOLLOW set of C is examined. Since] is an element of the FOLLOW set of C, then we know that we should expand C to the empty production, and that some other symbol of the sentential form will match the input symbol].

Since the FOLLOW set just gives the nonterminals for which a certain production can be used, it is much like a FIRST set as described earlier. The elements of a FOLLOW set must be disjoint with all of the FIRST sets of the productions of that nonterminal. If there is a common element between a FOLLOW set and one of its associated FIRST sets, the parser does not know whether to expand the nonterminal to the production specified by the FIRST set, or whether the nonterminal should be expanded to the empty right-hand side as specified by the FOLLOW set. This restriction constitutes the remainder of the definition of an LL(1) grammar.

The FOLLOW sets for the nullable nonterminals of the GAUSS grammar are given here for a reference.

FOLLOW (<declaration list>) = {<simpident>, <arrayident>,
    <procident>, RETURN, IF, LOOP, STOP, READ, WRITE}
FOLLOW (<procedure list>) = {#EOF}
FOLLOW (<const list>) = {;}
FOLLOW (<bound pair list>) = {)}
FOLLOW (<second bound>) = {), ,}
FOLLOW (<simple constant list>) = {)}
FOLLOW (<ident list>) = {;}
FOLLOW (<statement list>) = {ENDPROC, ELSE, ENDIF, WHILE,
    ENDLOOP}
FOLLOW (<parameter list>) = {<simpident>, <arrayident>,
    <procident>, FORWARD, INTEGER, STRING, LOGICAL,
    ARRAY, RETURN, IF, LOOP, STOP, READ, WRITE}
FOLLOW (<parameters>) = {)}
FOLLOW (<comma list>) = {)}
FOLLOW (<argument list>) = {;}
FOLLOW (<arguments>) = {)}
FOLLOW (<sublist>) = {), ,}
FOLLOW (<ret expression>) = {;}
FOLLOW (<else clause>) = {ENDIF}
FOLLOW (<substring>) = {:=, &, @, *, /, %, AND, +, –, OR, >, <,
    =, >=, <=, <>, ,,), |, ;, :, THEN, USING}

FOLLOW (<length>) = {)}
FOLLOW (<input goals>) = {;}
FOLLOW (<expression list>) = {USING}
FOLLOW (<expressions>) = {USING,)}
FOLLOW (<etail>) = {:, ,,), ;, |, THEN, USING}
FOLLOW (<ptail>) = {:, ,,), ;, |, <, <=, >, >=, =, <>,
     THEN, USING}
FOLLOW (<ttail>) = {+, -, OR, :, ,,), ;, |, <, <=, >, >=,
     =, <>, THEN, USING}
FOLLOW (<itail>) = {*, /, %, AND, +, -, OR, :, ,,), ;, |,
     <, <=, >, >=, =, <>, THEN, USING}
FOLLOW (<ctail>) = @, *, /, %, AND, +, -, OR, :, ,,), ;,
     |, <, <=, >, >=, =, <>, THEN, USING}

Now that we have the necessary sets of data to perform a parse, we can explore the parsing technique used when parsing languages given by LL(1) grammars.

2-3.3 Parsing Function

An LL(1) parser can be defined by a parsing function, $M(x,y)$, where x denotes the current symbol on top of the stack, and y is the current input symbol. M is defined as follows:

1. $M(a, a) = pop$, for all $a \in V_T$
2. $M(\#, \#) = accept$
3. $M(A, a) = (\alpha, i)$ for all $a \in$ FIRST (α)
   where $A \rightarrow \alpha$ is the ith production
4. $M(A, b) = (\alpha, i)$ for all $b \in$ FOLLOW (A)
   where $A \rightarrow \epsilon$ is the ith production
5. $M(z, a) = error$ for all $z \in V \cup \{\#\}$ and $a \in V_T \cup \{\#\}$
   such that none of 1, 2, 3, or 4 apply

In this definition, *pop* indicates that the top element of the parse stack should be popped off and the current input symbol should be replaced by the next input symbol. The *accept* action indicates that a successful parse has been completed. The *error* action occurs when there is an error in the input stream being parsed. The (α, i) action means that the right-hand side of production number i should replace the current symbol on top of the parse stack. The # symbol marks the bottom of the stack and the end of the input string.

With this definition, the parsing function can be obtained for the example grammar given earlier in this section. This parsing function is best represented by a table as shown in Fig. 2-5.

As a reference the LL(1) parsing table for the GAUSS compiler is given in Sec. 2-3.7. The table is called LL1_parsetab and each row is preceded by a comment containing the name of the corresponding symbol. All error entries in the table are marked '@error'. The '@pop' entries indicate that the top element of the parse stack should be removed. The '@accept' entry indicates a successful parse, i.e., the GAUSS program being compiled is syntactically valid. The entries marked by an integer x mean that the top symbol of the stack should be expanded according to production x of the revised grammar presented in Sec. 2-3.2.

Stack Symbol	Current Input Symbol						
	i	←	e	[	]	.	#
S′	(A#,1)						
A	(iB←e,1)						
B		(ε,3)		(SB,2)		(SB,2)	
S				([eC],4)		(.i,5)	
C			(eC,6)		(ε,7)		
i	pop						
←		pop					
e			pop				
[				pop			
]					pop		
.						pop	
#							accept

All blank entries are error entries

Fig. 2-5   LL(1) parsing table for an example grammar

During an expansion, the elements of the right-hand side of a certain production are pushed onto the parse stack. Because of this, it is necessary to store the right-hand side for each production of the LL(1) grammar. This is done in the *rhs_prod* table. This table is actually a vector, with the token values of each terminal, nonterminal, and action symbol used to represent the right-hand side. For example, the right-hand side of the production

<if stmt> ::= IF <expression> <then clause> <else clause> ENDIF

would appear in the table as

#if, $expression, ##(273), $then_clause, $else_clause, ##(275), #endif,

The right-hand sides appear one after the other in the order that they appear in the grammar. Note, however, that the right-hand side has been augmented by the action symbols ##(273) and ##(275). These symbols do not define any syntactic aspect of the language. They are simply cues to the parser that denote when particular action routines are to be invoked to perform some semantic activity such as generating object-code instructions. Throughout the remainder of our discussion on the parser we ignore action symbols. They are discussed later in Sec. 2-5, which describes the code generation process. They need not concern us at the present time because, typically, these action symbols are added to the grammar description after the parser has been implemented.

In order to reference a particular right-hand side, the *prod_index* table must be used. Each entry in this table gives the starting position in *rhs_prod* for the corresponding production. For example, in order to access the right-hand side of production 36, *prod_index (36)* provides an index into *rhs_prod* where the first symbol of the right-hand side of production 36 begins. Although the *prod_index* table is not really necessary, it allows an 'expand' entry in the LL(1) table to contain the actual production number to be applied, rather than an index into the *rhs_prod* table.

This makes the LL(1) table entries easier to comprehend, despite the added complexity of an extra indexing table. This is important later when action symbols must be added to the grammar as it is much less painful to alter the indices in the *prod_index* table then all the indices in the LL(1) parse table. In effect, we are able to insulate the LL(1) parse table from changes due to the addition of action symbols to the grammar.

2-3.4   Top-down Description of Parser

The parser determines whether or not a GAUSS program follows the syntax rules of the GAUSS language. The parsing procedure, *llparse*, can call three subordinate procedures: *action, err_hand*, and *list_err* as illustrated in the calling sequence of Fig. 2-6.

The purpose of the procedures are now discussed. Details about each procedure will be described in more detail later in this section.

The *action* routine performs semantic (i.e., context sensitive) checking and code generation. This routine is described in Sec. 2-5 on code generation.

The procedure *err_hand* recovers from a parsing error. The procedure looks for a terminal or nonterminal symbol on the stack that can generate the next input symbol. Any symbols above this in the stack are popped off the stack. Finally, the portion of the production that can produce the input symbol is pushed onto the stack. If this fails, the input symbol is deleted from the input.

The procedure *err_hand* can invoke two procedures, namely, *fixup* and *error*. The *fixup* routine is called to take the symbol on top of the stack and expand it until the top stack element is the same as that of the current input symbol. It is invoked by *err_hand* once a portion of a procedure has been pushed onto the stack. The error routine saves the error parameters in a buffer so they can be printed when the *list_err* procedure is invoked.

The *list_err* procedure prints all of the errors for a given input line. It may call procedure *llerror* to generate the error message if an error entry in the LL(1) parse table is found while parsing. Procedure *llerror* may call another procedure, *token_pr*, if the string representation is required.

Figure 2-6 illustrates the calling sequence of these procedures.

2-3.5   Implementation of the Parser

The algorithm for the LL(1) parser comes from Sec. 6-2.5 of Tremblay and Sorenson [1982]. Basically, the parser algorithm works as follows. A stack is used to contain the current sentential form of the parse. The parse starts by initializing the stack to contain the goal symbol of the grammar and the end-of-file marker. The top element of this stack and the current input symbol are used as indices into the parse table described earlier. The corresponding entry in the parse table tells the parser what action to perform. If the action denotes an expansion, then the top symbol of the stack (a nonterminal symbol) is replaced by the right-hand side of the production for this nonterminal. The parse table entry indicates which right-hand side is to be used. If the action is an accept action, then the parser is finished, since the input that has been read is a syntactically correct program. If the action to be performed is a pop operation, then the top element of the stack (a terminal symbol) and the current input symbol are the same. Since the input symbol has been

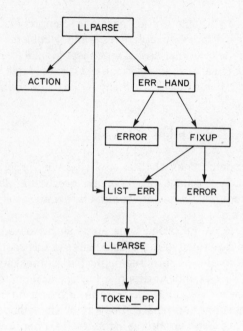

Fig. 2-6   Structure chart of the GAUSS parser

matched, the top element of the stack is removed, and the next input symbol is obtained from the input stream (i.e., from the scanner). If the action denotes an error, then the error handling routine is called to recover from the error. This is discussed further in the next subsection.

The parsing algorithm is given here for a more detailed description.

Algorithm IMPROVED_LL1: Given the parsing table LL1_PARSETAB for a particular grammar G, this algorithm parses strings to determine whether or not these strings belong to the language generated by the grammar. The input string is stored in the string variable INPUT-STRING. The variable CURSOR is the index in INPUT_STRING of the current input symbol. The parsing stack is a vector PARSE with associated stack top indices PARSE_TOP and TRUE_TOP. The variable STACK_SYMBOL is used to hold the current input symbol. P# is a list of production numbers which make up the parse of the input string. The identifier j is a local index variable Finally, we define CURRENT_RHS as the current right-hand side and CURRENT_P# as the current production number from the grammar. The goal symbol of the unaugmented grammar (the left-hand side of production 1) is initially in the variable START.

1.   [Initialize]
        INPUT_STRING ← INPUT_STRING o '#'
        CURSOR ← 1
        PARSE[1] ← '#'
        PARSE[2] ← START
        TRUE_TOP ← PARSE_TOP ← 2
        P# ← "

2. [Parse]
    Repeat while true
        STACK_SYMBOL ← PARSE[PARSE_TOP]
        CURRENT_INPUT ← SUB(INPUT_STRING, CURSOR, 1)
        If LL1_PARSETAB(STACK_SYMBOL, CURRENT_INPUT) =
               (CURRENT_RHS, CURRENT_P#)
        then PARSE_TOP ← PARSE_TOP – 1
           Repeat for j = LENGTH(CURRENT_RHS), ..., 1
               PARSE_TOP ← PARSE_TOP + 1
               PARSE[PARSE_TOP] ← SUB(CURRENT_RHS, j, 1)
           If CURRENT_RHS ≠ ϵ
           then TRUE_TOP ← PARSE_TOP
           P# ← P# o '◻' o CURRENT_P#
        else If LL1_PARSETAB(STACK_SYMBOL, CURRENT_INPUT) = 'pop'
        then PARSE_TOP ← TRUE_TOP ← PARSE_TOP – 1
           CURSOR ← CURSOR + 1
           else If LL1_PARSETAB(STACK_SYMBOL, CURRENT_INPUT) =
             'accept'
           then Write ('SUCCESSFUL PARSE')
               Exit
             else Call ERROR_HANDLER

The second stack pointer in this algorithm, TRUE_TOP, is used when it is necessary to recover from errors as will be explained in the next subsection.

The implementation of the IMPROVED_LL1 algorithm will be exhibited in Sec. 2-3.7. An important data structure in the implementation is the *parse* vector. This vector is used as a parse stack, which contains the current sentential form. The variable *parse_top* is used to point to the element of *parse* that is currently the top element of the stack. The stack is manipulated by two macro procedures *s_push* and *s_pop*. They were implemented as macro procedures in order to have the code in-line. The use of macros reduces execution time and permits modular code for the parser. Since a significant amount of execution time for a compilation is spent in the parser, efficient execution in this part of the compiler is necessary.

The *s_push* procedure is used to push the right-hand side of a production onto the parse stack. The argument that *s_push* receives is the number of the production whose right-hand side is to be stacked. This is used as an index into *prod_index* to find the location in *rhs_prod* of the beginning of this production. The production must be stacked in reverse order so that the first symbol of the right-hand side appears at the top of the stack when the operation is finished. This allows the procedure to find the beginning of the right-hand side of the next production, and then work backwards to the beginning of the production that needs to be stacked, stacking the items as it proceeds. The procedure also sets the *parse_top* pointer to the top of the stack as required. Checking is done in order to ensure that the limits of the parse stack are not overflowed.

The *s_pop* procedure is used to remove the top element from the parse stack *parse*. It checks for the presence of at least two elements on the stack, and, if successful, removes its top element by decrementing the stack top pointer, *parse_top*. There must be at least two elements in the stack before a pop can take place, since the bottom element is the end-of-file marker. This marker is only used to match the corresponding end-of-file marker that is received as an input token when the end of the GAUSS program is encountered. At this time the parser returns control to the procedure which called the parser.

To aid in the debugging of the parser, certain information is printed with each parse action if the *ll1_debug* flag is set to true. After each table reference in which the parser determines what action is required, the stack contents and the current input symbol are printed. Then, if the action is an expansion, the debugging code prints which nonterminal on top of the stack is being expanded. If the action is anything but an expansion, the debugging code simply prints what action is taken. The debugging output allows the programmer to determine what is actually happening during the parse. In particular, he or she can see what is happening to the stack, which elements are being popped, which elements are being expanded, what symbols the elements are being expanded to, and when an error occurs. This gives enough information to determine what is going wrong when the parser is not working correctly.

Now that the basics of building a parser for an LL(1) grammar have been discussed, one question still remains. If the compiler receives a syntactically erroneous program to be compiled, what should be done when the parser encounters an error entry from the parsing table? This question is discussed in the next subsection.

2-3.6 Syntactic Error Recovery

When the parser encounters an error entry in the parsing table, there are several different things that the compiler can do. One of the simplest approaches is to report the error and stop. This method of error recovery is simple to implement, but is not very useful as far as the user is concerned. To force the user to correct the single error detected and then resubmit the program to the compiler is an indication of a poor compiler implementation. Such an approach is unacceptable.

Another possibility is to correct the error and continue, so that the program will compile correctly. Unfortunately, this involves determining what the user intended to write as opposed to what was actually written. This problem has not been solved since it requires capabilities akin to telepathy. A reasonable compromise between these two methods of error recovery is what is known as error repair. This involves reporting the error, and then fixing the parse stack and the input program so that parsing can continue to the end of the program. This allows all errors to be detected and reported in one run, without having to decide exactly what the user had intended in place of the errors.

The error recovery strategy followed in this implementation is that of error repair. When an error occurs, the contents of the stack and the input stream must somehow be adjusted so that parsing can continue. The complexity of the error recovery system is related to its effectiveness. A system can be built which will repair errors very well, but the system is probably fairly complex. If a simple error repair system is implemented, the error repairs may not be as good, and avalanches of errors may occur. This happens when one error is incorrectly repaired, so that subsequent input which is actually correct is determined to be faulty by the parser.

The method used to recover from errors is loosely based on the Fisher, Milton and Quiring [1977] method. However, while the latter method modifies only the unparsed portion of the input string in making its repair, the method used here modifies the unparsed portion of the input string and the stack contents. The modification of the stack by the insertion or deletion of symbols indicates that the generation of code cannot be continued, since the parse actions required to obtain the stack contents of the modified stack are not readily available.

The most important part of the error recovery method is the *prefix* table. This table is used to determine whether it is possible to generate the given input symbol from a certain symbol on the stack. The elements of this table are integers. If an entry is zero, this means that it is not possible to generate the given input symbol from the stack symbol. If the entry is nonzero, then it is of the form xxxyy. The xxx portion of the entry indicates that if the stack symbol is expanded according to production xxx of the grammar, we can generate the given input symbol. The yy portion of the entry indicates that it is the yy symbol of this production which will generate the input symbol. This is required, since more than one symbol may have been omitted and the production may contain nullable symbols.

The basic algorithm works as follows. Starting at the top of the stack, use each element of the stack and the current input symbol as indices into the *prefix* table. If the entry is zero, continue to the next stack element and repeat the procedure. If the entry is nonzero, then the stack symbol has to be expanded according to the production specified in the *prefix* table entry. When this is done, the first part of the production before the specified element which is desired, is NOT placed on the stack. The remaining part of the production is placed on the stack as specified. Once this is done the top symbol is again expanded according to its *prefix* table entry, until the top symbol is a terminal symbol. This terminal symbol on the stack should then match the current input symbol, and parsing can be resumed. Note, that when no element of the parse stack can generate the input symbol, the input symbol is deleted and the parser is allowed to continue parsing, if possible. In this case, it is not necessary to stop the code generation, since the stack has not been altered.

In the source code for the parser, it will be seen that the *err_hand* procedure is the one that searches the stack for a symbol (terminal or nonterminal) which will generate the input symbol. This procedure also deletes the input symbol if such a stack symbol cannot be found. If, however, a stack symbol can be found, then the *fixup* routine performs the stacking of the appropriate productions so that parsing can be resumed.

Consider the following example, in which the input is

WHILE X = 3; ...

and the stack contents are

       <statement>
       ;
     <statement list>
        .
        .
        .

The programmer obviously wants a LOOP statement which starts with the LOOP keyword. This keyword, however, has been omitted. When the parser tries to parse this input, it will immediately detect the error and call the *err_hand* routine. This routine will first attempt the table access *prefix ($statement, #while)*

The value for this table element is 5701. Since this element is nonzero, it means that it is possible to obtain WHILE from the nonterminal <statement>. This number, and the location on the stack of the symbol <statement> are then passed to the *fixup* routine. This routine interprets the number 5701 as follows. The 57 indicates that it is production 57 of the grammar which we want to stack. Production 57 is given by

<statement> ::= <while statement>

The 01 indicates that it is the first element of the right-hand side of this production which can generate the given input symbol of WHILE. After the production is stacked, the *parse* stack will look as follows:

    <while stmt>
        ;
    <statement list>
        .
        .
        .

The input will still be as before.

Now, the *fixup* routine will take the top stack symbol (<while stmt>) and reference the *prefix* table with it and the input symbol WHILE. The value for this entry is 8003. This means that <while stmt> must be expanded according to production number 80, which is

<while stmt> ::= LOOP <statement list> WHILE <expression>;
            <statement list> ENDLOOP

The 03 means that it is the third element of this production which can generate the input symbol WHILE. Thus the production is stacked only from the third symbol onward. After this has been done, the stack will appear as follows:

        WHILE
    <expression>
        ;
    <statement list>
        ENDLOOP
        ;
    <statement list>
        .
        .
        .

The input string remains as before. Since the top element of the stack is now the same as the current input symbol, control is returned to the *err_hand* routine which in turn passes control to the parser, where parsing can continue.

Since the *prefix* table is so important in the error recovery scheme, it is presented in the program listing given in the next subsection. The generation of this table is not an easy task. The basic algorithm used is that given in Sec. 6-2.5 in Tremblay and Sorenson [1982], which computes the prefix table required for the Fisher, Milton and Quiring method of error recovery. This was done by hand, and the entries were not always made as computed, although not many changes were made. It was found in creating this table, however, that it was possible to obtain almost any input symbol from a given stack symbol. The algorithm would expand many productions, filling the stack with legal, but highly improbable parts of productions. This in turn led to an avalanche of errors. To correct this fault, it was necessary to go through the table and decide by examination of the grammar whether a given input symbol should be allowed to be generated from a given stack symbol when an error was being repaired. The entries that were in the table were correct—it was only necessary to change many of them to zero entries to allow only reasonable expansions to occur. This resulted in a recovery method which was more accurate, and would not cause such severe error avalanches.

For example, if the parser was currently parsing an IF statement, and the stack contents were

>   ELSE
>   <statement>
>   ;
>   .
>   .
>   .

and the input symbols were

>   ELSE TRUE ...

then the following processing takes place. The parser pops the ELSE from the stack and also deletes the ELSE from the input stream. Then it attempts to parse with <statement> on top of the stack and TRUE as the input symbol. This is, of course, an error. With the original table, the error recovery routine changes the stack contents to

>   TRUE
>   <ctail>
>   <itail>
>   <ttail>
>   <ptail>
>   <etail>
>   ;
>   .
>   .
>   .

The problem with this is that many symbols have been placed on the parse stack all of which must eventually be matched by symbols in the input stream. It has been our experience that expecting this many input symbols to appear after the original error is unlikely. In this case, the symbol TRUE will probably be deleted from the input stream, depending on what other symbols occur on the stack.

Since such an ad hoc method was used to construct this table, it was necessary to imbed checking into the error handler procedures in case the entries in the table were not properly constructed. If such an error does arise, it will cause a *complier error* message to be printed out.

In the next subsection the source code for the parser is given.

2-3.7 LL(1) Parser Source Code

The source code for the parser is given in Fig. 2-7.

```
/********************************************/
/*                                        */
/*            llparse                      */
/*                                        */
/********************************************/

/* This procedure is designed to parse GAUSS programs according to
   the LL(1) parsing method.  The algorithm for this procedure has
   been taken from Section 6-2.5 of Tremblay and Sorenson's
   'The Theory and Practice of Compiler Writing'.  The necessary tables
   etc. are described below.  The correspondence between
   the variables of the algorithm and those in this programs are as
   follows:
            algorithm name        program name
            PARSE                 parse
            PARSE_TOP             parse_top
            CURRENT_INPUT         next_token
            LL1_PARSETAB          ll1_parsetab
            TRUE_TOP              true_top
   */

llparse:  PROCEDURE RETURNS (BIT (1));

/* The following table embodies the LL(1) parse table as generated
   from the LL(1) grammar for gauss.  Each group of lines separated
   by double spaces represents one row of the table.  The entries
   marked by '@pop' indicate that the stack should be popped.  '@error'
   entries indicate the error entries, and '@accept' entries indicate
   an accept entry.  Entries with integer values between 1 and 136
   represent the grammar expansion that should be performed with
   the given symbol on the stack top and the current input symbol.
   For example, the entry 3 means that the third production of the
```

Fig. 2-7   Source code for the parser

grammar should be applied. The expansions are obtained from the 'prod_index' and the 'rhs_prod' tables. */

DECLARE ll1_parsetab (#_of_symbols, #_of_terminals) FIXED BIN (15)
STATIC INITIAL

/* and */	(@pop, (56) @error,
/* array */	@error, @pop, (55) @error,
/* const */	(2) @error, @pop, (54) @error,
/* else */	(3) @error, @pop, (53) @error,
/* endif */	(4) @error, @pop, (52) @error,
/* endloop */	(5) @error, @pop, (51) @error,
/* endproc */	(6) @error, @pop, (50) @error,
/* false */	(7) @error, @pop, (49) @error,
/* forward */	(8) @error, @pop, (48) @error,
/* if */	(9) @error, @pop, (47) @error,
/* integer */	(10) @error, @pop, (46) @error,
/* logical */	(11) @error, @pop, (45) @error,
/* loop */	(12) @error, @pop, (44) @error,
/* not */	(13) @error, @pop, (43) @error,
/* of */	(14) @error, @pop, (42) @error,
/* or */	(15) @error, @pop, (41) @error,
/* proc */	(16) @error, @pop, (40) @error,
/* read */	(17) @error, @pop, (39) @error,
/* return */	(18) @error, @pop, (38) @error,
/* string */	(19) @error, @pop, (37) @error,
/* stop */	(20) @error, @pop, (36) @error,

Fig. 2-7   Source code for the parser (cont'd.)

/* then */   (21) @error, @pop, (35) @error,

/* true */   (22) @error, @pop, (34) @error,

/* using */   (23) @error, @pop, (33) @error,

/* while */   (24) @error, @pop, (32) @error,

/* write */   (25) @error, @pop, (31) @error,

/* arrayident */   (26) @error, @pop, (30) @error,

/* arrayconident */ (27) @error, @pop, (29) @error,

/* := */   (28) @error, @pop, (28) @error,

/* : */   (29) @error, @pop, (27) @error,

/* , */   (30) @error, @pop, (26) @error,

/* & */   (31) @error, @pop, (25) @error,

/* / */   (32) @error, @pop, (24) @error,

/* eof */   (33) @error, @accept, (23) @error,

/* = */   (34) @error, @pop, (22) @error,

/* >= */   (35) @error, @pop, (21) @error,

/* > */   (36) @error, @pop, (20) @error,

/* @ */   (37) @error, @pop, (19) @error,

/* <= */   (38) @error, @pop, (18) @error,

/* # */   (39) @error, @pop, (17) @error,

/* literal */   (40) @error, @pop, (16) @error,

/* (*/   (41) @error, @pop, (15) @error,

/* < */   (42) @error, @pop, (14) @error,

/* - */   (43) @error, @pop, (13) @error,

/* * */   (44) @error, @pop, (12) @error,

/* % */   (45) @error, @pop, (11) @error,

Fig. 2-7 Source code for the parser (cont'd.)

```
/* <> */              (46) @error, @pop, (10) @error,

/* newident */        (47) @error, @pop, (9) @error,

/* number */          (48) @error, @pop, (8) @error,

/* + */               (49) @error, @pop, (7) @error,

/* procident */       (50) @error, @pop, (6) @error,

/* ) */               (51) @error, @pop, (5) @error,

/* ; */               (52) @error, @pop, (4) @error,

/* simpident */       (53) @error, @pop, (3) @error,

/* simpconident */    (54) @error, @pop, (2) @error,

/* | */               (55) @error, @pop, @error,

/* uminus */          (56) @error, @pop,

/* program */         @error, 1, (8) @error, 1, 1, (4) @error, 1, (2) @error,
                      1, (37) @error,

/* global */          @error, 3, (8) @error, 3, 3, (4) @error, 2, (2) @error,
                      3, (37) @error,

/* core */            (2) @error, 5, (13) @error, 4, (30) @error, 5,
                      (9) @error,

/* declaration list */ @error, 6, (7) @error, 7, 6, 6, 7, (4) @error, 7, 7,
                      6, 7, (4) @error, 7, 7, (23) @error, 7, (2) @error,
                      7, (3) @error,

/* procedure list */  (10) @error, 9, 9, (4) @error, 8, (2) @error, 9,
                      (13) @error, 10, (23) @error,

/* declaration */     @error, 11, (8) @error, 11, 11, (7) @error, 11,
                      (37) @error,

/* entity list */     (2) @error, 12, (44) @error, 13, (9) @error,

/* const list */      (30) @error, 14, (21) @error, 15, (4) @error,

/* type specifier */  @error, 17, (8) @error, 16, 16, (7) @error, 16,
                      (37) @error,

/* simple type */     (10) @error, 18, 20, (7) @error, 19, (37) @error,
```

Fig. 2-7 Source code for the parser (cont'd.)

```
/* array */          @error, 21, (55) @error,

/* bound pair list */ (30) @error, 22, (20) @error, 23, (5) @error,

/* bound pair */     (26) @error, (2) 24, (11) @error, (3) 24,
                     (6) @error, 24, @error, 24, (2) @error, 24, 24,
                     @error, 24,

/* second bound */   (29) @error, 25, 26, (20) @error, 26, (5) @error,

/* constant */       (7) @error, 27, (14) @error, 27, (17) @error, 27, 28,
                     (6) @error, 27, (7) @error, 27,

/* simple constant */ (7) @error, 33, (14) @error, 32, (17) @error, 31,
                     (7) @error, 30, (7) @error, 29,

/* array constant */ (41) @error, 34, (15) @error,

/* simple constant list */   (30) @error, 35, (20) @error, 36, (5) @error,

/* ident list */     (30) @error, 37, (21) @error, 38, (4) @error,

/* procedure */      (16) @error, 39, (40) @error,

/* procedure tail */ @error, 41, (6) @error, 40, (4) 41, (4) @error, (4) 41,
                     (4) @error, 41, 41, (23) @error, 41, (2) @error, 41,
                     (3) @error,

/* procedure body */ @error, 42, (7) @error, (4) 42, (4) @error, (4) 42,
                     (4) @error, 42, 42, (23) @error, 42, (2) @error, 42,
                     (3) @error,

/* statement list */ (3) @error, (4) 44, (2) @error, 43, (2) @error, 43,
                     (4) @error, 43, 43, @error, 43, (3) @error, 44, 43, 43,
                     (23) @error, 43, (2) @error, 43, (3) @error,

/* parameter list */ @error, 46, (6) @error, (5) 46, (4) @error, (4) 46,
                     (4) @error, 46, 46, (14) @error, 45, (8) @error, 46,
                     (2) @error, 46, (3) @error,

/* parameters */     (30) @error, 47, (20) @error, 48, (5) @error,

/* parameter */      @error, 49, (8) @error, 49, 49, (7) @error, 49,
                     (37) @error,

/* parameter type */ @error, 51, (8) @error, 50, 50, (7) @error, 50,
                     (37) @error,

/* comma list */     (30) @error, 52, (20) @error, 53, (5) @error,
```

Fig. 2-7 Source code for the parser (cont'd.)

/* statement */   (9) @error, 56, (2) @error, 57, (4) @error, 60, 55, @error, 58, (4) @error, 61, 59, (23) @error, 54, (2) @error, 59, (3) @error,

/* procedure call */ (50) @error, 62, (6) @error,

/* argument list */ (41) @error, 63, (10) @error, 64, (4) @error,

/* arguments */   (30) @error, 65, (20) @error, 66, (5) @error,

/* argument */   (26) @error, 68, (26) @error, 67, (3) @error,

/* sublist */   (30) @error, 70, (10) @error, 69, (9) @error, 70, (5) @error,

/* return stmt */   (18) @error, 73, (38) @error,

/* ret expression */ (7) @error, 74, (5) @error, 74, (8) @error, 74, (3) @error, 74, 74, (11) @error, (3) 74, (6) @error, 74, @error, 74, @error, 75, 74, 74, @error, 74,

/* if stmt */   (9) @error, 76, (47) @error,

/* then clause */   (21) @error, 77, (35) @error,

/* else clause */   (3) @error, 78, 79, (52) @error,

/* while stmt */   (12) @error, 80, (44) @error,

/* stop stmt */   (20) @error, 81, (36) @error,

/* assignment stmt */ (26) @error, 83, (26) @error, 82, (3) @error,

/* substring */   85, (14) @error, 85, (5) @error, 85, @error, 85, (4) @error, (5) 85, @error, (5) 85, (2) @error, 84, (5) 85, (2) @error, 85, @error, 85, 85, (2) @error, 85, @error,

/* start */   (26) @error, 86, 86, (11) @error, (3) 86, (6) @error, 86, @error, 86, (2) @error, 86, 86, @error, 86,

/* length */   (7) @error, 87, (5) @error, 87, (8) @error, 87, (3) @error, 87, 87, (11) @error, (3) 87, (6) @error, 87, @error, 87, 88, @error, 87, 87, @error, 87,

/* read stmt */   (17) @error, 89, (39) @error,

/* input goal list */ (26) @error, 90, (26) @error, 90, (3) @error,

Fig. 2-7   Source code for the parser (cont'd.)

```
/* input goals */     (30) @error, 91, (21) @error, 92, (4) @error,

/* input goal */      (26) @error, 94, (26) @error, 93, (3) @error,

/* write stmt */      (25) @error, 95, (31) @error,

/* expression list */ (7) @error, 96, (5) @error, 96, (8) @error, 96, 97,
                      (2) @error, 96, 96, (11) @error, 96, 96, 96, (6) @error,
                      96, @error, 96, (2) @error, 96, 96, @error, 96,

/* expressions */     (23) @error, 72, (6) @error, 71, (20) @error,
                      72, (5) @error,

/* expression */      (7) @error, 98, (5) @error, 98, (8) @error, 98,
                      (3) @error, 98, 98, (11) @error, (3) 98, (6) @error,
                      98, @error, 98, (2) @error, 98, 98, @error, 98,

/* etail */           (21) @error, 105, @error, 105, (5) @error, 105, 105,
                      (3) @error, 101, 102, 99, @error, 103, (3) @error,
                      100, (3) @error, 104, (4) @error, 105, 105, (2) @error,
                      105, @error,

/* part */            (7) @error, 106, (5) @error, 106, (8) @error, 106,
                      (3) @error, 106, 106, (11) @error, (3) 106, (6) @error,
                      106, @error, 106, (2) @error, 106, 106, @error, 106,

/* ptail */           (15) @error, 109, (5) @error, 110, @error, 110,
                      (5) @error, 110, 110, (3) @error, (3) 110, @error,
                      110, (3) @error, 110, 108, (2) @error, 110, (2) @error,
                      107, @error, 110, 110, (2) @error, 110, @error,

/* term */            (7) @error, 111, (5) @error, 111, (8) @error, 111,
                      (3) @error, 111, 111, (11) @error, (3) 111, (6) @error,
                      111, @error, 111, (2) @error, 111, 111, @error, 111,

/* ttail */           115, (14) @error, 116, (5) @error, 116, @error, 116,
                      (5) @error, 116, 116, @error, 113, @error, (3) 116,
                      @error, 116, (3) @error, 116, 116, 112, 114, 116,
                      (2) @error, 116, @error, 116, 116, (2) @error, 116,
                      @error,

/* factor */          (7) @error, 119, (5) @error, 117, (8) @error, 119,
                      (3) @error, 119, 119, (11) @error, (3) 119, (6) @error,
                      119, @error, 119, (2) @error, 119, 119, @error, 118,

/* index */           (7) @error, 121, (14) @error, 121, (3) @error,
                      121, 121, (11) @error, 120, 121, 121, (6) @error, 121,
                      @error, 121, (2) @error, 121, 121, (2) @error,
```

Fig. 2-7   Source code for the parser (cont'd.)

```
/* itail */          123, (14) @error, 123, (5) @error, 123, @error, 123,
                     (5) @error, 123, 123, @error, 123, @error, (3) 123,
                     122, 123, (3) @error, (5) 123, (2) @error, 123,
                     @error, 123, 123, (2) @error, 123, @error,

/* catena */         (7) @error, 124, (14) @error, 124, (3) @error,
                     124, 124, (12) @error, 124, 124, (6) @error, 124,
                     @error, 124, (2) @error, 124, 124, (2) @error,

/* ctail */          126, (14) @error, 126, (5) @error, 126, @error,
                     126, (5) @error, 126, 126, 125, 126, @error, (5) 126,
                     (3) @error, (5) 126, (2) @error, 126, @error,
                     126, 126, (2) @error, 126, @error,

/* primary */        (7) @error, 136, (14) @error, 135, (3) @error, 131,
                     132, (12) @error, 134, 127, (6) @error, 133, @error,
                     128, (2) @error, 129, 130, (2) @error,

/* proc_name */      (47) @error, 137, (2) @error, 138, (6) @error);
```

/* The following table is used to obtain the right-hand sides of the productions of the grammar. For example, if we want the right-hand side of production 43, then prod_index(43) will give an index into the rhs_prod table where this information can be found. This allows the use of the actual production numbers from the grammar to reference the right-hand sides, rather than an unrelated offset into the rhs_prod table. */

```
DECLARE prod_index (139) FIXED BIN (15) STATIC INITIAL
        (1, 3, 7, 10, 14, 18, 21, 21, 25, 31,
        31, 35, 41, 44, 50, 50, 52, 53, 54, 55,
        56, 64, 67, 67, 71, 74, 75, 77, 79, 82,
        84, 86, 88, 90, 95, 99, 99, 103, 103, 109,
        111, 112, 120, 124, 124, 128, 128, 131, 131, 134,
        136, 144, 147, 147, 148, 149, 150, 151, 152, 153,
        154, 155, 160, 164, 164, 167, 167, 169, 171, 178,
        179, 182, 182, 184, 186, 187, 194, 199, 205, 205,
        215, 217, 225, 237, 242, 243, 244, 246, 247, 249,
        251, 254, 254, 256, 264, 270, 272, 272, 274, 277,
        280, 283, 286, 289, 292, 292, 294, 298, 302, 307,
        307, 309, 313, 317, 321, 326, 326, 329, 332, 333,
        336, 338, 341, 341, 343, 347, 347, 350, 354, 358,
        362, 372, 382, 384, 386, 388, 390, 391, 392);
```

/* The following table contains the right-hand sides for each production of the LL(1) grammar for GAUSS. The table takes the form of a vector. The tokens for the first right-hand side of a production appear first, then the tokens for the

Fig. 2-7 Source code for the parser (cont'd.)

second production, etc. To find the tokens which represent
a particular right-hand side of a production, say 26, it is
necessary to use prod_index (26) which will give the index
into this table of where the right-hand side of production
26 begins. */

```
DECLARE rhs_prod (391) FIXED BIN (15) STATIC INITIAL
/* 1 -- <program> ::= */
     ($global, #eof,
/* 2 -- <global> ::= */
     ##(221), $procedure, #semi, $procedure_list,
/* 3 -- <global> ::= */
     ##(204), $type_specifier, $core,
/* 4 -- <core> ::= */
     ##(222), $procedure, #semi, $procedure_list,
/* 5 -- <core> ::= */
     $entity_list, ##(203), #semi, $global,
/* 6 -- <declaration list> ::= */
     $declaration, #semi, $declaration_list,
/* 7 -- <declaration list> ::= null */
/* 8 -- <procedure list> ::= */
     ##(221), $procedure, #semi, $procedure_list,
/* 9 -- <procedure list> ::= */
     $simple_type, ##(221), ##(205), $procedure, #semi,
     $procedure_list,
/* 10 -- <procedure list> ::= null */
/* 11 -- <declaration> ::= */
     ##(204), $type_specifier, $entity_list, ##(203),
/* 12 -- <entity list> ::= */
     #const, #newident, ##(201), #eq, $constant, $constant_list,
/* 13 -- <entity list> ::= */
     #newident, ##(202), $ident_list,
/* 14 -- <const list> ::= */
     #comma, #newident, ##(201), #eq, $constant, $constant_list,
/* 15 -- <const list> ::= null */
/* 16 -- <type specifier> ::= */
     $simple_type, ##(205),
/* 17 -- <type specifier> ::= */
     $array,
/* 18 -- <simple type> ::= */
     #integer,
/* 19 -- <simple type> ::= */
     #string,
/* 20 -- <simple type> ::= */
     #logical,
/* 21 -- <array> ::= */
     #array, #lparen, $bound_pair, $bound_pair_list,
     #rparen, #of, $simple_type, ##(216),
```

Fig. 2-7   Source code for the parser (cont'd.)

```
/* 22 -- <bound pair list> ::= */
        #comma, $bound_pair, $bound_pair_list,
/* 23 -- <bound pair list> ::= null */
/* 24 -- <bound pair> ::= */
        ##(206), $expression, ##(207), $second_bound,
/* 25 -- <second bound> ::= */
        #colon, $expression, ##(207),
/* 26 -- <second bound> ::= null */
        ##(208),
/* 27 -- <constant> ::= */
        $simple_constant, ##(209),
/* 28 -- <constant> ::= */
        $array_constant, ##(210),
/* 29 -- <simple constant> ::= */
        #uminus, #number, ##(211),
/* 30 -- <simple constant> ::= */
        #number, ##(212),
/* 31 -- <simple constant> ::= */
        #literal, ##(213),
/* 32 -- <simple constant> ::= */
        #true, ##(214),
/* 33 -- <simple constant> ::= */
        #false, ##(215),
/* 34 -- <array constant> ::= */
        #lparen, $simple_constant, ##(217), $simple_constant_list,
        #rparen,
/* 35 -- <simple constant list> ::= */
        #comma, $simple_constant, ##(217), $simple_constant_list,
/* 36 -- <simple constant list> ::= null */
/* 37 -- <ident list> ::= */
        #comma, #newident, ##(202), $ident_list,
/* 38 -- <ident list> ::= null */
/* 39 -- <procedure> ::= */
        #proc, $proc_name, ##(219), $parameter_list, ##(220),
        $procedure_tail,
/* 40 -- <procedure tail> ::= */
        #forward, ##(226),
/* 41 -- <procedure tail> ::= */
        $procedure_body,
/* 42 -- <procedure body> ::= */
        $declaration_list, ##(228), ##(289), $statement, #semi,
        $statement_list, #endproc, ##(229),
/* 43 -- <statement list> ::= */
        ##(289), $statement, #semi, $statement_list,
/* 44 -- <statement list> ::= null */
/* 45 -- <parameter list> ::= */
        #lparen, $parameter, $parameters, #rparen,
/* 46 -- <parameter list> ::= null */
```

Fig. 2-7   Source code for the parser (cont'd.)

```
/* 47 -- <parameters> ::= */
      #comma, $parameter, $parameters,
/* 48 -- <parameters> ::= null */
/* 49 -- <parameter> ::= */
      $parameter_type, #newident, ##(224),
/* 50 -- <parameter type> ::= */
      $simple_type, ##(205),
/* 51 -- <parameter type> ::= */
      #array, #lparen, ##(225), $comma_list, #rparen, #of,
      $simple_type, ##(205),
/* 52 -- <comma list> ::= */
      #comma, ##(225), $comma_list,
/* 53 -- <comma list> ::= null */
/* 54 -- <statement> ::= */
      $procedure_call,
/* 55 -- <statement> ::= */
      $return_stmt,
/* 56 -- <statement> ::= */
      $if_stmt,
/* 57 -- <statement> ::= */
      $while_stmt,
/* 58 -- <statement> ::= */
      $stop_stmt,
/* 59 -- <statement> ::= */
      $assignment_stmt,
/* 60 -- <statement> ::= */
      $read_stmt,
/* 61 -- <statement> ::= */
      $write_stmt,
/* 62 -- <procedure call> ::= */
      #procident, ##(248), $argument_list, ##(249), ##(270),
/* 63 -- <argument list> ::= */
      #lparen, $argument, $arguments, #rparen,
/* 64 -- <argument list> ::= null */
/* 65 -- <arguments> ::= */
      #comma, $argument, $arguments,
/* 66 -- <arguments> ::= null */
/* 67 -- <argument> ::= */
      #simpident, ##(260),
/* 68 -- <argument> ::= */
      #arrayident, $sublist,
/* 69 -- <sublist> ::= */
      ##(253), #lparen, $expression, $expressions, #rparen, ##(254),
      ##(261),
/* 70 -- <sublist> ::= null */
      ##(260),
/* 71 -- <expressions> ::= */
      #comma, $expression, $expressions,
```

Fig. 2-7   Source code for the parser (cont'd.)

```
/* 72 -- <expressions> ::= null */
/* 73 -- <return stmt> ::= */
      #return, $ret_expression,
/* 74 -- <ret expression> ::= */
      $expression, ##(271),
/* 75 -- <ret expression> ::= null */
      ##(272),
/* 76 -- <if stmt> ::= */
      #if, $expression, ##(273), $then_clause, $else_clause, ##(275),
      #endif,
/* 77 -- <then clause> ::= */
      #then, ##(289), $statement, #semi, $statement_list,
/* 78 -- <else clause> ::= */
      ##(274), #else, ##(289), $statement, #semi, $statement_list,
/* 79 -- <else clause> ::= null */
/* 80 -- <while stmt> ::= */
      ##(276), #loop, $statement_list, #while, $expression, ##(273),
      #semi, $statement_list, ##(277), #endloop,
/* 81 -- <stop stmt> ::= */
      #stop,##(280),
/* 82 -- <assignment stmt> ::= */
      #simpident, ##(284), $substring, ##(279), ##(281), #assign,
      $expression, ##(282),
/* 83 -- <assignment stmt> ::= */
      #arrayident, ##(253), #lparen, $expression, $expressions,
      #rparen, ##(254), $substring, ##(279), #assign, $expression,
      ##(283),
/* 84 -- <substring> ::= */
      #lparen, $start, #substr, $length, #rparen,
/* 85 -- <substring> ::= null */
      ##(265),
/* 86 -- <start> ::= */
      $expression,
/* 87 -- <length> ::= */
      $expression, ##(266),
/* 88 -- <length> ::= null */
      ##(267),
/* 89 -- <read stmt> ::= */
      #read, $input_goal_list,
/* 90 -- <input goal list> ::= */
      $input_goal, $input_goals,
/* 91 -- <input goals> ::= */
      #comma, $input_goal, $input_goals,
/* 92 -- <input goals> ::= null */
/* 93 -- <input goal> ::= */
      #simpident, ##(285),
/* 94 -- <input goal> ::= */
      #arrayident, ##(253), #lparen, $expression, $expressions,
```

Fig. 2-7 Source code for the parser (cont'd.)

```
            #rparen, ##(254), ##(286),
/* 95 -- <write stmt> ::= */
            #write, ##(287), $expression_list, #using, #literal, ##(288),
/* 96 -- <expression list> ::= */
            $expression, $expressions,
/* 97 -- <expression list> ::= null */
/* 98 -- <expression> ::= */
            $part, $etail,
/* 99 -- <etail> ::= */
            #gt, $part, ##(230),
/* 100 -- <etail> ::= */
            #lt, $part, ##(231),
/* 101 -- <etail> ::= */
            #eq, $part, ##(232),
/* 102 -- <etail> ::= */
            #ge, $part, ##(233),
/* 103 -- <etail> ::= */
            #le; $part, ##(234),
/* 104 -- <etail> ::= */
            #ne, $part, ##(235),
/* 105 -- <etail> ::= null */
/* 106 -- <part> ::= */
            $term, $ptail,
/* 107 -- <ptail> ::= */
            #plus, $term, ##(236), $ptail,
/* 108 -- <ptail> ::= */
            #minus, $term, ##(237), $ptail,
/* 109 -- <ptail> ::= */
            #or, ##(238), $term, ##(262), $ptail,
/* 110 -- <ptail> ::= null */
/* 111 -- <term> ::= */
            $factor, $ttail,
/* 112 -- <ttail> ::= */
            #mult, $factor, ##(239), $ttail,
/* 113 -- <ttail> ::= */
            #div, $factor, ##(240), $ttail,
/* 114 -- <ttail> ::= */
            #mod, $factor, ##(241), $ttail,
/* 115 -- <ttail> ::= */
            #and, ##(242), $factor, ##(262), $ttail,
/* 116 -- <ttail> ::= null */
/* 117 -- <factor> ::= */
            #not, $index, ##(243),
/* 118 -- <factor> ::= */
            #uminus, $index, ##(244),
/* 119 -- <factor> ::= */
            $index,
/* 120 -- <index> ::= */
```

Fig. 2-7   Source code for the parser (cont'd.)

```
              #length, $catena, ##(245),
/* 121 -- <index> ::= */
              $catena, $itail,
/* 122 -- <itail> ::= */
              #index, $catena, ##(246),
/* 123 -- <itail> ::= null */
/* 124 -- <catena> ::= */
              $primary, $ctail,
/* 125 -- <ctail> ::= */
              #concat, $primary, ##(247), $ctail,
/* 126 -- <ctail> ::= null */
/* 127 -- <primary> ::= */
              #lparen, $expression, #rparen,
/* 128 -- <primary> ::= */
              #procident, ##(248), $argument_list, ##(249),
/* 129 -- <primary> ::= */
              #simpident, ##(250), $substring, ##(251),
/* 130 -- <primary> ::= */
              #simpconident, ##(252), $substring, ##(251),
/* 131 -- <primary> ::= */
              #arrayident, ##(253), #lparen, $expression, $expressions,
              #rparen, ##(254), ##(259), $substring, ##(251),
/* 132 -- <primary> ::= */
              #arrayconident, ##(253), #lparen, $expression, $expressions,
              #rparen, ##(254), ##(259), $substring, ##(251),
/* 133 -- <primary> ::= */
              #number, ##(255),
/* 134 -- <primary> ::= */
              #literal, ##(256),
/* 135 -- <primary> ::= */
              #true, ##(257),
/* 136 -- <primary> ::= */
              #false, ##(258),
/* 137 -- <proc_name> ::= */
              #newident,
/* 138 -- <proc_name> ::= */
              #procident );
```

/* The following two macro procedures are used to push and pop
things onto the parse stack. */

```
        /*****************************************/
        /*                                       */
        /*            s_push                     */
        /*                                       */
        /*****************************************/
```

/* The push procedure pushes the tokens of the right-hand side of the

Fig. 2-7   Source code for the parser (cont'd.)

given production number onto the top of the parse stack. */

```
*MACRO
     s_push (prod_no) =
     BEGIN;
          DECLARE
               i FIXED BIN (15);   /* index into the rhs_prod table */
          i = prod_index (prod_no + 1) - 1;
          DO WHILE (i >= prod_index (prod_no));
               IF (parse_top >= parse_limit)
               THEN DO;
                    CALL error (6, 0, 0, 0);
                    CALL list_err;
                    STOP;
               END;
               parse_top = parse_top + 1;
               parse (parse_top) = rhs_prod (i);
               i = i - 1;
          END;
     END %;
*MEND
```

```
/******************************************/
/*                                        */
/*               s_pop                    */
/*                                        */
/******************************************/
```

/* This procedure will pop the top element off of the parse
stack, checking for underflow. */

```
*MACRO
     s_pop =
          IF (parse_top <= 1)
          THEN DO;
               CALL error (7, 0, 0, 0);
               CALL list_err;
               STOP;
          END;
          parse_top = parse_top - 1;
     %;
*MEND
```

```
          DECLARE
               parse (parse_limit) FIXED BIN (15),  /* parse stack */
               parse_top FIXED BIN (15),    /* top of parse      */
               true_top FIXED BIN (15),     /* actual stack top
                                             pointer       */
```

Fig. 2-7   Source code for the parser (cont'd.)

```
            parse_string(159 : 161) CHAR (7) VARYING INITIAL ('pop',
                'accept', 'error'),
            parse_action FIXED BIN (15),/* from parse table  */
            i FIXED BIN (15);

    /* now do the initializations */
    parse_top, true_top = 2;
    next_token = scanner;
    parse (1) = #eof;     /* initialize the stack to the right_ */
    parse (2) = $global;  /* hand_side of first prod. and #eof */

DO forever;

            DO WHILE ( parse ( parse_top ) > ##(200) );
                /* call semantic routines */
                CALL action ( parse ( parse_top ) );
                parse_top = parse_top - 1;
            END;

            IF (ll1_debug)
            THEN DO;
                CALL stack_pr (parse, parse_top, true_top);
                PUT SKIP LIST ('input symbol is ', token_str
                    (next_token));
            END;

            parse_action = ll1_parsetab (parse (parse_top),
                                    next_token);
            IF (parse_action >= 1 & parse_action < @pop)
            THEN DO;
                IF (ll1_debug)
                THEN
                    PUT SKIP EDIT ('parse action = expand',
                        ' ''', token_str (parse
                        (parse_top)), '''')(A,A,A,A);
                s_pop;
                s_push (parse_action);

                /* reset true_top if this production does
                   not expand to a null right-hand side */
                i = prod_index (parse_action + 1) -
                    prod_index (parse_action);
                IF (i > 1)
                THEN true_top = parse_top;
                ELSE
                IF (rhs_prod (prod_index (parse_action))
                    < ##(200) & i = 1)
                THEN true_top = parse_top;
            END;
```

Fig. 2-7   Source code for the parser (cont'd.)

```
                ELSE DO;
                IF (ll1_debug)
                THEN
                        PUT SKIP EDIT ('parse action = ',
                            parse_string (parse_action))(A, A);
                IF (parse_action = @pop)
                THEN DO;
                        s_pop;
                        DO WHILE ( parse ( parse_top ) > # #(200) );
                                /* call semantic routines */
                                CALL action ( parse ( parse_top ) );
                                parse_top = parse_top - 1;
                        END;
                        true_top = parse_top;
                        next_token = scanner;
                END;

                ELSE
                        IF (parse_action = @accept)
                        THEN DO;
                                IF (line_errors > 0)
                                THEN
                                        CALL list_err;
                                RETURN ('1'B);
                        END;
                        ELSE
                                CALL err_hand (parse, parse_top,
                                    true_top, next_token);
                END;
        END;


        /**********************************************/
        /*                                            */
        /*            err_hand                         */
        /*                                            */
        /**********************************************/
```

/* The err_hand procedure is used to recover from a parsing error while
doing the ll(1) parse of the program. Basically, the method involves
looking for a symbol (terminal or nonterminal) on the stack which can
generate the next input symbol. The symbols above this symbol on the
stack are then removed, and the portion of the production which can
produce the given input symbol is then stacked onto the stack. If
this fails, then the input symbol is deleted from the input, and
the parser is allowed to continue parsing, if possible. For a complete
description of this method, see Sec. 6-2.5 of Tremblay and Sorenson's
The Theory and Practice of Compiler Writing . */

Fig. 2-7   Source code for the parser (cont'd.)

err_hand: PROCEDURE (parse, parse_top, true_top, next_token);

    DECLARE
        parse (*) FIXED BIN (15),   /* the parse stack */
        parse_top FIXED BIN (15),   /* top of the parse stack */
        true_top FIXED BIN (15),   /* real top of parse stack */
        next_token FIXED BIN (15);   /* the input token */

    DECLARE
        (s, i, j) FIXED BIN (15);   /* index variables */

    /* The prefix table is used to determine if the symbol on the
    stack can produce the given input symbol. 0 entries indicate
    that this is not possible. All other entries are of the form
    xxxyy where xxx indicates the production that the stack symbol
    should be expanded to, and yy indicates which element of
    the expansion produces the given input symbol. */
    BEGIN;
    DECLARE prefix (#_of_terminals + 1: #_of_symbols,
        #_of_terminals) FIXED BIN (15) INITIAL

/* program */   (0, (2) 101, (7) 0, (2) 101, (4) 0, 101, (2) 0, 101,
                     (13) 0, 102, (23) 0,

/* global */   0, 301, 201, (7) 0, 301, 301, (4) 0, 201, (2) 0,
                     301, (13) 0, 201, (23) 0,

/* core */   0, 503, 501, (7) 0, 503, 503, (4) 0, 401, 0, 0, 503,
                     (13) 0, 401, (23) 0,

/* declaration list */0, (2) 601, (7) 0, (2) 601, (7) 0, 601, (37) 0,

/* procedure list */ 0, (2) 801, (7) 0, (2) 901, (4) 0, 801, (2) 0, 901,
                     (37) 0,

/* declaration */   0, 1101, 1102, (7) 0, 1101, 1101, (7) 0, 1101,
                     (6) 0, (2) 1101, (19) 0, 1102, (2) 0, 1102, (2) 0,
                     1102, 1102, (2) 0,

/* entity list */   (2) 0, 1201, (31) 0, 1203, (22) 0,

/* constant list */ (7) 0, 1404, (14) 0, 1404, (7) 0, 1401, (3) 0, 1403,
                     (6) 0, 1404, (5) 0, 1402, (3) 0, 1404, (5) 0,

/* type specifier */ 0, 1701, (8) 0, (2) 1601, (7) 0, 1601, (9) 0, 1701,
                     1701, (10) 0, 1701, (9) 0, 1701, (5) 0,

/* simple type */   (10) 0, 1801, 2001, (7) 0, 1901, (37) 0,

Fig. 2-7 Source code for the parser (cont'd.)

```
/* array */        0, 2101, (8) 0, 2107, 2107, 0, 0, 2106, (4) 0, 2107,
                   (9) 0, 2103, 2104, (10) 0, 2102, (9) 0, 2105, (5) 0,

/* bound pair list */ (29) 0, 2202, 2201, (10) 0, 2202, 0, 2202, 2202,
                   (3) 0, 2202, 2202, 0, 2202, 0, 2202, 2202, 0, 2202,

/* bound pair */   (29) 0, 2402, 2401, (10) 0, 2401, 0, 2401, 2401,
                   (3) 0, 2401, 2401, 0, 2401, 0, 2401, 2401, 0, 2401,

/* second bound */ (29) 0, 2501, 2502, (10) 0, 2502, 0, 2502, 2502,
                   (3) 0, 2502, 2502, 0, 2502, 0, 2502, 2502, 0, 2502,

/* constant */     (7) 0, 2701, (14) 0, 2701, (17) 0, 2701, 2801,
                   (6) 0, 2701, 0, 0, 2801, (4) 0, 2701,

/* simple constant */(7) 0, 3301, (14) 0, 3201, (17) 0, 3101, (7) 0, 3001,
                   (7) 0, 2901,

/* array constant */(7) 0, 3402, (14) 0, 3402, (7) 0, 3403, (9) 0, 3402,
                   3401, (6) 0, 3402, 0, 0, 3404, (4) 0, 3402,

/* simple constant list */  (7) 0, 3502, (14) 0, 3502, (7) 0, 3501, (9) 0,
                   3502, (7) 0, 3502, (7) 0, 3502,

/* ident list */   (30) 0, 3701, (16) 0, 3702, (9) 0,

/* procedure */    0, 3903, 3904, (7) 0, (2) 3903, (7) 0, 3903,
                   (27) 0, 3902, (2) 0, 3902, (6) 0,

/* procedure tail */ (8) 4101, 4001, (7) 4101, 0, (16) 4101, 0, (23) 4101,

/* procedure body */4202, 4201, 4201, (3) 4202, 4205, 4202, 0, 4202, 4201,
                   4201, 4202, 4202, 4201, 4202, 0, 4202, 4202, 4201,
                   (9) 4202, 4201, 4201, 4202, 4202, 0, (13) 4202, 4201,
                   (4) 4202, 4203, (4) 4202,

/* statement list */ (9) 0, 4301, (2) 0, 4301, (4) 0, (2) 4301, 0, 4301,
                   (3) 0, 4301, 4301, 0, 0, 4301, (2) 0, (2) 4301, 0,
                   (13) 4301, 0, (4) 4301, 4302, (4) 4301,

/* parameter list */ 0, 4502, (8) 0, (2) 4502, 0, 0, 4502, (4) 0, 4502,
                   (10) 0, 4503, (10) 0, 4501, (5) 0, 4502, (3) 0, 4504,
                   (5) 0,

/* parameters */   0, 4702, (8) 0, (2) 4702, 0, 0, 4702, (4) 0, 4702,
                   (10) 0, 4701, (16) 0, 4702, (9) 0,

/* parameter */    0, 4901, (8) 0, (2) 4901, 0, 0, 4901, (4) 0, 4901,
                   (27) 0, 4902, (9) 0,
```

Fig. 2-7 Source code for the parser (cont'd.)

/* parameter type */ 0, 5101, (8) 0, (2) 5001, 0, 0, 5105, (4) 0, 5001,
(10) 0, 5103, (10) 0, 5102, (9) 0, 5104, (5) 0,

/* comma list */ (30) 0, 5201, (26) 0,

/* statement */ (9) 0, 5601, 0, 0, 5701, 5901, 0, 5901, 0, 6001, 5501,
0, 5801, 0, 5901, 0, 5701, 6101, (3) 5901, 0, (3) 5901,
0, (13) 5901, 0, (2) 5901, 5401, 5901, 5601, (4) 5901,

/* procedure call */ (50) 0, 6201, (6) 0,

/* argument list */ (26) 0, 6302, (3) 0, 6303, (10) 0, 6301, (9) 0, 6304,
0, 6302, (3) 0,

/* arguments */ (26) 0, 6502, (3) 0, 6501, (22) 0, 6502, (3) 0,

/* argument */ (26) 0, 6801, (26) 0, 6701, (3) 0,

/* sublist */ (30) 0, 6903, 0, 6902, (8) 0, 6901, 0, 6902, 6902,
(3) 0, 6902, 6902, 0, 6904, 0, 6902, 6902, 0, 6902,

/* return stmt */ (18) 0, 7301, (38) 0,

/* ret expression */ 7401, (6) 0, 7401, (5) 0, 7401, 0, 7401, (6) 0, 7401,
(3) 0, 7401, 7401, 0, 0, (3) 7401, 0, (13) 7401, 0,
(4) 7401, 0, (4) 7401,

/* if stmt */ (9) 0, 7601, (47) 0,

/* then clause */ (9) 0, 7702, 0, 0, 7702, (4) 0, (2) 7702, 0, 7702, 7701,
0, 0, (3) 7702, 0, 7702, (21) 0, 7702, 0, 7703, 7702,
(3) 0,

/* else clause */ (3) 0, 7801, (5) 0, 7802, 0, 0, 7802, (4) 0, (2) 7802,
0, 7802, (3) 0, (3) 7802, 0, 7802, (21) 0, 7802, 0,
7803, 7802, (3) 0,

/* while stmt */ (5) 0, 8007, (3) 0, 8002, 0, 0, 8001, (4) 0, (2) 8002,
0, 8002, (3) 0, 8003, (2) 8002, 0, 8002, (21) 0, 8002,
0, 8005, 8002, (3) 0,

/* stop stmt */ (20) 0, 8101, (36) 0,

/* assignment stmt */ 8204, (6) 0, 8204, (5) 0, 8204, 0, 8204, (6) 0, 8204,
(3) 0, 8301, 8204, 8203, 0, (3) 8204, 0, (7) 8204,
8302, (5) 8204, 0, (3) 8204, 8305, 0, 8201, 8204, 8202,
8204,

Fig. 2-7 Source code for the parser (cont'd.)

/* substring */   (32) 0, 8402, (8) 0, 8401, 0, 8402, 8402, (3) 0,
                     (2) 8402, 0, 8405, 0, (2) 8402, 8403, 8402,

/* start */   (32) 0, 8601, (8) 0, 8601, 0, 8601, 8601, (3) 0,
                     (2) 8601, 0, 8601, 0, (2) 8601, 0, 8601,

/* length */   (32) 0, 8701, (8) 0, 8701, 0, 8701, 8701, (3) 0,
                     (2) 8701, 0, 8701, 0, (2) 8701, 0, 8701,

/* read stmt */   (17) 0, 8901, (8) 0, 8902, (3) 0, 8902, (10) 0,
                     8902, (9) 0, 8902, 0, 8902, (3) 0,

/* input goal list */ (26) 0, 9001, (3) 0, 9002, (22) 0, 9001, (3) 0,

/* input goals */   (26) 0, 9102, (3) 0, 9101, (22) 0, 9102, (3) 0,

/* input goal */   (26) 0, 9401, (14) 0, 9402, (9) 0, 9405, 0, 9301,
                     (3) 0,

/* write stmt */   9502, (6) 0, 9502, (5) 0, 9502, 0, 9502, (6) 0, 9502,
                     9503, 0, 9501, 9502, 9502, 0, 0, (3) 9502, 0, (13) 9502,
                     0, (4) 9502, 0, (4) 9502,

/* expression list */ 9601, (6) 0, 9601, (5) 0, 9601, 0, 9601, (6) 0, 9601,
                     (3) 0, 9601, 9601, 0, 0, 9602, 9601, 9601, 0, (13) 9601,
                     0, (4) 9601, 0, (4) 9601,

/* expressions */   7102, (6) 0, 7102, (5) 0, 7102, 0, 7102, (6) 0, 7102,
                     (3) 0, 7102, 7102, 0, 0, 7101, 7102, 7102, 0, (13) 7102,
                     0, (4) 7102, 0, (4) 7102,

/* expression */   9801, (6) 0, 9801, (5) 0, 9801, 0, 9801, (6) 0, 9801,
                     (3) 0, 9801, 9801, (3) 0, (2) 9801, 0, (3) 9802, 9801,
                     9802, (3) 9801, 9802, (3) 9801, 9802, 0, (4) 9801,
                     0, (4) 9801,

/* etail */   9902, (6) 0, 9902, (5) 0, 9902, 0, 9902, (6) 0, 9902,
                     (3) 0, 9902, 9902, (3) 0, (2) 9902, 0, 10101, 10201,
                     9901, 9902, 10301, (3) 9902, 10001, (3) 9902, 10401,
                     0, (4) 9902, 0, (4) 9902,

/* part */   10601, (6) 0, 10601, (5) 0, 10601, 0, 10602, (6) 0,
                     10601, (3) 0, 10601, 10601, (3) 0, (2) 10601, 0,
                     (9) 10601, 10602, (3) 10601, 0, 10601, 10602, 10601,
                     10601, 0, (4) 10601,

/* ptail */   10702, (6) 0, 10702, (5) 0, 10702, 0, 10901, (6) 0,
                     10702, (3) 0, 10702, 10702, (3) 0, (2) 10702, 0,

Fig. 2-7   Source code for the parser (cont'd.)

(9) 10702, 10801, (3) 10702, 0, 10702, 10701, 10702,
10702, 0, (4) 10702,

/* term */   11102, (6) 0, 11101, (5) 0, 11101, 0, 11101, (6) 0,
11101, (3) 0, 11101, 11101, (3) 0, 11101,
11102, 0, (10) 11101, 11102, 11102, 11101, 0, (4) 11101,
0, (4) 11101,

/* ttail */   11501, (6) 0, 11201, (5) 0, 11202, 0, 11202, (6) 0,
11202, (3) 0, 11202, 11202, (3) 0, 11202, 11303,
0, (10) 11202, 11201, 11401, 11202, 0, (4) 11202,
0, (4) 11202,

/* factor */   11901, (6) 0, 11901, (5) 0, 11701, 0, 11901, (6) 0,
11901, (3) 0, 11901, 11901, (3) 0, (2) 11901, 0,
(13) 11901, 0, (4) 11901, 0, (3) 11901, 11801,

/* index */   12101, (6) 0, 12101, (5) 0, 12101, 0, 12101, (6) 0,
12101, (3) 0, 12101, 12101, (3) 0, (2) 12101, 0,
(5) 12101, 12001, (7) 12101, 0, (4) 12101, 0, (4) 12101,

/* itail */   12202, (6) 0, 12202, (5) 0, 12202, 0, 12202, (6) 0,
12202, (3) 0, 12202, 12202, (3) 0, (2) 12202, 0,
(3) 12202, 12201, (9) 12202, 0, (4) 12202, 0, (4) 12202,

/* catena */   12402, (6) 0, 12401, (5) 0, 12402, 0, 12402, (6) 0,
12401, (3) 0, 12401, 12401, (3) 0, (2) 12402, 0,
(6) 12402, (2) 12401, (5) 12402, 0, 12401, 12402, 12401,
12401, 0, (3) 12401, 12402,

/* ctail */   12502, (6) 0, 12502, (5) 0, 12502, 0, 12502, (6) 0,
12502, (3) 0, 12502, 12502, (3) 0, 12501,
12502, 0, (13) 12502, 0, (4) 12502, 0, (4) 12502,

/* primary */ 12702, (6) 0, 13601, (5) 0, 12702, 0, 12702, (6) 0,
13501, (3) 0, 13101, 13201, (3) 0, 12702, 12702,
0, (6) 12702, 13401, 12701, (5) 12702, 0, 13301,
12702, 12801, 12703, 0, 12901, 13001, 12902, 12702,

/* proc_name */   (47) 0, 13701, (2) 0, 13801, (6) 0);

/* The main loop of the procedure goes down the stack, looking
for a symbol which can produce the current input symbol. */

CALL error (8, parse (parse_top), next_token, 0);

DO i = true_top TO 1 BY -1;
    s = parse (i);

Fig. 2-7   Source code for the parser (cont'd.)

```
               IF (s > ##(200))
               THEN no_code = '1'B;
               ELSE
               IF (s = next_token)
               THEN DO;
                       true_top, parse_top = i;
                       RETURN;
               END;
               ELSE
               IF (s > #_of_terminals)
               THEN
                       IF (prefix (s, next_token) ¬= 0)
                       THEN DO;
                               CALL fixup(parse,i, next_token);
                               true_top, parse_top = i;
                               RETURN;
                       END;
          END;

     /* couldn't find anything on the stack which could produce
     the given input symbol.  Delete the input symbol.  */

     IF (ll1_debug)
     THEN
             PUT SKIP EDIT ('****  ', token_pr (next_token),
             ' has been deleted from the input',
             ' stream')(A, A, A, A);
     no_code = '0'B;
     next_token = scanner;

/*******************************************/
/*                                         */
/*              fixup                       */
/*                                         */
/*******************************************/
```

/* This procedure will take the symbol on top of the stack,
and expand the portions of it until the top stack symbol is
the same as that of the current input symbol. */

```
fixup:  PROCEDURE (parse, i, next_token);

        DECLARE
               parse (*) FIXED BIN(15),      /* parse stack */
               i FIXED BIN (15),            /* index into parse */
               next_token FIXED BIN (15);  /* input symbol */

        DECLARE
```

Fig. 2-7   Source code for the parser (cont'd.)

```
p FIXED BIN (15),      /* prefix entry */
prod FIXED BIN (15),  /* production part of p */
symbol FIXED BIN (15),      /* symbol part of p */
lo FIXED BIN (15),      /* lo and hi indicate the */
hi FIXED BIN (15),      /* bounds of the prod. to be
                             stacked. */
j FIXED BIN (15);      /* index variable */

DO WHILE (parse (i) ¬= next_token);

      /* make sure parse(i) is a nonterminal.  The ad hoc
       prefix table may contain this type of error in it. */

      IF (parse (i) <= #_of_terminals)
      THEN DO;
            CALL error (14, 0, 0, 0);
            CALL list_err;
            STOP;
      END;

      /* first obtain the production number and the symbol
       of the production which can produce the given input
       symbol using the prefix table.  */

      p = prefix (parse (i), next_token);

      /* check for an error in the table */

      IF (p = 0)
      THEN DO;
            CALL error (14, 0, 0, 0);
            CALL list_err;
            STOP;
      END;

      prod = TRUNC (p / 1e2);
      symbol = MOD (p, 100);
      i = i - 1;
      lo = prod_index (prod);
      DO j = 1 TO symbol;
            IF (rhs_prod (lo) > #_of_terminals)
            THEN no_code = '1'B;
            DO WHILE (rhs_prod (lo) > ##(200));
                  lo = lo + 1;
            END;
            lo = lo + 1;
      END;
      lo = lo - 1;
```

Fig. 2-7   Source code for the parser (cont'd.)

```
                hi = prod_index (prod + 1) - 1;

                /* now stack the remainder of the production
                which can produce the given input symbol.  */

                DO j = hi TO lo BY -1;
                        i = i + 1;
                        parse (i) = rhs_prod (j);
                END;
        END;
END fixup;
END;
END err_hand;


        /* * * * * * * * * * * * * * * * * * * * * * * * * * * * * * * * * */
        /*                                                              */
        /*                    stack_pr                                  */
        /*                                                              */
        /* * * * * * * * * * * * * * * * * * * * * * * * * * * * * * * * * */

/* This procedure is used to print out the contents of the parse stack
and indicate where the parse stack top and the true top pointers
are located.  */

stack_pr:  PROCEDURE (parse, parse_top, true_top);

        DECLARE
                (parse (*),     /* the parsing stack */
                parse_top,     /* working top of the stack */
                true_top,      /* actual top of the stack */
                i)              /* index variable */
                        FIXED BIN (15);

        PUT SKIP (2) LIST ('stack contents:');
        PUT SKIP EDIT ('true_top --> ')(A);

        DO i = true_top TO 1 BY -1;
                IF (parse (i) < ##(200))
                THEN PUT EDIT (token_str (parse (i)))(COL (15), A);
                ELSE PUT EDIT ('action',parse (i))(COL (15), A, F(3));
                IF (i = parse_top)
                THEN PUT EDIT (' <-- parse_top')(A);
                PUT SKIP;
        END;
END stack_pr;
END llparse;
```

Fig. 2-7   Source code for the parser (cont'd.)

```
/*******************************************/
/*                                         */
/*              error                      */
/*                                         */
/*******************************************/
```

/* This procedure is used to insert the given error number
and corresponding parameters into the error_buf, so that
they can be printed out when the list_err procedure is
called. A maximum of ten errors per line is allowed. */

```
error:  PROCEDURE (err_numb, parm1, parm2, parm3);
        DECLARE
                (err_numb,      /* which error occurred */
                parm1,          /* the first parameter */
                parm2,          /* the second parameter */
                parm3)          /* the third parameter */
                        FIXED BIN (15);


        DECLARE
                digit CHAR (1);         /* indicates how many errors for
                                        this line */


        /* if more than 10 errors, exit, otherwise insert in table */


        IF (line_errors >= 10)
        THEN DO;
                line_errors = line_errors + 1;
                RETURN;
        END;


        ELSE DO;
                IF (¬ll1_debug & SUBSTR (error_mark, begin_tok, 1)
                        ¬= ' ')
                THEN
                        RETURN;
                PUT STRING (digit) EDIT (line_errors)(F(1));
                SUBSTR (error_mark, begin_tok, 1) = digit;
                error_buf (line_errors, 1) = err_numb;
                error_buf (line_errors, 2) = parm1;
                error_buf (line_errors, 3) = parm2;
                error_buf (line_errors, 4) = parm3;
                line_errors = line_errors + 1;
        END;
END error;
```

Fig. 2-7   Source code for the parser (cont'd.)

```
/*********************************************/
/*                                           */
/*              list_err                     */
/*                                           */
/*********************************************/
```

/* This procedure is used to print all of the errors for a given
line. The error numbers have been saved in the error_buf structure.
The error number is used as an index into the err_mesg_tab. The
entry in this table for a given error, is an index into the
pat_space table. This table contains indices into the dict table
which contains the actual words to be printed out. From these
words in the dictionary table, this procedure will generate the
appropriate error message, and reinitialize the error_buf table
for the next input line of source code. */

```
list_err:  PROCEDURE;

        DECLARE
               (i, j) FIXED BIN (15);  /* index variables */

        /* print line if it hasn't already been printed, and
         print the associated error indicators beneath the line.  */

        IF (list_flag)
        THEN
                PUT SKIP EDIT (line_num, ':', line_buf)
                              (F(4), A, X(2), A(80));
        PUT SKIP EDIT (error_mark)(X(7), A(80));

        /* now generate the message for each error in error_buf.  */

        DO i = 0 TO min (9, line_errors - 1);
                PUT SKIP EDIT ('**** error (', i, '): ')
                                (A, F(1), A);
                IF (error_buf (i, 1) = 8)
                THEN  /* an ll(1) parsing error - special message */
                        CALL llerror (error_buf (i, 2),
                                        error_buf (i, 3));
                ELSE DO;
                        j = err_mesg_tab (error_buf (i, 1));
                        DO WHILE(j < err_mesg_tab(error_buf(i, 1) + 1));
                                PUT EDIT (' ', dict (pat_space (j)))
                                        (A, A);
                                j = j + 1;
                        END;
                        PUT EDIT ('.')(A);
                END;
        END;
END;
```

Fig. 2-7   Source code for the parser (cont'd.)

```
        IF (line_errors > 10)
        THEN
                PUT SKIP EDIT ('**** ', line_errors - 10,
                            'errors not reported.')(A, F(3), A);

        error_num = error_num + line_errors;
        line_errors = 0;
        error_mark = '';
END list_err;
```

```
        /******************************************/
        /*                                        */
        /*              llerror                    */
        /*                                        */
        /******************************************/
```

/* This procedure is used to generate the error message for errors
which occur as a result of an error entry in the LL(1) parse table.
The symbol on top of the stack and the input symbol at the time of
the error are required in order to determine what error message
should be printed. Generating an appropriate error message
consists of printing all the possible tokens that could have
appeared in the input, and the token which did appear in the input.
This is accomplished by having all possible input tokens for a given
nonterminal in a table, and then printing these out. The tables used
for this purpose are explained below. */

llerror: PROCEDURE (stack_top, input);

/* ffset and fftoken are tables used to facilitate the
  printing of parser syntax error messages. ffset
  is a vector of integers. It contains one entry for
  each nonterminal symbol of the grammar. This entry
  is the index of the first of a series of tokens
  in fftoken. These are the tokens which could
  validly appear where the nonterminal is required.
  The end of the series of tokens is one less than the
  value of the next entry in ffset.   */

```
DECLARE ffset (#_of_terminals + 1 : #_of_symbols + 1)
            FIXED BIN (15) STATIC INIT
        (1, 6, 11, 14, 27, 32, 36, 38, 40, 44, 47, 48, 50, 63, 66, 72,
        77, 78, 80, 82, 83, 97, 110, 124, 139, 141, 145, 149, 151,
        160, 161, 163, 165, 167, 170, 171, 185, 186, 187, 189, 190,
        191, 193, 215, 228, 242, 243, 245, 247, 249, 250, 264, 267, 280,
        293, 205, 321, 334, 354, 367, 378, 399, 409, 431, 441, 443);
```

Fig. 2-7 Source code for the parser (cont'd.)

DECLARE fftoken (1 : 442) FIXED BIN (15) STATIC INIT

/* program */   (#proc, #integer, #string, #logical, #array,

/* global */   #proc, #integer, #string, #logical, #array,

/* core   */   #proc, #const, #newident,

/* declaration list */#integer, #string, #logical, #array, #simpident,
                     #arrayident, #procident, #return, #if, #loop, #stop,
                     #read, #write,

/* procedure list */ #proc, #integer, #string, #logical, #eof,

/* declaration */   #integer, #string, #logical, #array,

/* entity list */   #const, #newident,

/* const list */   #comma, #semi,

/* type specifier */ #integer, #string, #logical, #array,

/* simple type */   #integer, #string, #logical,

/* array */   #array,

/* bound pair list */ #comma, #rparen,

/* bound pair */   #not, #true, #false, #uminus, #length,
                     #lparen, #literal, #number, #simpident,
                     #arrayident, #simpconident,
                     #arrayconident, #procident,

/* second bound */ #colon, #rparen, #comma,

/* constant */   #uminus, #true, #false, #number, #literal, #lparen,

/* simple constant */#uminus, #number, #literal, #true, #false,

/* array constant */ #lparen,

/* simple const list*/ #comma, #rparen,

/* ident list */   #comma, #semi,

/* procedure */   #proc,

/* procedure tail */ #forward, #integer, #string, #logical, #array,

Fig. 2-7   Source code for the parser (cont'd.)

```
                        #simpident, #arrayident, #procident, #return,
                        #if, #loop, #stop, #read, #write,

/* procedure body */ #integer, #string, #logical, #array, #simpident,
                        #arrayident, #procident, #return, #if, #loop,
                        #stop, #read, #write,

/* statement list */  #simpident, #arrayident, #procident, #return,
                        #if, #loop, #stop, #read, #write, #endproc,
                        #else, #endif, #while, #endloop,

/* parameter list */  #lparen, #simpident, #arrayident, #procident,
                        #forward, #integer, #string, #logical, #array,
                        #return, #if, #stop, #loop, #read, #write,

/* parameters */      #comma, #rparen,

/* parameter */       #integer, #string, #logical, #array,

/* parameter type */ #integer, #string, #logical, #array,

/* comma list */      #comma, #rparen,

/* statement */       #procident, #return, #if, #loop, #stop,
                        #simpident, #arrayident, #read, #write,

/* procedure call */ #procident,

/* argument list */  #lparen, #semi,

/* arguments */       #comma, #rparen,

/* argument */        #simpident, #arrayident,

/* sublist */         #lparen, #rparen, #comma,

/* return stmt */     #return,

/* ret expression */ #not, #uminus, #length, #lparen, #true, #false,
                        #literal, #number, #simpident, #simpconident,
                        #arrayident, #arrayconident, #procident, #semi,

/* if stmt */         #if,

/* then clause */     #then,

/* else clause */     #else, #endif,

/* while stmt */      #loop,
```

Fig. 2-7 Source code for the parser (cont'd.)

```
/* stop stmt */        #stop,

/* assignment stmt */ #simpident, #arrayident,

/* substring */        #lparen, #assign, #concat, #index, #mult, #div,
                       #mod, #and, #plus, #minus, #or, #lt, #gt, #eq, #ge, #le,
                       #ne, #comma, #rparen, #substr, #semi, #colon,

/* start */            #not, #uminus, #length, #lparen, #true, #false,
                       #literal, #number, #simpident, #simpconident,
                       #arrayident, #arrayconident, #procident,

/* length */           #not, #uminus, #length, #lparen, #true, #false,
                       #literal, #number, #simpident, #simpconident,
                       #arrayident, #arrayconident, #procident,
                       #rparen,

/* read stmt */        #read,

/* input goal list */ #simpident, #arrayident,

/* input goals */      #comma, #semi,

/* input goal */       #simpident, #arrayident,

/* write stmt */       #write,

/* expression list */ #not, #uminus, #length, #lparen, #true, #false,
                       #literal, #number, #simpident, #simpconident,
                       #arrayident, #arrayconident, #procident,
                       #using,

/* expressions */      #comma, #using, #rparen,

/* expression */       #not, #uminus, #length, #lparen, #true, #false,
                       #literal, #number, #simpident, #simpconident,
                       #arrayident, #arrayconident, #procident,

/* etail */            #gt, #lt, #eq, #ge, #le, #ne, #colon, #comma, #rparen,
                       #semi, #substr, #then, #using,

/* part */             #not, #uminus, #lparen, #true, #false, #literal,
                       #number, #simpident, #simpconident, #arrayident,
                       #arrayconident, #procident,

/* ptail */            #plus, #minus, #or, #colon, #comma, #rparen, #semi,
                       #substr, #lt, #le, #gt, #ge, #eq, #ne, #then, #using,
```

Fig. 2-7   Source code for the parser (cont'd.)

```
/* term */          #not, #uminus, #length, #lparen, #true, #false,
                    #literal, #number, #simpident, #simpconident,
                    #arrayident, #arrayconident, #procident,


/* ttail */         #mult, #div, #mod, #and, #plus, #minus, #or, #colon,
                    #comma, #rparen, #semi, #substr, #lt, #le, #gt, #ge,
                    #eq, #ne, #then, #using,


/* factor */        #not, #uminus, #length, #lparen, #true, #false,
                    #literal, #number, #simpident, #simpconident,
                    #arrayident, #arrayconident, #procident,


/* index */         #length, #lparen, #true, #false, #literal, #number,
                    #simpident, #simpconident, #arrayident, #arrayconident,
                    #procident,


/* itail */         #index, #mult, #div, #mod, #and, #plus, #minus, #or,
                    #semi, #comma, #rparen, #semi, #substr, #lt, #le, #gt,
                    #ge, #eq, #ne, #then, #using,


/* catena */        #lparen, #simpident, #simpconident, #arrayident,
                    #arrayconident, #procident, #true, #false, #literal,
                    #number,


/* ctail */         #concat, #index, #mult, #div, #mod, #and, #plus, #minus,
                    #or, #semi, #comma, #rparen, #semi, #substr, #lt, #le,
                    #gt, #ge, #eq, #ne, #then, #using,


/* primary */       #lparen, #procident, #simpident, #simpconident,
                    #arrayident, #arrayconident, #number, #literal,
                    #true, #false,


/* proc_name */     #newident, #procident);


     DECLARE
            (stack_top,     /* symbol that was on top of stack */
            input,          /* symbol that was the current input */
            i,              /* index variable for printing tokens */
            last,           /* last token of ffset to be printed */
            token,          /* the token to be printed  */
            col)            /* column indicator for printing */
            FIXED BIN (15);


     PUT EDIT (' expecting ')(A);


     /* print the tokens that could have appeared in the input */


     IF (stack_top <= #_of_terminals)
```

Fig. 2-7   Source code for the parser (cont'd.)

```
THEN PUT EDIT (token_pr (stack_top))(A);
ELSE DO;
      col = 27;
      i = ffset (stack_top);
      last = ffset (stack_top + 1) - 1;

      DO WHILE (i <= last);
            token = fftoken (i);
            PUT EDIT (token_pr (token))(A);
            col = col + length (token_str (token));
            IF (i < last)
            THEN DO;
                  PUT EDIT (' or ')(A);
                  col = col + 4;
                  IF (col >= 60)
                  THEN DO;
                        PUT SKIP EDIT (' ')(X(26), A);
                        col = 27;
                  END;
            END;
            i = i + 1;
      END;
END;

PUT SKIP EDIT ('but found ', token_pr (input))(X(17), A, A);
END llerror;

/*********************************************/
/*                                           */
/*             token_pr                      */
/*                                           */
/*********************************************/
```

/* This procedure returns the string representation of the given
token. It also determines whether the token should be quoted or not
depending on the type of token to be returned. */

```
token_pr: PROCEDURE (token) RETURNS (CHAR(26) VARYING);

      DECLARE
            token FIXED BIN (15);  /* token to be returned */

      IF (token = #simpident | token = #simpconident |
            token = #arrayident | token = #arrayconident |
            token = #procident | token = #newident |
            token = #literal | token = #number | token = #eof)
      THEN
            RETURN (token_str (token));
```

Fig. 2-7   Source code for the parser (cont'd.)

```
            ELSE
                 RETURN ('''' || token_str (token) || '''');

        END token_pr;
END init;
END compile;
*data
```

Fig. 2-7   Source code for the parser (cont'd.)

2-4   TABLE HANDLER

This section describes the routines used to implement the symbol table for the GAUSS compiler. A symbol table is used to store useful information about identifiers while the program is being compiled. This information is found in the declaration statements for identifiers. The type of information that is required is the type of the identifier (i.e., INTEGER, STRING, LOGICAL, ARRAY, or PROC), the number of dimensions of the identifier (0 for simple identifiers, the number of parameters for PROC identifiers), whether the identifier is a constant or a variable, and whether the identifier has a local or global scope. This information is used by the code generation routines to emit the correct code to reference a variable, and also for semantic checking. In Sec. 2-4.1 some of the problems connected with developing a symbol table for a GAUSS compiler are introduced. Section 2-4.2 describes the organization of the symbol table and Sec. 2-4.3 presents a topdown description of the table handler. Section 2-4.4 gives a description of the routine which inserts and searches for symbols in the symbol table. Section 2-4.5 describes the process of removing local symbols from the table after a procedure has been parsed. Finally, Sec. 2-4.6 contains the PL/I source code which implements the functions required for the creation and maintenance of the symbol table.

2-4.1   Introduction

The table-handling routines for the GAUSS compiler are used to perform all the required operations on the symbol table. The operations required for the symbol table are insertion, lookup, and deletion. The insertions occur when a declaration is being processed. This is done in the semantic portion of the compiler. The lookup operations are done by the scanner, which determines the type of the identifier being searched for, in order to return the correct token. The scanner also returns the symbol table index of the required identifier. The semantic routines in the parser use this index value. The deletion operations are performed on the local symbol table after each procedure is processed. The semantic routines invoke the deletion procedure.

The scoping rules of identifiers in GAUSS require that the table handler differentiate between local symbols and global symbols. Therefore, the symbol table is partitioned: one part for the local symbols, which appear in the symbol table only during the processing of the corresponding procedure; and another part for global symbols (including procedure identifiers), which remain in the symbol table during the entire compilation of the program.

The symbol table structure used in this implementation employs a hash-table method for indexing, the division method for the hashing function, and separate chaining for collision resolution. For a complete description of this type of symbol table organization, see Tremblay and Sorenson [1982].

Because of this type of symbol table organization, and the properties required of the symbol table in parsing a GAUSS program, two procedures are used to perform the needed operations, namely the *lookup* and *sym_rem* procedures. The *lookup* procedure performs both the insertions and the lookups in the symbol table. The *sym_rem* procedure removes the local symbols from the symbol table when the compilation of a procedure has been finished.

2-4.2 Symbol Table Organization

The organization of the symbol table is very important to the efficiency of the operations performed on this table. Since there are two types of symbols (i.e., global and local), a single symbol table can be difficult to use. If the global and local symbols are interspersed in the table, the deletion of the local symbols from the table can cause problems, since many pointers may have to be reset in the linked list (or chain) of elements that have been hashed into the same location. Using two separate symbol tables can be wasteful of space, since one table can be full, causing a symbol table overflow error, even though there may be unused elements in the other table.

Considering these problems, the following symbol table organization was derived. There is one symbol table used for both global and local symbols. The local symbols will be found at one end of the table, while the global symbols are found at the other end. With this table, there are two hash tables, one for local symbols and one for global symbols. Since the symbols are separated according to their scope, the deletion of local symbols will be a trivial matter. Also, since only one symbol table is used, the only time a symbol table overflow error can occur is when there is absolutely no more space for any type of symbol. In the remainder of this discussion, when we speak of the local or global symbol tables, we will actually be referring to that part of the symbol table which contains the local symbols or global symbols, respectively.

The symbol table for the following program segment is illustrated in Figs. 2-8 and 2-9. In Fig. 2-8 the symbol table is depicted as it would be after the declarations for the first procedure have been processed. Figure 2-9 shows the symbol table just after the processing of the declarations for the second procedure. Note that at this time, the symbol table is full, and the addition of another element would cause a symbol table overflow error. When the local symbol table is cleared, however, there will be space to insert more symbols.

```
INTEGER INT, QUEUE;
STRING A;

PROC MAIN
      LOGICAL FLAG;
         .
         .
         .
ENDPROC;
```

PROC F1 (INTEGER Q)
STRING B;

.
.
.

ENDPROC;

For the purposes of this example, it is assumed that the hashing function for the variables is as follows:

INT, FLAG and B are hashed into 1
MAIN is hashed into 2
Q is hashed into 3
A is hashed into 4
QUEUE and F1 are hashed into 5

The size of the hash tables is 5.

A cross-reference table is maintained in a similar fashion to the symbol table. A vector called *xr* is split into nodes of size *xrnode* (i.e., 5 in the current implementation). Nodes at one end of the vector are used for local symbols while nodes at the other end are used for global symbols. The first *xrnode* – 1 (i.e., 4) slots in a node are used to store the line numbers on which a symbol is referenced. The last slot is used to point to the next cross-reference node for the same symbol. Each entry in the symbol table has an attribute pointing to its first and last cross-reference slot.

In order to do type checking on procedure parameters, it is necessary to augment the symbol table with a *procinfo* table. This table contains the type and dimension of each parameter in a procedure. Although such information is recorded in the local symbol table while a procedure is being compiled, it is deleted after the procedure has been compiled (see Sec. 2-4.5). The *address* attribute of a procedure in the symbol table is used to point to a segment in the *procinfo* table.

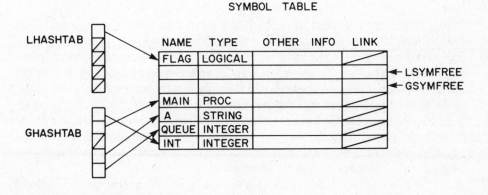

Fig. 2-8 Symbol table contents (after declarations of first procedure)

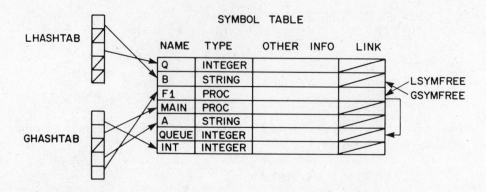

Fig. 2-9 Symbol table contents (after declarations of second procedure)

The first location in the segment contains the actual address of the procedure. The other locations contain the type and dimension of parameters in the procedure. Therefore, if a procedure contains p parameters, then the *procinfo* segment contains 1 + 2 * p locations. Section 2-5.4.4 describes the allocation of *procinfo* segments and Sec. 2-5.5 details their use.

2-4.3 Top-down Description of Table Handler

The table handler consists of two procedures, *lookup* and *sym_rem* as shown in Fig. 2-10. The procedure *lookup* is invoked to perform insert and search operations in the symbol table. The procedure may call the procedure *error* to print error messages if a search has failed. The procedure *error* was described in Sec. 2-3. The other table handling procedure, *sym_rem*, deletes the local symbol table entries from the symbol table at the end of a procedure. The local hash table is also reinitialized by this procedure.

2-4.4 LOOKUP Procedure

This routine is used to do both the insert and search operations in the symbol table. It receives three arguments from the calling routine, namely *name*, *flag*, and *scope*. *name* is the identifier name that is to be inserted or searched for. *flag* indicates whether the operation is to be an insertion or a lookup, and *scope* indicates whether the operation should take place in the local symbol table or the global symbol table. Note that the value of *scope* is used only for insertions, since during a lookup operation it is not known in which part of the symbol table that the identifier is located. Thus for a lookup operation, *scope* is set to indicate where the identifier was found, but for an insertion, *scope* indicates which part of the symbol table that the identifier should be inserted.

The *lookup* procedure accesses several global data structures. The most important of these are the symbol table and the two hash tables, *lhashtab* and *ghashtab*, which provide access to the symbol table. Since the symbol table is filled from both ends, there are two pointers into the symbol table, *lsymfree* and *gsymfree*. These pointers indicate the next available slot in the symbol table for local and global symbols, respectively.

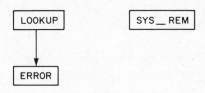

Fig. 2-10   Structure chart for the GAUSS table handler

The first step in the *lookup* procedure is to calculate the hash value of the identifier in *name*. The hash value is derived from the addition of the EBCDIC values of the first and last characters of *name* to the length of *name*. The result of this summation modulus the size of the appropriate hash table is used as the hash value. If the indicated operation is a lookup, then the local symbol table is searched. This is accomplished by examining each element in the chain pointed to by *lhashtab(hash)*, where *hash* is the hash value computed for the given identifier. If the identifier is found, the address of its location in the symbol table is returned to the calling procedure. Otherwise, the global symbol table is searched by examining each element in the chain pointed to by *ghashtab(hash)*. The address of the symbol table entry is returned if the identifier is found. If the identifier cannot be found in either of the symbol tables, -1 is returned to indicate that the identifier is not in the symbol table.

For an insertion operation, the method is similar for global and local symbols. First, a check is made to ensure that there is room in the symbol table for another entry. If there is no room, an error message is generated. Otherwise, depending on the value of *scope*, the next free element for the local or global symbol tables is found. This element is then entered as the head of the chain pointed at by the appropriate hash table. The name field of the symbol table entry is initialized to *name*, and the other fields are initialized to 0. Notice that this procedure does not test whether there already exists a symbol table entry with the same name as *name*. This is not necessary since the scanner distinguishes between identifiers that are in the symbol table and those that are not. The semantic routines invoke the *lookup* procedure for insertion only when the identifier is not found in the symbol table.

2-4.5   SYM_REM Procedure

This procedure is used to remove the symbols from the local symbol table. To do this, it is necessary to reset *lsymfree* to 1, which indicates that the next local identifier will be inserted at the beginning of the local symbol table. After this is done, the link field of the elements in the local hash table are all set to null. Since the chains of symbol table elements are no longer accessible, the symbols can be considered removed.

Before this removal is done, however, it is necessary to check if a listing of the symbol table has been requested (i.e., the *sym_debug* flag is *true*). Since the local symbol table is cleared at the end of the completion of each local procedure, it is necessary to print the local symbol table entries after the processing of each procedure. This is done by examining each element of the local hash table, and, if it contains a pointer to a list of elements, the list is traversed, printing the entries as it is processed. Once all entries have been printed, they can be removed as described earlier.

A similar listing operation is done for the global symbol table at the end of the program if the *sym_debug* flag is true. This listing is done in the procedure *init*, after control has been returned from the parser.

The following section gives the PL/I source code which implements the table handling functions just described.

2-4.6   Table Handler Source Code

The source code for the table handler is given in Fig. 2-11.

```
/ * * * * * * * * * * * * * * * * * * * * * * * * * * * * * * * * * * * * * * * * * * /
/ *                                                                        * /
/ *                    lookup                                              * /
/ *                                                                        * /
/ * * * * * * * * * * * * * * * * * * * * * * * * * * * * * * * * * * * * * * * * * * /


/* This procedure is designed to do the lookups
into the symbol table.  The symbol table organization used is
the hash table method.  There are two hash tables, lhashtab and
ghashtab, which are used for local and global symbols, respectively.
Both of these tables contain pointers to the heads of chains
of symbols hashed into that location.  The actual symbol table
consists of only one table, with the local symbols occupying
the lower limits of the table, and the global symbols occupying
the upper limits of the table.  The parameter 'name' contains
the name to be inserted or looked up.
The hash method used is the division method, with the addition of
the EBCDIC values of the first character and the last character of
'name' to the length of the 'name' used as the
preconditioning method. */

lookup:  PROCEDURE (name) RETURNS (FIXED BIN (15));
         DECLARE name CHAR(*) VARYING; /* ident to be inserted */

         DECLARE
               hash FIXED BIN(31),  /* hash location  */
               symptr FIXED BIN (15),       /* symbol table pointer  */
               i FIXED BIN (15),
               temp FIXED BIN (15),
               xrptr FIXED BIN (15);


         /* compute the hash value of the identifier */
```

Fig. 2-11   Source code for the table handler

```
hash = LENGTH ( name );
UNSPEC (temp) = '00000000'B ||
            UNSPEC (SUBSTR (name, hash, 1));

hash = hash + temp;
UNSPEC (temp) = '00000000'B ||
            UNSPEC (SUBSTR (name, 1, 1));
hash = MOD (hash + temp, nhash) + 1;

/* first search the local table */
/* then search the global table */
DO symptr = lhashtab (hash), ghashtab (hash);

DO WHILE (symptr ¬= null);
     IF (symtab (symptr).name = name)
     THEN DO;
            /* identifier found */
            symtab (symptr).xrtail =
               symtab (symptr).xrtail + 1;

        IF ( mod (symtab (symptr).xrtail, xrnode) = 0)
        THEN DO;
            /* get another xrnode */
            IF (lxrptr > gxrptr)
            THEN DO;
               CALL error (13, 0, 0, 0);
               lxrptr = lxrptr - xrnode;
            END;
            IF (scope = 'l')
            THEN DO;
               /* local identifier */
               xrptr = lxrptr;
               lxrptr = lxrptr + xrnode;
            END;
            ELSE DO;
               /* global identifier */
               xrptr = gxrptr;
               gxrptr = gxrptr - xrnode;
            END;

            /* set link to next xrnode */
            xr ( symtab (symptr).xrtail ) = xrptr;

            /* set xrtail to front of next list */
            symtab (symptr).xrtail = xrptr;
        END;

            /* insert line number in cross reference list */
```

Fig.2-11   Source code for the table handler (cont'd.)

```
                          xr ( symtab (symptr).xrtail ) = line_num;
                          RETURN (symptr);
                END;
                symptr = symtab (symptr).link;
        END;

        END;

        /* lookup has failed */

        IF (lsymfree > gsymfree)
        THEN DO;
                CALL error (12, 0, 0, 0);
                IF ( scope = 'g' )
                THEN STOP;
                lsymfree = lsymfree - 1;
        END;

        IF (lxrptr > gxrptr)
        THEN DO;
                CALL error (13, 0, 0, 0);
                lxrptr = lxrptr - xrnode;
        END;

        IF (scope = 'l')
        THEN DO;
                /* local identifier */
                symptr = lsymfree;
                lsymfree = lsymfree + 1;
                symtab (symptr).link = lhashtab (hash);
                lhashtab (hash) = symptr;
                xrptr = lxrptr;
                lxrptr = lxrptr + xrnode;
        END;
        ELSE DO;
                /* global identifier */
                symptr = gsymfree;
                gsymfree = gsymfree - 1;
                symtab (symptr).link = ghashtab (hash);
                ghashtab (hash) = symptr;
                xrptr = gxrptr;
                gxrptr = gxrptr - xrnode;
        END;

        /* now set the fields of the new entry */
        symtab (symptr).name = name;
        symtab (symptr).use = #newident;
        symtab (symptr).type = 0;
```

Fig.2-11   Source code for the table handler (cont'd.)

```
          symtab (symptr).xrhead = xrptr;
          symtab (symptr).xrtail = xrptr;
          xr (xrptr) = line_num;
          RETURN (symptr);
END lookup;

          /*****************************************/
          /*                                       */
          /*              sym_rem                  */
          /*                                       */
          /*****************************************/

sym_rem:  PROCEDURE;

/* This procedure is designed to remove the local symbol table
entries from the symbol table at the end of a procedure.  At the
same time, the local hash table, lhashtab, is reinitialized so that
all the elements of this table are null.  If the 'sym_debug' flag
is on, then the structure of the local symbol table is displayed.
If the 'xref_flag' is on, the contents of the symbol table
are printed out before they are removed. */

DECLARE (i, j, k) FIXED BIN (15),
        ptr FIXED BIN (15),
        lowname CHAR (1);


IF (sym_debug)
THEN DO;
        PUT SKIP (2) EDIT ('symbol table debug of ',
                symtab (procidptr).name) (A,A);
        PUT SKIP (2) EDIT ('name','hash loc.','link','address')
                (A, COL(18), A, COL(31), A, COL(39), A);
        PUT SKIP;

        DO i = 1 TO nhash;
                ptr = lhashtab (i);
                DO WHILE (ptr ¬= null);
                        PUT SKIP EDIT (symtab (ptr).name,
                                i, symtab (ptr).link,
                                symtab (ptr).address)
                                (A(16), COL(18), F(3),
                                COL(31), F(3), COL(39), F(4));
                        ptr = symtab (ptr).link;
                END;
        END;
        PUT SKIP;
END;
```

Fig.2-11   Source code for the table handler (cont'd.)

```
IF (xref_flag)
THEN DO;
        PUT SKIP (2) EDIT ('cross reference of ',
                symtab (procidptr).name) (A,A);
        PUT SKIP(2) EDIT ('name', 'type', 'use', 'dimen',
                'references') (A, COL(18), A, COL(32), A,
                COL(63), A, COL(70), A);
        PUT SKIP;

        DO i = 1 TO lsymfree - 1;
                lowname = '0';
                DO j = 1 TO lsymfree - 1;
                        IF (symtab(j).name < lowname)
                        THEN DO;
                                ptr = j;
                                lowname = symtab (j).name;
                        END;
                END;
                PUT SKIP EDIT (symtab (ptr).name,
                        token_str (symtab (ptr).type),
                        token_str (symtab (ptr).use),
                        symtab(ptr).dimen)
                        (A(16), COL(18), A(9),
                        COL(32), A(26), COL(63), F(4));
                j = symtab (ptr).xrhead;
                PUT EDIT (xr(j)) (COL(70), F(3));
                j = j + 1;
                k = 1;
                DO WHILE (j ¬= symtab (ptr).xrtail + 1);
                        IF (mod(j,xrnode) = 0)
                        THEN j = xr(j);
                        IF (k = 10)
                        THEN DO;
                                PUT EDIT (',', xr(j))
                                (A, COL(70), F(3));
                                k = 1;
                        END;
                        ELSE DO;
                                PUT EDIT (',', xr(j))
                                (A, X(1), F(3));
                                k = k + 1;
                        END;
                        j = j + 1;
                END;
                symtab (ptr).name = '0';
        END;
        PUT SKIP;
    END;
```

Fig.2-11   Source code for the table handler (cont'd.)

```
        localptr = -3;
        lhashtab = null;
        lsymfree = 1;
        lxrptr = 1;
        END sym_rem;
```

Fig.2-11   Source code for the table handler (cont'd.)

2-5   CODE GENERATOR

This section describes the routines used to implement code generation and semantic checking. In Sec. 2-5.1, we introduce the run-time environment assumed for the GAUSS intermediate code. In Sec. 2-5.2, the general code generation strategy is described. A top-down description of the code generator is given in Sec. 2-5.3. Section 2-5.4 discusses the handling of declarations including procedure declarations and Sec. 2-5.5 explains procedure calls and returns. Sections 2-5.6 and 2-5.7 discuss the handling of expressions and the assignment statement respectively. Section 2-5.8 describes the implementation of control structures. Input and output are described in Secs. 2-5.9 and 2-5.10, respectively. Section 2-5.11 outlines semantic error recovery. Section 2-5.12 lists the action routines used by the code generator. Finally, Sec. 2-5.13 gives a list of compilation errors for the compiler.

2-5.1   Intermediate Code Environment

The GAUSS compiler does not generate object code for any real machine. It generates intermediate code for a hypothetical stack machine. There are at least two advantages in producing intermediate language code: the extra pass in translating the intermediate code to machine code affords an opportunity to perform some simple optimization, and an intermediate language form allows the compiler to have some degree of portability (i.e., an intermediate code to machine code translator can be written for each of a series of target machines).

A description of the GAUSS intermediate code is given in Appendix A. Throughout this chapter, however, an attempt is made to motivate the use of the intermediate language instructions as they are required in the compilation process. The remainder of the section describes the environment necessary to support the intermediate code. In particular the hypothetical machine organization, activation records, addressing modes, and string storage are discussed.

Before proceeding, it should be pointed out that the execution of a compiled GAUSS program into intermediate code can take place in one of two ways. The first alternative is to construct an intermediate language interpreter which interprets the generated intermediate code. Of course, this form of execution would be quite slow. The second possibility is to translate the intermediate code into machine code or threaded code for a particular target machine (e.g., PDP-11). Regardless of the method of execution, the discussion throughout this chapter is applicable to both techniques.

A final introductory comment relates to the use of the term "run time" throughout this section. If an interpretive form of execution is used, run time means the time at which the intermediate code is interpreted. If machine code is executed, then run time applies to the time at which the machine code is executed.

2-5.1.1 Hypothetical Machine Organization

In describing the "hypothetical machine organization" we are really describing the organization of a hypothetical machine that supports the execution or interpretation of intermediate language instructions. The organization of this machine consists primarily of a code area and a data area. While these two areas need not be adjacent, it is important that the storage locations within each be contiguous.

The code area contains the intermediate language instructions generated during compilation. An intermediate language instruction is composed of an operation part and an operand part. The operand part may contain zero or more operands depending on the nature of the instruction. A storage location in the code area is associated with each of the components of an intermediate language instruction. Therefore, for example, an instruction with two operands would require a total of three locations. The size of the code area is known after compilation.

The data area is broken into three parts, as exhibited in Fig. 2-12, and contains the storage allocated for the variables and constants of a GAUSS program. The sizes of the parts are determined externally by adjusting the values of system parameters prior to the compilation of a program. One section is a string area; another part is devoted to the run-time stack. A third area stores global variables and string descriptors. If either the string area or the run-time stack use all of their allocated space, then the program has insufficient storage and is terminated abnormally.

Global variables, constant arrays, and string constants are stored in the global area which is fixed in size at compile time. Local variables are stored in the local storage area which is variable in size at run time. An exception to this rule occurs for strings created at run time. The descriptors for these strings are stored in the string descriptor area of the local string area, and the characters of the string are stored in the string area of the local string area. A more detailed discussion of strings will be postponed until Sec. 2-5.1.4.

2-5.1.2 Activation Records

The local area must be shared between all executing procedures. A procedure is executing if it has been called but has not yet returned (nor terminated). The storage requirements of an executing procedure is organized into a single contiguous area called an *activation record*. The structure of an activation record is given in Fig. 2-13.

A special location called the *activation base pointer (abp)* contains the base address of the activation record of the currently executing procedure. The other locations in the most current activation record are referenced relative to this base address.

The construction of the activation record can be separated into two phases. The first phase takes place when a procedure is invoked. At that time, the activation base pointer is updated and the implicit parameters (i.e., the old activation base pointer and the return address) and the explicit parameters are stored. The second phase occurs when the local variable declarations are handled. At this time, space is allocated in the activation record to hold the values of the local variables.

The activation records are stacked on top of each other in the local area to reflect the calling sequence. If procedure A calls procedure B, B calls C, and C calls D, then the order of the activation records is DCBA from the top of the local area to the bottom. If procedure D returns, C returns, and B calls E, then the order is EBA.

2-5.1.3 Addressing

GAUSS intermediate code uses two modes of addressing: relative and absolute. The *absolute address* of a location in the data area is its position number in the global storage area. The *relative address of a location in the global area* is its absolute address. The *relative address of a location in the local area* is the negation of the offset from the activation base pointer. Therefore, when the relative address is positive, it refers to the global area; otherwise, it refers to the local area.

2-5.1.4 Strings

Strings in GAUSS are handled by using string references. The string reference r of a string s is simply a pointer (i.e., address) to a location in the string descriptor area. A string descriptor is stored in three adjacent locations. The first location, which is the location pointed to by reference r, contains the current length of the string s. The second and third locations hold a two-word pointer into the string area where the characters composing the string are stored contiguously — two characters per location. The pointer, itself, references the location holding the first two characters of the string. This method of string storage is illustrated in Fig. 2-14 for a local string variable s which has a current value of "GAUSS".

There still exists the nontrivial problem of recovering storage allocated to strings through reassignment. The allocation of a separate descriptor and string area simplifies significantly the garbage collection problem. A fourth location in the string descriptor is used to simplify garbage collection. The storage management facilities necessary for the string area will be discussed later in Chap. 3.

2-5.2 Code Generation and Semantic Analysis Strategy

In this subsection, the code generation and semantic analysis strategy is outlined for the GAUSS compiler. The strategy that is adopted is to augment the LL(1) grammar with special symbols called *action symbols*. The LL(1) parser is altered to handle the recognition of these action symbols by invoking a set of action routines — one routine for each action symbol. In effect, the LL(1) parser is changed to act as a rudimentary attributed translation parser. The parser is rudimentary in the sense that the inherited and synthesized attributes are not handled as parameters that are passed to and between action routines as described in Chap. 11 of Tremblay and Sorenson [1982]. Instead they are placed on, referenced, and removed from a semantic stack through explicit assignments and tests in the action routines.

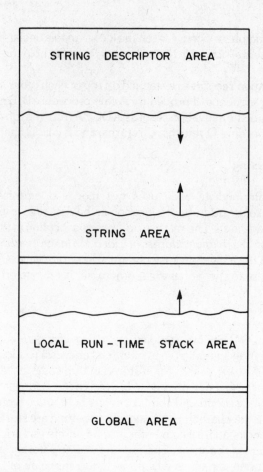

Fig. 2-12   Data area in the GAUSS compiler

There are two main advantages in using this approach. Firstly, the basic LL(1) grammar can be easily modified to contain the action symbols without changing the parsing tables except for the *rhs_prod* table. Secondly, it is a relatively simple procedure to alter the LL(1) parsing algorithm so that it detects an action symbol and invokes the corresponding action routine. An examination of the source statements for the parser, as given in Sec. 2-3.5, indicates how minor these modifications are.

The major disadvantage with this approach to attribute translation is the ad hoc method in which the action routines create and reference the inherited and synthesized attributes to generate code. Clearly, using an attributed translation system that automatically handles the creation and synthesizing of attributes would be preferable; however, such systems are not necessarily readily available. By handling the attributes explicitly on a stack, the student may acquire a better understanding of the correspondence between parsing actions and semantic analysis activities.

In the remainder of this section some of the facilities that are required for code generation and semantic analysis are described. In particular the compile-time environment is outlined in Sec. 2-5.2.1 and the processing of an augmented translation grammar is illustrated in Sec. 2-5.2.2.

TEMPORARIES ARRAYS	VARIABLE PORTION OF ACTIVATION RECORD
SIMPLE IDENTIFIERS ARRAY POINTERS TEMPLATE POINTERS ARRAY TEMPLATES	FIXED PORTION OF ACTIVATION RECORD
ADDRESS OF ARGUMENT N **...** ADDRESS OF ARGUMENT 1	EXPLICIT PARAMETERS
RETURN ADDRESS OLD ACTIVATION BASE POINTER	← ACTIVATION BASE POINTER

Fig. 2-13   Activation record area in GAUSS compiler

2-5.2.1 Compile-time Environment

The major components of the compile-time environment are the semantic stack and the various code and data areas required to hold the generated intermediate code and program constants. The semantic stack, simulated by an array called *sem*, is used to store information necessary for code generation and semantic analysis. The contents can be information from the parsed part of the GAUSS program, variables controlling the state of the compiler, and references to other data structures such as the symbol table or other elements in the semantic stack. Information on the semantic stack is accessed relative to the top of stack pointer *sem_top*.

The other significant information structures used at compile time are the code area and the global area. The code area is stored in the array *code* which is indexed using the variable *codeptr*. The global area is handled using the array *global* with its associated index *globalptr*. Although the local area is not created at compile time, the index *localptr* is used as a relative address operand for various instructions that are generated at compile time. Note that because of the type of intermediate code addressing that has been adopted, *globalptr* is always positive and *localptr* is always negative.

2-5.2.2 Augmented Grammar

In this subsection the activities of the parser are described with particular emphasis given to a discussion of how action symbols are handled. The use of the semantic stack is illustrated with an example involving the generation of code for an "if" statement.

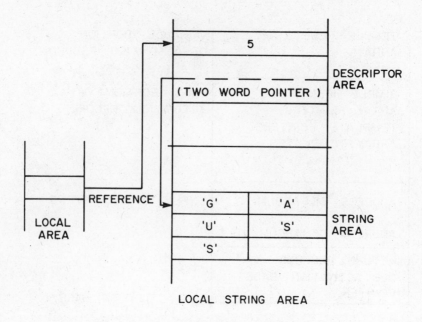

Fig. 2-14   Storage structure for strings in GAUSS compiler

The parser stacks productions of the LL(1) grammar on the parse stack according to the parsing function. In order to specify at what point code is to be generated, the LL(1) grammar can be augmented with action symbols. When the parser reaches an action symbol on the parse stack, the appropriate action routine is called in order to carry out the semantic analysis and code generation associated with that particular part of the parse. The following example gives a segment of the augmented grammar for the "if" statement. This example is used to illustrate how action symbols can be used to invoke semantic action routines. The grammar description that is used is taken from the initialization statements of the *rhs_prod* array. For ease of reading, the production number and left-hand side are included as a comment. The symbols of the right-hand side are separated by commas.

```
/* 76 — <if stmt> ::= */
        #if, $expression, ##(273), $then_clause,
        $else_clause, ##(275), #endif,
/* 77 — <then clause> ::= */
        #then, $statement, #semi, $statement_list,
/* 78 — <else clause> ::= */
        ##(274), #else, $statement, #semi, $statement_list,
/* 79 — <else clause> ::= null */
```

There are three types of grammar symbols: terminals, nonterminals, and action symbols. Symbols of the form ##(2dd), where dd denotes two digits, are action symbols. Symbols which begin with $ are nonterminals and the remaining symbols which begin with # are terminals. Terminals and nonterminals are given well-chosen macro names instead of the integer values they represent. This makes compiler writing and modification easier. Action symbols were not given macro names because the function of the action routines defy brief description. Instead, they are numbered so that the action routines can be ordered for easy reference.

It should be noted that the augmented grammar is still LL(1). Because the action symbols are only cues for triggering the execution of a semantic routine, they are handled separately from the syntactic analysis activity.

The parsing algorithm can be altered by adding a simple test to detect if the top symbol of the parse stack is an action symbol. If it is, then the associated action routine is called. For example, action ##(273) tells the parser that code for the expression before the <then clause> has been generated. The semantic analysis and code generation corresponding to this action symbol is as follows:

```
1       routine (##(273)):
2             /* production 76 */
3             /* production 80 */
4             /* if or while condition */
5              if (sem (sem_top) ~= #logical)
6             then do;
7                   call sem_err('expecting logical expression');
8                   call code_fix (1,1);
9             end;
10            code (codeptr) = $$branchf;
11            sem (sem_top) = codeptr + 1;
12            codeptr = codeptr + 2;
13            return;
```

Line 1 is the label of the action routine. When the *action* procedure is called with ##(273) as an argument, a multibranch GO TO statement transfers control to this label.

Lines 2 and 3 indicate that action symbol ##(273) is found in productions 76 and 80. Line 4 implies that the routine is called after the if or while condition has been recognized.

Line 5 tests the type of the expression used for the condition. The action routine that handles the expression should have previously placed the type on top of the semantic stack.

Line 7 reports a semantic error by calling the *sem_err* procedure. Line 8 recovers from this error by calling the *code_fix* procedure with arguments (1,1) to generate code that replaces the one illegal value on top of the run-time stack by one legal value.

Line 10 generates a branch-on-false instruction *$$branchf*. (All intermediate language instructions are assigned a mnemonic macro name beginning with $$.) Since the operand of the instruction is not known, line 11 saves the address of the operand on top of the semantic stack. The operand, which is a label, is resolved later by a different action routine. Line 12 increments the *codeptr* by two: one for the instruction and one for the operand.

Other action symbols and their associated action routines are described in the following sections.

The grammar, which is stored in the array called *rhs_prod*,, can be augmented by inserting the action symbols at the appropriate location. The alterations to *rhs_prod* changes the relative position of the right-hand side symbols within a production. Therefore the index numbers in *prod_index* must also be altered. These two arrays have been described previously in Sec. 2-3.3. As the action routines are designed and debugged, it is unavoidable that *rhs_prod* is changed several times. After making a few of these changes manually, it became obvious that the creation of a program which automatically generated the *prod_index* array from the *rhs_prod* was necessary and therefore done.

2-5.3   Top-down Description of Code Generator

The code generator routine, *action*, generates code and performs context sensitive checking. It has a number of subordinate procedures: *template, store_lit, format–lit, relation, bin_op, unary_op, split, sem_err*, and *code_fix*. The calling sequence of these procedures is illustrated in Fig. 2-15. The purpose of each subordinate procedure is briefly outlined with more detailed discussions left for later subsections.

The *template* routine creates array templates, placing an array template in the global area if it can be computed at compile time. Otherwise a skeleton of the template is placed in the local area.

The procedure *store_lit* stores string literals in the global area. The procedure returns the location where the string descriptor is saved.

The *format_lit* procedure generates the code for write statements, including code to handle any specified formatting.

The procedure *relation* performs semantic checking and generates code for the relation operations (i.e., $>$, $<=$, etc.).

The *bin_op* and *unary_op* routines perform semantic checking and code generation for binary operations and unary operations respectively. The semantic checking ensures that the operands are of the correct type for the operation.

Another routine, *split*, tests if the type of the first operand for the logical conjunction and disjunction operators is logical. It then generates the appropriate code.

The *sem_err* routine prints a semantic error message when a context sensitive error has been detected.

The *code_fix* procedure generates code that pops and pushes values on the run-time stack. This is done as a run-time response to a compilation error, hopefully improving run-time debugging by salvaging as much code as is possible.

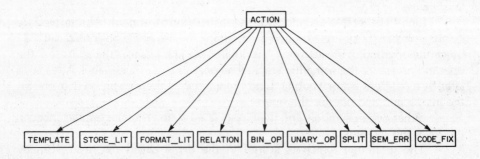

Fig. 2-15   Structure chart of the code generator

2-5.4   Declaration Semantics

This section describes the declaration semantics for variables, constants and procedures. Since arrays may be either variable or constant in size, an introduction on arrays precedes the discussion of both types. The section concludes with an example illustrating how declarations are handled in a sample program.

2-5.4.1   Arrays

An array is a set of data elements all of the same type that share a common name. To reference uniquely each element of the array, a subscript list is appended. When an array declaration is handled, a *template* is built in the data area so that array elements can be dereferenced during execution.

We will now consider the contents of the template. Let n be the number of dimensions of an array. Let $L(i)$ be the lower bound of dimension i and $U(i)$ be the upper bound of dimension i. Clearly these values, i, $L(i)$, and $U(i)$, should be in the template to detect a subscript out of range or the wrong number of subscripts. In fact these values are sufficient to calculate the address of an array element relative to the base location of the area allocated to the array. Let *loc* be the base location of this area. Then the absolute address of an array element with subscripts represented as $V(1)$, $V(2)$, ..., $V(n)$ is given below.

$$The\ absolute\ address\ =\ loc\ +\ \sum_{i=1}^{n} [V(i) - L(i)]\ P(i-1)$$

$$where\ P(0) = 1\ and\ P(i) = \prod_{j=1}^{i} [U(j) - L(j) + 1].$$

$$Let\ RC = -\ \sum_{i=1}^{n} L(i)\ P(i-1).$$

$$Then\ the\ absolute\ address = loc + RC + \sum_{i=1}^{n} V(i)\ P(i-1).$$

$$Let\ AC = RC + loc.$$

$$Then\ the\ absolute\ address = AC + \sum_{i=1}^{n} V(i)\ P(i-1).$$

We call RC the relative constant part of the address calculation and AC the absolute part of the address calculation. A detailed discussion of array addressing functions can be found in Tremblay and Sorenson [1982].

The structure of a template is given in Fig. 2-16.

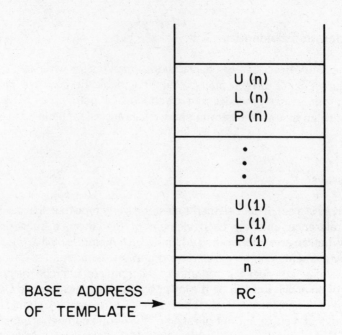

Fig. 2-16   Data template for arrays in GAUSS compiler

The templates for global arrays are generated at compile time and are stored in the global area. Because $L(i)$, $U(i)$, and $P(i)$ are not necessarily known at compile time, the templates for local arrays are generated during program execution and are stored in the local area. In both cases, arrays which are declared in the same declaration statement share the same template. Clearly they have the same type, dimension, and bounds and therefore have the same RC (relative constant part) value. Hence, if x is the absolute constant address associated with an array identifier, then the contents of location x is the address of the template and the contents of address $x + 1$ is the absolute part of the address calculation. These two locations are filled in at compile time for global array variables and at execution time for local array variables.

2-5.4.2   Variable Declarations

Let us begin by considering the declaration of a simple variable. A simple variable, whether it be of type integer or logical, requires a single word of storage for its representation. Similarly string references require a single word. As a result, the semantics associated with simple variable declarations are almost trivial. If a simple global variable is declared, the address field of its symbol table entry is set to the value of *globalptr* which is then incremented by one in preparation for handling the next global variable. In a similar manner, if the declared simple variable is local, the address field of its symbol table entry is set to *localptr* which is then decremented by one in accordance with the addressing scheme for local variables described earlier.

In general, to handle the declaration of an array variable, space must be allocated for the array, the template, the template pointer, and the array pointer.

However, because some inherent differences do exist, let us examine the cases of global and local variables separately.

From the definition of GAUSS as described in Chap. 1, the bounds of global variable arrays must be known at compile time. As a result, all the following actions can be completed at compile time:

> building the template
> allocating space for the array
> setting the address field of the symbol table entry to *globalptr*
> saving the template pointer at location *globalptr*
> saving the absolute constant part of the address calculation
>   at location *globalptr + 1*
> incrementing *globalptr* by two

The *globalptr* is incremented by two to reflect the fact that the template pointer and the absolute constant part of the address calculation are stored in the global area.

In GAUSS, the bounds of local variable arrays need not be known at compile time. If they are known, then the template can be built at compile time and placed in the global area. If the bounds are not known, then a number of actions must take place. First, code (in particular the intermediate language instruction *$$template*) must be generated to build the template at run time. Then, the address field of the symbol table entry is set to *localptr* which is then decremented by two to allow for the template pointer and the absolute part. Finally, code must be generated so that run-time space for the local array is allocated and the template pointer and the absolute constant part of the address calculation are created. This is achieved by generating the *$$allocate* instruction whose operands are the relative address of the template and the relative address of the array identifier.

The augmented grammar for variable declarations is as follows:

```
/* 1 — <program> ::= */
      $global, #eof,
/* 3 — <global> ::= */
      ##(204), $type_specifier, $core,
/* 5 — <core> ::= */
      $entity_list, ##(203), #semi, $global,
/* 6 — <declaration list> ::= */
      $declaration, #semi, $declaration_list,
/* 7 — <declaration list> ::= null */
/* 11 — <declaration> ::= */
      ##(204), $type_specifier, $entity_list, ##(203),
/* 13 — <entity list> ::= */
      #newident, ##(202), $ident_list,
/* 16 — <type specifier> ::= */
      $simple_type, ##(205),
/* 17 — <type specifier> ::= */
      $array,
/* 18 — <simple type> ::= */
      #integer,
/* 19 — <simple type> ::= */
```

```
            #string,
/* 20 — <simple type> ::= */
            #logical,
/* 21 — <array> ::= */
            #array, #lparen, $bound_pair, $bound_pair_list,
            #rparen, #of, $simple_type, ##(216),
/* 22 — <bound pair list> ::= */
            #comma, $bound_pair, $bound_pair_list,
/* 23 — <bound pair list> ::= null */
/* 24 — <bound pair> ::= */
            ##(206), $expression, ##(207), $second_bound,
/* 25 — <second bound> ::= */
            #colon, $expression, ##(207),
/* 26 — <second bound> ::= null */
            ##(208),
/* 37 — <ident list> ::= */
            #comma, #newident, ##(202), $ident_list,
/* 38 — <ident list> ::= null */
```

The first action symbol of a declaration is ##(204) (in productions 03 and 11). When this action symbol is encountered, the invoked action routine places seven elements on top of the semantic stack. The top of the semantic stack is organized as shown in Fig. 2-17.

The type and dimension locations are used for all identifiers. The remaining elements are generated only for array declarations. In particular, the address of the template, the size of the array and the relative constant part are all required when handling global arrays and local arrays with array bounds that are known at compile time. The final two elements, the pointer to the allocated area and the end of the allocated area, are used only in storing string constant arrays and for checking to see if the number of string constants agree with the specified array bounds.

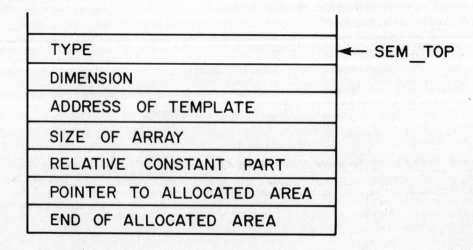

Fig. 2-17   Semantic stack description for arrays

The next set of action symbols handle the type specification. If it is a simple type, then the action routine associated with the action symbol ##(205) in production 16 places the type on top of the semantic stack; otherwise, <array> must be handled in production 21.

The first step in handling <array> is to process each <bound pair> as described in production 24. Action routine ##(206) is called at the start of a <bound pair> and it increments the dimension location on the semantic stack and prepares for bound <expression>s. Action routine ##(207) is invoked in productions 24 and 25 to handle the explicit bound <expression>s. Action routine ##(208), called in production 26, recognizes the default lower bound of 1. After the <bound pair> has been processed, intermediate language instructions will have been generated to place the lower- and upper-bound values on top of the run-time stack. In addition, the <expression>s are tested to ensure they are integers and whether or not they can be evaluated at compile time.

The final step in handling <array> is achieved by action routine ##(216) of production 21. The type is saved in the type location on the semantic stack. The *template* procedure is then called. If all the bounds of the declared array are known at compile time, then the template is built in the global area, the code which places the value of the bounds on the run-time stack is deleted, and the address of the template, the size of the array, and the relative constant part of the address calculation are placed in their respective locations on the semantic stack; otherwise, code must be generated to build the template at run time in the local area. The intermediate language instruction emitted to perform this is *$$template* whose operand is the number of dimensions of the array. The address of the template is determined and it is placed in its location on the semantic stack (see Fig. 2-17).

Now that the <type specifier> has been handled, all that remains is the <entity list> as described in production 13. After handling each new identifier action routine ##(202) is called. This routine copies the type and dimension from the top of the semantic stack to the symbol table entry of the identifier. Then it allocates storage as previously described.

The seven locations on the semantic stack are reclaimed after the declaration is completed. This is signalled by action symbol ##(203) in productions 5 and 11.

2-5.4.3   Constant Declarations

Although global and local constants differ in scope, they are handled in the same way. For simple constants, the value is simply stored in the address field of the symbol table. This reduces space requirements and eliminates the necessity of having to load constants onto the run-time stack. Constant arrays are similar to global variable arrays except that the constants are inserted directly into the allocated space in the global area. When handling string constants, space must be allocated for all the string references before the string characters are read. Therefore, the compiler stores the string reference at the next available location in the allocated area. The string descriptor and then the characters forming the string are loaded into the global area above the string reference. In the case of an array of string constants, the descriptors and characters are loaded into an area above the space allocated for the set of string references that are associated with the array elements.

The augmented grammar required to handle constant declarations is as follows:

```
/* 12 — <entity list> ::= */
    #const, #newident, ##(201), #eq, $constant, $constant_list,
/* 14 — <const list> :: */
    #comma, #newident, ##(201), #eq, $constant, $constant_list,
/* 15 — <const list> ::= null */
/* 27 — <constant> ::= */
    $simple_constant, ##(209),
/* 28 — <constant> ::= */
    $array_constant, ##(210),
/* 29 — <simple constant> ::= */
    #uminus, #number, ##(211),
/* 30 — <simple constant> ::= */
    #number, ##(212),
/* 31 — <simple constant> ::= */
    #literal, ##(213),
/* 32 — <simple constant> ::= */
    #true, ##(214),
/* 33 — <simple constant> ::= */
    #false, ##(215),
/* 34 — <array constant> ::= */
    #lparen, $simple_constant, ##(217), $simple_constant_list, #rparen,
/* 35 — <simple constant list> ::= */
    #comma, $simple_constant, ##(217), $simple_constant_list,
/* 36 — <simple constant list> ::= null */
```

The <type specifier> of a constant declaration is the same as the <type specifier> of a variable declaration. In fact, the first indication of a constant declaration arises when the keyword *const* is recognized at the start of the <entity list> in production 12. After the identifier in the <entity list> or each identifier in the <constant list> is recognized, action routine ##(201) is called. This routine fills in the symbol table entry of the identifier and allocates space as previously described. The pointer to the allocated area and the end address of the allocated area are placed in the semantic stack at the locations shown in Fig. 2-17. The pointer to the allocated area is initially set to the beginning of the area allocated to string array constants and this pointer is incremented by one each time a descriptor for a new string constant is created. All that remains is to handle the <constant>.

Recall from Sec. 2-2.5 that the scanner synthesizes constants by placing the value of an integer constant in the variable *value*, by placing the value of a string constant in the variable *strbuf*, and by passing tokens to the parser that represent the values *true* and *false* for logical constants. Negative number constants are handled in action routine ##(211) which negates the value in *value* and then proceeds to action routine ##(212). Action routine ##(212) is invoked as well when unsigned integer constants are handled in production 30. This action routine simply checks to see if the identifier declared for the constant is of type integer.

Similarly, action routine ##(213), which is invoked during the expansion of production 31, checks if the identifier for the constant is declared to be of type string. If it is, the procedure *store_lit* is called which assigns to *value* the reference for the string constant. The reference is a pointer to the next open location in the global area. The string descriptor and the characters of the string are then loaded into the global area beginning at the reference location.

Logical constants are handled in productions 32 and 33. Action routine ##(214) places a 1 in *value* (representing a logical value of *true*) while action routine ##(215) places a 0 in *value* (representing a logical value of *false*). Both action routines also verify that the identifier for the logical constant is declared to be of type logical (i.e., semantic analysis is again performed).

The <simple constant> can be used in two ways. If it is used as the <constant> in production 27, then action routine ##(209) checks if the identifier is simple and saves *value* in the address field of the symbol table entry. If it is used as part of <array constant> in production 34, then *value* is stored at the first available location in the allocated area.

In the case of an array of string constants, the space that is initially allocated is filled up with string references. As string constants are defined, the string descriptors and the characters in the strings are placed in the next available space in the global area which would be above the space allocated for the string reference.

At the end of production 28 for <constant>, action routine ##(210) checks if the constant identifier is an array and matches the number of constants initialized with the size of the array. This final check involves a test to see if there is a match between the pointer to the allocated area and the end of allocated area parameters, which are both on the semantic stack. If there is not a match, an erroneous constant-array declaration has occurred.

2-5.4.4   Procedure Declarations

There are two forms of procedure declarations: the forward declaration and the procedure definition. Examples of each were given in Sec. 1-4.1. They are processed in a similar fashion except that in a forward declaration a dummy procedure address of 0 is used in the *procinfo* segment as opposed to a true procedure address. The first time a particular procedure is declared, the symbol table entry and the segment in the *procinfo* array are filled in. Subsequent declarations of that procedure are then compared to the first declaration but no changes are made. Inconsistencies in procedure dimension, parameter type, and parameter dimension are detected and error messages are produced. Redefinition of the procedure is also considered an error.

The following augmented productions recognize and handle procedure declarations:

```
/* 1 — <program> :: */
      $global, #eof,
/* 2 — <global> ::= */
      ##(221), $procedure, #semi, $procedure_list,
/* 3 — <global> ::= */
      ##(204), $type_specifier, $core,
/* 4 — <core> ::= */
      ##(222), $procedure, #semi, $procedure_list,
/* 8 — <procedure list> ::= */
```

##(221), $procedure, #semi, $procedure_list,
/* 9 — <procedure list> ::= */
    $simple_type, ##(221), ##(205), $procedure, #semi, $procedure_list,
/* 10 — <procedure list> ::= null */
/* 39 — <procedure> ::= */
    #proc, $proc_name, ##(219), $parameter_list, ##(220),
    $procedure_tail,
/* 40 — <procedure tail> ::= */
    #forward, ##(226),
/* 41 — <procedure tail> ::= */
    $procedure_body,
/* 45 — <parameter list> ::= */
    #lparen, $parameter, $parameters, #rparen,
/* 46 — <parameter list> ::= null */
/* 47 — <parameters> ::= */
    #comma, $parameter, $parameters,
/* 48 — <parameters> ::= null */
/* 49 — <parameter> ::= */
    $parameter_type, #newident, ##(224),
/* 50 — <parameter type> ::= */
    $simple_type, ##(205),
/* 51 — <parameter type> ::= */
    #array, #lparen, ##(225), $comma_list, #rparen, #of, $simple_type,
    ##(205),
/* 52 — <comma list> ::= */
    #comma, ##(225), $comma_list,
/* 53 — <comma list> ::= null */
/* 137 — <proc_name> ::= */
    #newident,
/* 138 — <procname> ::= */
    #procident,

When commencing the parsing of a procedure declaration statement as described in production 2, action routine ##(221) reserves space (using the variable *codesave*) for a *$$incrsp* instruction in the code area. The operand of this instruction is the amount of space that must be allocated in the local area of the run-time stack for the fixed part of the local variables (i.e., the space for the simple variables, string references, and array templates). Of course, the exact amount of space needed will not be known until all the procedure parameters and local variable declarations have been processed. When this is known (see the discussion in Sec. 2-5.5.2 of action routine ##(228) in production 42), the *$$incrsp* instruction and its operand are generated at the location denoted as *codesave*.

Action routine ##(221) then causes two locations to be allocated on top of the semantic stack. The top location is to contain the type of the procedure. It is initialized to zero to indicate that it does not return a value. The next location is reserved for the dimension (number of parameters) of the procedure. If indeed the procedure returns a value, then action routine ##(205) places the type on top of the semantic stack. It should be noted that action routine ##(222) is similar to ##(221) followed by ##(205) except that it compensates for having handled the <type specifier>.

After the procedure name is recognized in production 39, action routine ##(219) is called. If the procedure has not been previously declared, then the type and address fields of the symbol table entry and the procedure address and symbol table entry pointer locations of the *procinfo* segment are initialized. If the procedure has been declared previously, then the type field of the symbol table entry is tested to be consistent with the type on top of the semantic stack. To prepare for parameters, two more locations are allocated on top of the semantic stack, one for the type and the other for the dimension. The parameter dimension location is initialized to zero.

Parameters, as described in productions 49, 50, and 51, are handled one at a time. Action routine ##(225) increments the parameter dimension location. Action routine ##(205) saves the type in the parameter type location. Then action routine ##(224) fills in the symbol table entry of the parameter identifier, increments the procedure dimension count, and resets the parameter dimension to zero.

Once all the parameters have been handled in a procedure declaration as described in production 39, action routine ##(220) is called. If the procedure has not been previously declared, then the symbol table entry of the procedure identifier and the *procinfo* segment are completed; otherwise, more consistency checks are made concerning the size of the parameter list.

Consider, finally, the <procedure tail>. If the procedure declaration is a forward declaration, then action routine ##(226) calls the *sym_rem* procedure to remove the local symbol table entries that are created for the parameters of the procedure because these entries are not accessible by any part of the program. Otherwise, <procedure body> is handled as described in Sec. 2-5.4.

One might wonder why two action routines, namely ##(221) and ##(205), are adjacent in the augmented grammar description. The parser will simply call one action routine and then immediately call the second routine. Why not have a single routine that performs both ##(221) and ##(205)? We have chosen not to do this because action routine ##(205) fulfills a utility role in the sense that it is required in several other productions (e.g., productions 50 and 51) and therefore, it is more storage efficient to retain it as a separate routine. There are several other instances of utility action routines in the augmented grammar (e.g., ##(289) and ##(254)).

2-5.4.5 Declaration Examples

We will use the following example program to illustrate the code generation and semantic analysis associated with declarations:

```
LOGICAL CONST FOUND = TRUE, NOT_FOUND = FALSE;
        $$ global simple constants
STRING NEXT_MONTH;
        $$ global simple identifier
ARRAY(3) OF INTEGER CONST DAYS_IN_MONTH = (31, 28, 31);
        $$ global array of constants
ARRAY(0:2) OF STRING FIRST_NAME, LAST_NAME;
        $$ global arrays
PROC MAIN
        INTEGER CONST NEW = 1, OLD = 0;
        $$ local constants
        LOGICAL DEBUG: INTEGER I;
```

```
          $$ local simple identifiers
          ARRAY(3) OF STRING CONST MONTH = ("JAN", "FEB", "MAR");
          $$ local array of constants
          ARRAY(9, -3:10) OF LOGICAL LOG1;
          $$ local array
          DEBUG := TRUE;
     ENDPROC;
```

An indication of the changes in the compile-time organization due to the above sample program is given in Fig. 2-18.

2-5.5 Procedure Semantics

This section is concerned with how procedures are handled in GAUSS. The section is subdivided into three topic areas: the procedure call, the procedure body, and the procedure return. Each topic is discussed separately, but, clearly, their interdependence must be acknowledged.

2-5.5.1 Procedure Call

All parameter passing in GAUSS is pass-by-reference. Expressions, constants, and constant identifiers may not be used as arguments in a procedure call. Thus, only simple identifiers, array identifiers, and array elements may be used as arguments. If it is desirable that a pass-by-value type of parameter passing be used, then the argument can be assigned to a dummy variable and the dummy variable can be used as the input parameter to the called procedure.

The procedure call must be consistent with the procedure declaration. If a procedure is declared to return a value, then the procedure call must be used as an expression; otherwise, the procedure call must be used as a statement. The number of arguments in the call must match the number of parameters in the declaration. The type and dimension of each argument must match the type and dimension of the corresponding parameter (correspondence is by relative position).

The code generated from a procedure call transfers control to the called procedure and constructs a segment of the activation record as illustrated in Fig. 2-19.

Let us examine the action routines associated with a procedure call to find out how this run-time stack configuration is reached. The augmented grammar for a procedure call follows:

```
     /* 62 — <procedure call> ::= */
          #procident, ##(248), $argument_list, ##(249), ##(270),
     /* 63 — <argument list> ::= */
          #lparen, $argument, $arguments, #rparen,
     /* 64 — <argument list> ::= null */
     /* 65 — <arguments> ::= */
          #comma, $argument, $arguments,
     /* 66 — <arguments> ::= null */
     /* 67 — <argument> ::= */
          #simpident, ##(260),
```

```
/* 68 — <argument> ::= */
      #arrayident, $sublist,
/* 69 — <sublist> ::= */
      ##(253), #lparen, $expression, $expressions, #rparen, ##(254),
      ##(261),
/* 70 — <sublist> ::= null */
      ##(260),
/* 128 — <primary> ::= */
      #procident, ##(248), $argument_list, ##(249),
```

The first action symbol in the description of a procedure call, as given in production 62, is ##(248). Its action routine has two functions. The first function is to generate code which saves the activation base pointer and the return address of the calling procedure. The activation base pointer of the calling procedure is in a special run-time location. Therefore an intermediate language instruction, $$saveabp, is required to copy the activation base pointer on top of the run-time stack. The return address of the calling procedure can be determined at compile time. Therefore, all that is required is an intermediate language instruction which causes its operand to be pushed on top of the run-time stack. The $$push instruction accomplishes this. However, the return address is not known until the argument list has been handled. Hence, the code address of the operand of the $$push instruction is saved temporarily on the semantic stack and is filled in later by action routine ##(249). This action routine is invoked after handling argument lists during the processing of production 62 (a procedure call) or production 128 (a function call).

The second function of action routine ##(248) is to place information on the semantic stack in order to prepare for the handling of arguments. On top of the semantic stack is the remaining number of arguments that are expected. This location is initialized to the "dimension" of the called procedure. Second on the semantic stack is an index into the *procinfo* segment. The index points to the description of the parameter corresponding to the next argument. Third is the symbol table entry pointer of the called procedure. It is used later to resolve the entry address of the procedure.

The next step is to handle the arguments of the argument list as defined in productions 67 and 68. If the argument is a simple identifier or an identifier for an array, then action routine ##(260) is called from productions 67 and 70. This routine checks that the type and dimension of the argument match the type and dimension of the corresponding parameter. Then code is generated to place the absolute address of the argument on top of the run-time stack. The relative address of the identifier is known and stored in the address field of the symbol table entry. If the argument is a parameter of the calling procedure, then the run-time contents of the relative address is the absolute address of the variable it represents. Therefore, a $$load instruction is generated to place the contents of the designated relative address on top of the run-time stack. If the argument is not a parameter of the calling procedure, then the $$absolute instruction is generated to place the absolute address of the designated relative address on top of the run-time stack.

If the argument is an array element as described in production 68, then the <sublist> must be handled. Productions containing a subscript list are 69, 86, 94, 131, and 132. The processing of these subscript lists are similar, although not identical. Action routines ##(253) and ##(254) perform the common processing.

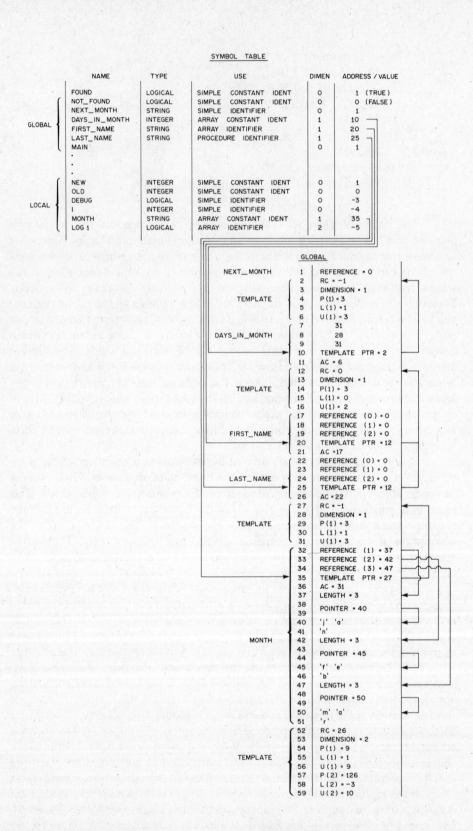

Fig. 2-18   Code generation and semantic analysis trace of declarations

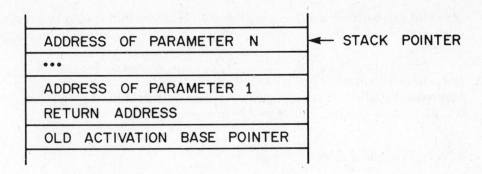

Fig. 2-19 Segment of activation record for a procedure call

Other action routines are later called upon to perform activities which are special to the type of sublist being considered — whether they be subscript lists in arrays or lists of parameters in a call statement. In the case of parameter passing, action routine ##(261) fulfills the role of handling the special case.

At the start of processing a subscript list, as described in production 69, the action routine ##(253) is called. This routine allocates two locations on the semantic stack. The top location is a marker (value of -1) that indicates the beginning of the lists of subscripts and the second location saves the symbol table entry pointer of the array identifier. Each expression in the subscript list is handled by generating code to place the value of the expression on top of the run-time stack at run time and the type on top of the semantic stack at compile time. Action routine ##(254) is called at the end of the subscript list. It counts the number of expressions while checking if they have the right type. Then code is generated to dereference (calculate the absolute address of) the array element. The method to do this is given in Sec. 2-5.2 but a single intermediate language instruction has been selected to perform this action. If the array identifier is a parameter, then the instruction is $$derefi; otherwise, $$deref is emitted. Both instructions use the relative address of the array identifier as an operand. If the array identifier is a parameter, then the run-time contents of the designated relative address is the absolute address of the array identifier it represents. In this way the template and the absolute constant part of the address calculation can be found.

As mentioned previously, the particular processing required to handle the <sublist> is accomplished by action routine ##(261). It checks that the type and dimension of the array element match the type and dimension of the corresponding parameter.

The last action routine in a procedure call is ##(249) as indicated in productions 62 and 128. It checks that the number of arguments found matches the number of arguments required. Then code is generated to set the new activation base pointer and instruction counter. This is accomplished by emitting the intermediate language instruction $$jump which has two operands. The first operand is the address of the procedure and the second operand is the number of arguments. Unfortunately, the address of the procedure is not always known at the time the call is made. When the addresses of the procedures are unknown, the one operand is used to maintain a linked list of the unresolved address locations. The second operand indicates the procedure. Once compilation is completed, the linked list can be traversed, replacing the first operand with the address of the procedure and the second operand with the number of arguments in the procedure.

Since a procedure call may be used as an expression, the type of the procedure is left on top of the semantic stack to be used later for type checking. If the procedure call is used as a statement, then the type must be the dummy value of 0. This is tested in action routine ##(270) in production 62.

2-5.5.2 Procedure Body

The code generated from a procedure body completes the construction of the activation record. The augmented grammar for the procedure body follows:

```
/* 42 — <procedure body> ::= */
    $declaration_list, ##(228), ##(289), $statement, #semi,
    $statement_list, #endproc, ##(229),
```

Action routine ##(228) is invoked after the declaration list is processed. At this point, storage requirements for the fixed-length part of the local variables are known. This storage must be allocated even before the code associated with the declaration list is executed. For example, the storage must be allocated before the code that allocates space for the elements of a dynamic array is executed. Therefore, the action routine ##(228) inserts a $$incrsp instruction immediately before the code generated by the declaration list. The operand of the instruction is the amount of storage needed. This operand *fix-up* is made easily since two locations in the code area are deliberately reserved before the code for the declaration list is generated (see discussion in Sec. 2-5.4.4). *codesave* points to the first location. Action routine ##(289) is a utility routine that generates the $$line instruction. This instruction simply saves a line number value at run time. This value is output as part of a run-time error message if a run-time error occurs in the next statement that is executed.

The code generated by the declaration list causes templates to be built and storage to be allocated for arrays. This completes the second phase in the construction of the activation record, i.e., the allocation of storage for local variables. At the end of the procedure body, action routine ##(229) is called. This routine ensures that the last statement of the procedure body is treated as a return statement.

2-5.5.3 Procedure Return

The return statement in a procedure must be consistent with the procedure declaration. If a procedure is declared to return a value of a certain type, then the return statement must return an expression of that type; otherwise, the return statement must not return a value.

The code generated from a procedure return removes the activation record of the returning procedure and returns control to the calling procedure. The augmented grammar for a procedure return follows:

```
/* 73 — <return stmt> ::= */
    #return, $ret_expression,
```

```
/* 74 — <ret expression> ::= */
    $expression, ##(271),
/* 75 — <ret expression> ::= null */
    ##(272),
```

Action routine ##(272) is called if the return statement does not return a value. Code must be generated to set the instruction counter to the return address, the stack pointer to the present activation base pointer, and the activation base pointer to the previous activation base pointer (i.e., the activation base pointer of the calling procedure). The intermediate language instruction $$return is designed to accomplish these tasks.

Action routine ##(271) is called if the return statement does return a value. In addition to the functions of the $$return instruction, the value of the return expression must be moved on top of the new run-time stack. All of this is accomplished by the intermediate language instruction $$returnval.

2-5.6 Expressions

Code generation and the semantic checking of expressions can be divided into two topics: primaries and operations. Each topic is now considered.

2-5.6.1 Primaries

Primaries are the atomic parts of an expression in the sense that they contain no operation on subexpressions. Code is generated to place the value of primary on top of the run-time stack. The type of the primary is placed on top of the semantic stack for subsequent type checking once the use of the primary is known. The augmented grammar for primaries follows:

```
/* 128 — <primary> ::= */
    #procident, ##(248), $argument_list, ##(249),
/* 129 — <primary> ::= */
    #simpident, ##(250), $substring, ##(251),
/* 130 — <primary> ::= */
    #simpconident, ##(252), $substring, ##(251),
/* 131 — <primary> ::= */
    #arrayident, ##(253), #lparen, $expression, $expressions,
    #rparen, ##(254), ##(259), $substring, ##(251),
/* 132 — <primary> ::= */
    #arrayconident, ##(253), #lparen, $expression, $expressions,
    #rparen, ##(254), ##(259), $substring, ##(251),
/* 133 — <primary> ::= */
    #number, ##(255),
/* 134 — <primary> ::= */
    #literal, ##(256),
/* 135 — <primary> ::= */
    #true, ##(257),
/* 136 — <primary> ::= */
    #false, ##(258),
```

```
/* 84 — <substring> ::= */
       #lparen, $start, #substr, $length, #rparen,
/* 85 — <substring> ::= null */
       ##(265),
/* 86 — <start> ::= */
       $expression,
/* 87 — <length> ::= */
       $expression, ##(266),
/* 88 — <length> ::= null */
       ##(267),
```

The procedure call which is included as a primary in production 128 has already been discussed in Sec 2-5.5. The other primaries can be classified into three categories: constants, simple identifiers, and array elements. After the discussion of these categories, substring designation is described. Substring designation may follow simple identifiers and array elements.

Let us first consider the constant primaries listed in productions 133 to 136. The value of the constant is known at compile time. Either it is explicitly placed in the variable *value* by the scanner or it is implicitly assigned by the action routine. Therefore, to have access to a constant, intermediate code must be generated which places the constant's value on top of the run-time stack. The intermediate language instruction which performs this stacking is *$$push*. The operand of the *$$push* instruction is the value of the constant. Action routine ##(255), which is invoked when production 133 is expanded, emits code that pushes the value of the number on the run-time stack. It also places the type "#integer" on top of the semantic stack. Similarly action routine ##(256), which is associated with production 134, pushes the reference value of the literal string on the run-time stack. In addition, the type "#string" is placed on top of the semantic stack. Finally, action routines ##(257) and ##(258) emit code that push the value 1 and 0, respectively, on the run-time stack. These routines also place the type "#logical" on top of the semantic stack.

The simple identifier primaries given in productions 129 and 130 are considered next. The value of a simple constant identifier is known at compile time and stored in the address field of the symbol table entry. Therefore, action routine ##(252) of production 130 pushes the value on top of the run-time stack and places the type of the simple constant identifier on top of the semantic stack. The value of a simple variable identifier is not known at compile time (unless perhaps by folding using global flow analysis which is not employed in this GAUSS compiler). However, its relative address is known and stored in the address field of the symbol table entry. If the identifier is a parameter, then the run-time contents of the relative address must be the absolute address of the variable it represents; otherwise, the content is the value of the variable. Two intermediate language instructions which use the relative address of a simple variable identifier as an operand have been defined. The *$$load* instruction is used for standard simple identifiers and it places the contents of the specified relative address on top of the run-time stack. The *$$loadi* instruction is required for parameters and it uses the contents of the specified relative address as an absolute address and places the contents of the designated absolute address on top of the run-time stack. In action routine ##(250) of production 129 either the *$$loadi* instruction or the *$$loadsi* instruction is generated if the identifier is a parameter, depending on whether the identifier is a string identifier. Otherwise the *$$load* instruction or the *$$loads* instruction is generated. The instructions *$$loads* and *$$loadsi* differ from their corresponding counterparts *$$load* and *$$loadi* as a temporary copy of the string is generated and its descriptor is pushed onto the run-time stack. This eases the task of garbage collection as the operands of all string operators are temporary if they are not from the global area and can be freed after use. This discussion also holds for the *$$loadsa* and *$$loada* instructions. Once the appropriate instruction has been generated the type of the identifier is placed on top of the semantic stack.

Finally, we consider the array primaries given in productions 131 and 132. The subscripts of an array are themselves expressions, so the need exists to handle expressions recursively. The constant array elements and variable array elements are handled in an almost identical manner. As described earlier in the discussion of procedure calls, action routines ##(253) and ##(254) generate code to place the absolute address of the array element on top of the run-time stack. In this case, the routines are invoked when productions 132 and 133 are expanded. To load the value of the array element, the absolute address on top of the stack must be replaced by the contents of the absolute address. The action routine ##(259) performs the loading of the contents of the absolute address. It generates the *$$loadsa* instruction if the array is a string array and the *$$loada* instruction otherwise. The routine then places the type of the array element on top of the semantic stack.

Primaries of type string may be followed by a substring designation. If they are, additional code is required to calculate the substring and place the new string reference on top of the run-time stack. Two steps are required to detect and handle this situation.

The first step is to process <substring>. If there is no substring designation, action routine ##(265) of production 85 signals this by placing the value 0 on top of the semantic stack. If there is a substring designation, then code is generated to place the value of the start expression on top of the run-time stack. If there is no length expression, then this is designated in action routine ##(267) of production 88 by placing the value 1 on top of the semantic stack. Otherwise, code is generated to place the value of the length expression on top of the run-time stack. Action routine ##(266) of production 87 then places the value 2 on top of the semantic stack to indicate the presence of a length expression.

The second step is to generate code to isolate the substring, if necessary. Action routine ##(251) is called when productions 130, 131, or 132 are expanded. If the top of the semantic stack is 0, then there is no substring designation and no code is generated. Otherwise, the type of the primary is tested to be string and the type of the start expression to be integer. If the top of the semantic stack is 1, then the *$$substring* instruction is generated; otherwise, the type of the length expression is tested to be integer and the *$$substringl* instruction is generated. Again through semantic analysis an error message is generated if an improper type is discovered.

2-5.6.2 Operations

The intermediate language is designed so that all the operands of an instruction that is associated with arithmetic, string, or logical operations in GAUSS should be placed on top of the run-time stack prior to the execution of the instruction. In other words, the GAUSS compiler generates postfix code for expressions. The types of the operands are placed on top of the semantic stack. Therefore, once the types have been checked, they are removed from the semantic stack and the type yielded by the operation is placed on the semantic stack. Similarly the intermediate language instruction generated will, when executed, replace the values of the operands on the run-time stack by the result for the operation. The augmented grammar for the operations in GAUSS follows:

```
/* 98 — <expression> ::= */
      $part, $etail,
/* 99 — <etail> ::= */
      #gt, $part, ##(230),
/* 100 — <etail> ::= */
      #lt, $part, ##(231),
/* 101 — <etail> ::= */
      #eq, $part, ##(232),
/* 102 — <etail> ::= */
      #ge, $part, ##(233),
/* 103 — <etail> ::= */
      #le, $part, ##(234),
/* 104 — <etail> ::= */
      #ne, $part, ##(235),
/* 105 — <etail> ::= null */
/* 106 — <part> ::= */
      $term, $ptail,
/* 107 — <ptail> ::= */
      #plus, $term, ##(236), $ptail,
/* 108 — <ptail> ::= */
      #minus, $term, ##(237), $ptail,
/* 109 — <ptail> ::= */
      #or, ##(238), $term, ##(262), $ptail,
/* 110 — <ptail> ::= null */
/* 111 — <term> ::= */
      $factor, $ttail,
/* 112 — <ttail> ::= */
      #mult, $factor, ##(239), $ttail,
/* 113 — <ttail> ::= */
      #div, $factor, ##(240), $ttail,
/* 114 — <ttail> ::= */
      #mod, $factor, ##(241), $ttail,
/* 115 — <ttail> ::= */
      #and, ##(242), $factor, ##(262), $ttail,
/* 116 — <ttail> ::= null */
/* 117 — <factor> ::= */
      #not, $index, ##(243),
/* 118 — <factor> ::= */
      #uminus, $index, ##(244),
/* 119 — <factor> ::= */
      $index,
/* 120 — <index> ::= */
      #length, $catena, ##(245),
```

```
/* 121 — <index> ::= */
      $catena, $itail,
/* 122 — <itail> ::= */
      #index, $catena, ##(246),
/* 123 — <itail> ::= null */
/* 124 — <catena> ::= */
      $primary, $ctail,
/* 125 — <ctail> ::= */
      #concat, $primary, ##(247), $ctail,
/* 126 — <ctail> ::= null */
```

The operations can be classified into three categories: relations, other binary operations, and unary operations. Because of the similarity of action routines for the operators within a category, a general procedure is written to handle the operations for each category. An action routine then invokes the appropriate procedure with a set of arguments that identify the operation being synthesized. The remainder of this section describes the three general procedures and provides an example action routine from each category.

First, let us consider the relations greater than, less than, equal, greater than or equal, less than or equal, and not equal, in productions 99 to 104. Their corresponding action routines call the *relation* procedure with three arguments: the token representing the relation; the instruction required to handle the string relation; and the instruction required to handle the integer relation. Clearly, the comparison between strings and between integers must be handled differently. However, a separate set of instructions for comparisons between logicals is not necessary. The allowable relations between logicals are handled as though they were relations between integers.

The first step of the *relation* procedure is to test if the relation is semantically correct. That is, the types of the operands, as stored on top of the semantic stack, must be the same. The relations between logical operands are limited to equality and inequality. The second step is to generate the correct intermediate language instruction. If the operands are strings, then the corresponding string instruction is generated; otherwise, the integer instruction is generated. Then the type #logical is placed on top of the semantic stack.

As an example consider action routine ##(232) of production 101 which handles the equality relation. It calls the *relation* procedure with the arguments #eq, $$seq, and $$ieq. #eq is the token representing the equality relation. $$seq is generated if the relational expression involves a test for equality of strings and $$ieq is generated if the test is on the equality of integers or logicals.

The binary operations of logical conjunction and disjunction are handled separately from other binary operations because the value of the operation can be determined from the value of the first operand. Therefore, the code generation and semantic analysis is split into two components. If the token #or is encountered, action routine ##(238) calls the *split* procedure with the argument $$or. The $$or instruction causes a branch if the value on top of the run-time stack is *true* (i.e., 1). If the token #and is encountered, action routine ##(242) calls the *split* procedure with the argument $$and. The $$and instruction causes a branch if the value on top of the run-time stack is *false* (i.e., 0). The *split* procedure tests if the type of the first operand, found on top of the semantic stack, is logical. Then it generates the appropriate opcode. Since the destination operand is not known until the second operand of the operation is encountered, the address of the instruction operand is saved on top of the semantic stack. The second component is action routine ##(262) which is invoked after the second operand of the operation is encountered. It tests if the type of the second operand is logical and sets the destination operand of the previous operation to *codeptr*.

Next consider the other binary operations addition, subtraction, multiplication, division, remainder-on-division, index-into-string, and concatenation, in productions 107 to 108, 112 to 114, 122, and 125 respectively. Their corresponding action routines call the *bin_op* procedure with two arguments: the type of the operands expected and the intermediate language instruction to be generated. The first step of the *bin_op* procedure is to test if the operands have the correct type. The next step is to generate the instruction. The type of the result is assumed to be the type of the operands but the action routines override this when necessary.

As an example, consider the action routine ##(247) of production 125 which handles the binary operation of concatenation. Its primary activity is to call the *bin_op* procedure with arguments #*string* and $$*concat*.

Consider, finally, the unary operations logical negation, arithmetic negation, and length-of-string, in productions 117, 118, and 120 respectively. Their corresponding action routines call the *unary_op* procedure with two arguments: the type of the operand expected and the intermediate language instruction to be generated. The *unary_op* procedure behaves like the *bin_op* procedure except for the obvious difference in number of operands. For example, action routine ##(243) of production 117 handles logical negation by calling the *unary_op* procedure with the arguments #*logical* and $$*not*.

2-5.7 Assignment Semantics

The augmented grammar for the assignment statement follows:

```
/* 82 — <assignment stmt> ::= */
        #simpident, ##(284), $substring, ##(279), ##(281), #assign,
        $expression, ##(282),
/* 83 — <assignment stmt> ::= */
        #arrayident, ##(253), #lparen, $expression, $expressions, #rparen,
        ##(254), $substring, ##(279), #assign, $expression, ##(283),
/* 84 — <substring> ::= */
        #lparen, $start, #substr, $length, #rparen,
/* 85 — <substring> ::= null */
        ##(265),
/* 86 — <start> ::= */
        $expression,
/* 87 — <length> ::= */
        $expression, ##(266),
/* 88 — <length> ::= null */
        ##(267),
```

The possibility of a substring designation on the left-hand side of an assignment statement introduces complications. Rather than developing the definition of intermediate language instructions to handle substring assignment, we begin by introducing the instructions and provide the motivation for these instructions after more discussion.

The *$$replace* instruction is used when the length expression is omitted from the substring designation. It requires three operands on top of the run-time stack: the string reference for the replacement string, the value of the start expression, and the absolute address of the left-hand variable. The *$$replacel* instruction is used when the length expression is present in the substring designation. It requires four operands: the three operands of the previous instruction, and the value of the length expression. Both of the previous instructions create a reference for the new string and store it at the absolute address of the left-hand variable.

When no substring designation is given during assignment to a string variable, the *$$replace* instruction must still be used in order that string space can be marked as free. In the event that garbage collection takes place, the free space is reused. In effect, we are handling

STRINGX := some right-hand side;

as

SUBSTR(STRINGX,1) := some right-hand side;

Action routine ##(279) is responsible for generating the code to load the value 1 on the run-time stack and resetting the semantic stack as if the substring designation actually occured.

Let us now examine assignment to a simple identifier. Action routine ##(284) of production 82 saves the identifier on top of the semantic stack and reserves two locations in the code area that are filled in later when <substring> is processed. After <substring> is processed, as described in Section 2-5.6, action routine ##(281) is called. If indeed a substring was not designated, then the two locations allocated previously are recovered. If the identifier is a parameter then the address of the parameter is loaded with simply a *$$load* instruction. In all other cases, the absolute address of the identifier must be generated by using the *$$absolute* instruction.

After code is generated to place the value of the right-hand side expression on top of the run-time stack, action routine ##(282) is called. It checks that the type of the right-hand side matches the type of the left-hand side. If a string was designated, then the *$$replace* or *$$replacel* instruction is generated depending on the substring designation. Otherwise, code must be generated to assign to the variable the value on top of the run-time stack. The intermediate language instructions which accomplish this are now discussed.

Given the relative address of an identifier, we wish to store the top of the run-time stack at the absolute address of the variable. If the identifier is a parameter, then the run-time contents of the relative address is the absolute address of the variable it represents; otherwise, the contents is the value of the variable. Therefore, the relative address is used as an operand for the following instructions. The *$$store* instruction stores the value on the top of the run-time stack at the specified relative address. The *$$storei* instruction is used in the case where the identifier is a parameter. This instruction uses the contents of the specified relative address as an absolute address and stores the top of the run-time stack at the designated absolute address.

Let us now consider the assignment to an array element. Action routines ##(253) and ##(254) generate code to place the absolute address of the array element on top of the run-time stack. After <substring> is processed and code is generated to place the value of the right-hand side expression on top of the run-time stack, action routine ##(283) is called. If a substring was designated, then either the $$replace or $$replacel instruction is generated; otherwise, code must be generated to store the top of the run-time stack at the absolute address stored on the run-time stack. The $$storea instruction accomplishes this.

2-5.8 Control Structure Semantics

Assuming that all of the other GAUSS constructs have been handled as described previously, the implementation of control structures is straightforward. By using the semantic stack to store code addresses, control structures can be nested to an arbitrary depth subject only to limitations on the semantic stack size.

2-5.8.1 If-then-else

Let us begin our discussion of control structures by examining the if statement. The augmented grammar for the if statement follows:

```
/* 76 — <if stmt> ::= */
     #if, $expression, ##(273), $then_clause, $else_clause, ##(275), #endif,
/* 77 — <then clause> ::= */
     #then, $statement, #semi, $statement_list,
/* 78 — <else clause> ::= */
     ##(274), #else, $statement, #semi, $statement_list,
/* 79 — <else clause> ::= null */
```

Code generation begins with the expansion of production 76. Once code for the conditional <expression> has been generated, action routine ##(273) is called. It checks the type of the expression to ensure that it is logical and generates a branch-on-false intermediate language instruction $$branchf. Since the destination operand for the emitted $$branch instruction is not yet known, the code address of the operand is stored on top of the semantic stack. The operand is to be filled in later by either action routines ##(274) or ##(275) depending on the presence of the <else clause>.

Next, notice that there are no special action routines associated with the <then clause> construct. Code is simply generated for each statement associated with the then part of the if statement.

Two situations exist with respect to the <else clause> — either the <else clause> is nonempty as depicted in production 78 or empty as shown in production 79. Suppose the <else clause> is nonempty. In processing production 78, action routine ##(274) is called immediately. It appends an unconditional branch instruction $$branch after the code generated from the <then clause>. Since the destination operand of the $$branch instruction is not yet known, the code address of the operand is saved on top of the semantic stack. However, prior to performing this save, the operand of the branch-on-false instruction emitted previously should be resolved. Once the operand is resolved, the same location on the semantic stack is used to hold the code address for the unresolved $$branch instruction.

After the <else clause>, action routine ##(275) is called as part of the activities associated with processing production 76. The operand of the previous branch instruction can now be filled in with the present value of the *codeptr*. The resolution of the latest unresolved branch can take place irrespective of whether the <else clause> was empty or not. That is, if the <else clause> was empty, the operand for the *$$branchf* instruction would be filled in; otherwise, the operand of the *$$branch* instruction is filled in.

2-5.8.2   Loop-while

The augmented grammar for the while statement follows:

```
/* 80 — <while stmt> ::= */
      ##(276), #loop, $statement_list, #while, $expression,
      ##(273), #semi, $statement_list, ##(277), #endloop,
```

At the beginning of the loop action routine ##(276) causes the present value of the *codeptr* to be saved on top of the semantic stack so it can be used as the destination of a branch which is emitted later.

Once code for the <statement list> and the conditional <expression> has been generated action routine ##(273) is called. It checks the type of the expression and generates a branch-on-false instruction *$$branchf*. Since the destination operand is not yet known, the *code* address of the operand is stored on top of the semantic stack. The operand is filled in later by action routine ##(277).

After code for another <statement list> has been generated, action routine ##(277) is called. It generates an unconditional branch instruction *$$branch* to the *code* address at the beginning of the loop. This address is found at the second location from the top of the semantic stack. Then, the present value of the *codeptr* is used as an operand for the branch-on-false instruction, which has its address on top of the semantic stack.

2-5.8.3   Stop

The augmented grammar for the stop statement follows:

```
/* 81 — <stop stmt> ::= */
      #stop, ##(280),
```

Action routine ##(280) generates the intermediate language instruction *$$stop*. The execution of this instruction immediately terminates the execution of the compiled program.

2-5.9   Input Semantics

The augmented grammar for the read statement follows:

```
/* 89 — <read stmt> ::= */
      #read, $input_goal_list,
/* 90 — <input goal list> ::= */
      $input_goal, $input_goals,
```

```
/* 91 — <input goals> ::= */
        #comma, $input_goal, $input_goals,
/* 92 — <input goals> ::= null */
/* 93 — <input goal> ::= */
        #simpident, ##(285),
/* 94 — <input goal> ::= */
        #arrayident, ##(253), #1paren, $expression, $expressions, #rparen,
        ##(254), ##(286),
```

The read statement acts on a list of items. Our strategy is to generate code after each item. Therefore, the code generated from the source statement "READ X,Y;" is the same as the code generated from "READ X; READ Y;".

When an <input goal> is found, code is generated to place the absolute address of the item on top of the run-time stack. Then code is generated to read a value into the address stored on top of the run-time stack. $$readint, $$readlog, and $$readstr are the intermediate language instructions to read an integer, logical, and string variable, respectively.

If the <input goal> is a simple identifier, then action routine ##(285) is called in production 93. If the identifier is a parameter, then a $$load instruction is generated; otherwise, the $$absolute instruction is generated. Both instructions use the relative address of the identifier as an operand. Then the type of the item is tested and one of the read intermediate language instructions is generated.

If the <input goal> is an array element, action routines ##(253) and ##(254) are called in production 94 to generate the code to place the absolute address of the array element on top of the run-time stack. Then the type of the item is tested and one of the read intermediate language instructions is generated by action routine ##(286).

2-5.10   Output Semantics

The augmented grammar for the write statement is as follows:

```
/* 95 — <write stmt> ::= */
        #write, ##(287), $expression_list, #using, #literal, ##(288),
/* 96 — <expression list> ::= */
        $expression, $expressions,
/* 97 — <expression list> ::= null */
```

At the beginning of the write statement action routine ##(287) causes a marker (value of –1) to be placed on top of the semantic stack. Each expression in the <expression list> causes code to be generated which places the value of the expression on top of the run-time stack and in addition the type of the expression is placed on top of the semantic stack. At the end of the write statement action routine ##(288) calls the *format_lit* procedure to generate a write instruction and check matching types. $$writeint, $$writelog, and $$writestr are the intermediate language instructions to write an integer, logical, and string value respectively. $$newline, $$space, and $$tab are the other intermediate language instructions used for formatting.

Due to the structure of the write statement, the format literal is not reached until all of the expressions have been handled. But write instructions cannot be generated until the format literal is reached. This dilemma can be solved by the following simple but inelegant technique.

A special run-time location called the *write counter* (*wc*) is set aside to store the address of the next value to be written. After every write instruction the write counter is incremented. The only problem is to initialize the write counter. Clearly, this will have to be done before generating any write instructions. Therefore, the first step of the *format_lit* procedure is to generate a $$write instruction whose operand is the number of expressions to be written. From this, the address of the first value can be determined and placed into the write counter.

The previous discussion illustrates a construct which is awkward to compile but natural to program. Such situations are sometimes unavoidable and should be ruled in favor of the language user unless the compiled code is extremely inefficient.

2-5.11 Semantic Error Recovery

The action routines are responsible for local semantic error recovery. For example, recall the *code_fix* procedure discussed in Sec. 2-5.2.2. It is used to recover from operations on illegal types. This section examines the recovery of semantic information due to syntactic errors.

Note, when the parser recovers from a syntactic error (see Sec. 2-3.6) by deleting a terminal from the input stream, then clearly no semantic recovery is required since no semantic processing must be undone. In addition, if the parser recovers by skipping a terminal on the parse stack, then no semantic recovery is needed. However, if the parser skips an action symbol, then semantic recovery is necessary and the parser sets the *no_code* flag to *true*.

When the action procedure is invoked, the *no_code* flag is tested. If the flag is *false*, then processing continues normally. If the flag is *true*, then semantic processing is ignored until an action symbol is encountered which marks the beginning of a new statement. When such a symbol is encountered, then the semantic stack and code area are restored to the state they were in immediately preceding the processing of the statement with the syntactic error.

Action symbols which denote the start of a new statement are ##(204), ##(221), and ##(289). The productions which contain these action symbols are as follows:

```
/* 2 — <global> ::= */
        ##(221), $procedure, #semi, $procedure_list,
/* 3 — <global> ::= */
        ##(204), $type_specifier, $core,
/* 8 — <procedure list> ::= */
        ##(221), $procedure, #semi, $procedure_list,
/* 9 — <procedure list> ::= */
        $simple_type, ##(221), ##(205), $procedure, #semi, $procedure_list,
/* 11 — <declaration> ::= */
        ##(204), $type_specifier, $entity_list, ##(203),
/* 42 — <procedure body> ::= */
        $declaration_list, ##(228), ##(289), $statement, #semi,
        $statement_list, #endproc, ##(229),
/* 43 — <statement list> ::= */
        ##(289), $statement, #semi, $statement_list,
/* 77 — <then clause> ::= */
```

```
            #then, ##(289), $statement, #semi, $statement_list,
/* 78 — <else clause> ::= */
            ##(274), #else, ##(289), $statement, #semi, $statement_list,
```

The action routines associated with the action symbols save the present value of *codeptr* and *sem_top* in *codesave* and *semsave*, respectively. In addition, they perform semantic processing according to their local context. For example, action routine ##(289) also generates code for recording line numbers at execution time.

In summary, semantic recovery is necessary only if syntactic recovery causes an action symbol to be deleted. The result of such semantic recovery is to ignore all semantic processing until the start of the next statement. Then *codeptr* and *sem_top* are restored to *codesave* and *semsave*, respectively. At the start of every statement, *codesave* and *semsave* are reset.

2-5.12   Action Routines Source Listing

The source code for the action routines is given in Fig. 2-20.

```
/********************************************/
/*                                          */
/*              action                      */
/*                                          */
/********************************************/
```

```
/* The action routines are used for context sensitive syntax
 checking and code generation. */

action: PROCEDURE (action_number);
        DECLARE
              action_number FIXED BIN(15);

        DECLARE
              routine (##(201):##(289)) LABEL,
              i FIXED BIN (15);

        IF (code_debug )
        THEN DO;
              PUT SKIP EDIT ('action routine =',action_number,
                       'sem_top =',sem_top,
                       'codeptr =',codeptr)
                       ( (3) (A,F(3),X(5)) );
        END;

        IF (no_code)
        THEN DO;
```

Fig. 2-20   Source code for the action routines

```
            IF (action_number = ##(289)
            | action_number = ##(204)
            | action_number = ##(221))
            THEN DO;
                    codeptr = codesave;
                    sem_top = semsave;
                    no_code = '0'b;
            END;
            ELSE RETURN;
     END;

     GO TO routine (action_number);

/********************* declarations *********************/
/*******************************************************************/

routine (##(201)):
     /* production 12 */
     /* production 14 */

     /* insert constant identifier into symbol table */
     symtab (idptr).type = sem (sem_top);
     symtab (idptr).dimen = sem (sem_top - 1);

     IF (symtab (idptr).dimen > 0)
     THEN DO;
            /* constant array identifier */
            symtab (idptr).use = #arrayconident;

            IF (sem (sem_top - 2) < 0)
            THEN DO;
                    /* bounds not known at compile time */
                    CALL sem_err ('dimen bound not known');
                    /* save relative address */
                    symtab (idptr).address = localptr;
                    localptr = localptr - 2;
                    /* allocate space for local array */
                    code (codeptr) = $$allocate;
                    code (codeptr + 1) = symtab (idptr).address;
                    code (codeptr + 2) = sem (sem_top - 2);
                    codeptr = codeptr + 3;
            END;

            ELSE DO;
                    /* allocate space for array */
                    sem (sem_top - 5) = globalptr;
                    globalptr = globalptr + sem (sem_top - 3);
                    sem (sem_top - 6) = globalptr;
```

Fig. 2-20   Source code for the action routines (cont'd.)

```
                    /* save relative address */
                    symtab (idptr).address = globalptr;

                    /* put template pointer into the global area */
                    global (globalptr) = sem (sem_top - 2);
                    /* put constant part into the global area */
                    global (globalptr + 1) = sem (sem_top - 5) +
                            sem (sem_top - 4);
                    globalptr = globalptr + 2;
            END;
        END;

        ELSE DO;
                /* simple constant */
                symtab (idptr).use = #simpconident;
        END;

        RETURN;

routine (##(202)):
        /* production 13 */
        /* production 37 */

        /* insert identifier into symbol table */
        symtab (idptr).type = sem (sem_top);
        symtab (idptr).dimen = sem (sem_top - 1);

        IF (symtab (idptr).dimen > 0)
        THEN DO;
                /* array identifier */
                symtab (idptr).use = #arrayident;
                IF (scope = 'g')
                THEN DO;
                        /* allocate space for global array */
                        i = globalptr;
                        globalptr = globalptr + sem (sem_top - 3);
                        /* save relative address */
                        symtab (idptr).address = globalptr;
                        /* put template pointer into the global area */
                        global (globalptr) = sem (sem_top - 2);
                        /* put constant part into the global area */
                        global (globalptr + 1) = i + sem (sem_top - 4);
                        globalptr = globalptr + 2;
                END;

                ELSE DO;
                        /* save relative address */
                        symtab (idptr).address = localptr;
```

Fig. 2-20   Source code for the action routines (cont'd.)

```
                localptr = localptr - 2;
                /* allocate space for local array */
                code (codeptr) = $$allocate;
                code (codeptr + 1) = symtab (idptr).address;
                code (codeptr + 2) = sem (sem_top - 2);
                codeptr = codeptr + 3;
        END;
    END;

    ELSE DO;
            /* simple identifier */
            symtab (idptr).use = #simpident;
            IF (scope = 'g')
            THEN DO;
                    /* save relative address of global ident */
                    symtab (idptr).address = globalptr;
                    globalptr = globalptr + 1;
            END;
            ELSE DO;
                    /* save relative address of local ident */
                    symtab (idptr).address = localptr;
                    localptr = localptr - 1;
            END;
    END;
    RETURN;

routine (##(203)):
    /* production 03 */
    /* production 11 */
    /* end of a declaration */
    /* clear semantic stack */
    sem_top = sem_top - 7;
    RETURN;

routine (##(204)):
    /* production 03 */
    /* production 11 */
    /* beginning of a declaration */
    codesave = codeptr;
    semsave = sem_top;
    /* build semantic stack */
    sem_top = sem_top + 7;
        /* sem (sem_top)             type */
            sem (sem_top - 1) = 0;       /* dimension */
        /* sem (sem_top - 2)        template pointer */
        /* sem (sem_top - 3)        size */
        /* sem (sem_top - 4)        constant part */
```

Fig. 2-20   Source code for the action routines (cont'd.)

```
                sem (sem_top - 5) = 0;            /* data area start */
                sem (sem_top - 6) = 0;            /* data area end */
        RETURN;

routine (##(205)):
        /* production 11 */
        /* production 16 */
        /* production 50 */
        /* production 51 */
        /* place identifier type on top of semantic stack */
        sem (sem_top) = next_token;
        RETURN;

routine (##(206)):
        /* production 24 */
        /* increment identifier dimension count */
        sem (sem_top - 1) = sem (sem_top - 1 ) + 1;
        /* prepare for bound expressions */
        sem_top = sem_top + 2;
        sem (sem_top) = codeptr;
        sem (sem_top - 1) = codeptr;
        RETURN;

routine (##(207)):
        /* production 24 */
        /* production 25 */
        /* check dimension bound expression */
        i = sem (sem_top - 1);
        IF ( code (i) ¬= $$push & scope = 'g')
        THEN DO;
                CALL sem_err ('dimen bound not known');
                code (i) = $$push;
                code (i + 1) = 1;
                codeptr = i + 2;
        END;
        IF (sem (sem_top) ¬= #integer )
        THEN DO;
                CALL sem_err ('dimen bound not integer');
                code (i) = $$push;
                code (i + 1) = 1;
                codeptr = i + 2;
        END;
        sem_top = sem_top - 1;
        IF (i = sem (sem_top - 1))
        THEN sem (sem_top) = codeptr;
        ELSE sem_top = sem_top - 2;
        RETURN;
```

Fig. 2-20 Source code for the action routines (cont'd.)

```
routine (##(208)):
        /* production 26 */
        /* insert default lower bound of 1 */
        DO i = codeptr - 1 TO sem (sem_top - 1) BY -1;
                code (i + 2) = code (i);
        END;
        i = sem (sem_top - 1);
        code (i) = $$push;
        code (i + 1) = 1;
        codeptr = codeptr + 2;
        sem_top = sem_top - 2;
        RETURN;


routine (##(209)):
        /* production 27 */
        /* simple constant found */
        IF (sem (sem_top - 1 ) > 0 )
        THEN CALL sem_err('array constant expected');
        ELSE symtab (idptr).address = value;
        RETURN;


routine (##(210)):
        /* production 28 */
        /* array of constants found */
        IF (sem (sem_top - 1) = 0 )
        THEN DO;
                CALL sem_err('simple constant expected');
                symtab (idptr).address = value;
        END;
        ELSE DO;
                IF (sem (sem_top - 5) ¬= sem (sem_top - 6))
                THEN CALL sem_err ('constant count wrong');
        END;
        RETURN;


routine (##(211)):
        /* production 29 */
        /* unary minus encountered before integer */
        value= -value;


routine (##(212)):
        /* production 30 */
        /* integer constant found */
        IF (sem (sem_top) ¬= #integer )
        THEN DO;
                CALL sem_err ('wrong constant type');
                value = 1;
        END;
        RETURN;
```

Fig. 2-20   Source code for the action routines (cont'd.)

```
routine (##(213)):
        /* production 31 */
        /* string constant found */
        IF (sem (sem_top) ¬= #string )
        THEN DO;
                CALL sem_err ('wrong constant type');
                strbuf = '';
        END;
        value = store_lit;
        RETURN;

        /**********************************************/
        /*                                            */
        /*              store_lit                     */
        /*                                            */
        /**********************************************/

store_lit: PROCEDURE;

/* this procedure is responsible for storing a literal
in the global area and returning the value of its reference */

DECLARE (value, z, i) FIXED BIN(15);

value = globalptr;
z = length (strbuf);
global (globalptr) = globalptr + 1;
global (globalptr + 1) = z;
global (globalptr + 2) = 0;
global (globalptr + 3) = globalptr + 4;
globalptr = globalptr + 4;
DO i = 1 TO z - 1 BY 2;
        UNSPEC (global (globalptr)) = UNSPEC
                (SUBSTR (strbuf,i,2));
        globalptr = globalptr + 1;
END;
IF (i = z)
THEN DO;
        UNSPEC (global (globalptr)) = UNSPEC
                (SUBSTR (strbuf,z,1) || ' ');
        globalptr = globalptr + 1;
END;
RETURN (-value);
END store_lit;


routine (##(214)):
        /* production 32 */
        /* logical constant true found */
```

Fig. 2-20   Source code for the action routines (cont'd.)

```
        IF (sem (sem_top) ¬= #logical )
        THEN CALL sem_err ('wrong constant type');
        value = 1;
        RETURN;

routine (# #(215)):
        /* production 33 */
        /* logical constant false found */
        IF ( sem (sem_top) ¬= #logical )
        THEN DO;
                CALL sem_err ('wrong constant type');
                value = 1;
        END;
        ELSE value = 0;
        RETURN;

routine (# #(216)):
        /* production 21 */
        /* array declaration encountered */
        sem (sem_top) = next_token;
        CALL template;
        RETURN;

        /* * * * * * * * * * * * * * * * * * * * * * * * * * * * * * * * * * * */
        /*                                                        */
        /*                 template                               */
        /*                                                        */
        /* * * * * * * * * * * * * * * * * * * * * * * * * * * * * * * * * * * */

template: PROCEDURE;

/* this procedure is responsible for the creation of array templates.
the address of the template will be in sem (sem_top - 2).
The template will be in the global area if it can be computed
at compile-time; otherwise, it will be in the local area. */

        DECLARE
                i FIXED BIN(15),
                size FIXED BIN(15),
                constant FIXED BIN(15),
                temp FIXED BIN(15);

IF (scope = 'l')
THEN DO i = codesave TO codeptr - 2 BY 2;
        IF (code (i) ¬= $$push)
        /* expression can not be evaluated at compile time */
        THEN DO;
                /* write code to generate template at run time */
```

Fig. 2-20   Source code for the action routines (cont'd.)

```
                code (codeptr) = $$template;
                code (codeptr + 1) = localptr;
                code (codeptr + 2) = sem (sem_top - 1);
                codeptr = codeptr + 3;
                /* save space in local area for template */
                sem (sem_top - 2) = localptr;
                localptr = localptr - 3 * sem (sem_top - 1) - 2;
                RETURN;
        END;
    END;

    /* generate a template */
    sem (sem_top - 2) = globalptr;
    globalptr = globalptr + 2;
    constant = 0;

    DO i = codesave TO codeptr - 4 BY 4;
            global (globalptr) = code (i + 3) - code (i + 1) + 1;
            IF (global (globalptr) < 1)
            THEN DO;
                    CALL sem_err('lower bound exceeds upper bound');
                    global (globalptr) = 1;
                    code (i + 3) = code (i + 1);
            END;
            global (globalptr + 1) = code (i + 1);
            global (globalptr + 2) = code (i + 3);
            constant = constant * global (globalptr) - code (i + 3);
            globalptr = globalptr + 3;
    END;

    size = global (globalptr - 3);
    DO i = globalptr - 6 TO sem (sem_top - 2) + 2 BY -3;
            temp = global(i);
            size = size * temp;
            global(i) = size;
    END;

    i = sem (sem_top - 2);
    global (i) = constant;
    global (i + 1) = sem (sem_top - 1);
    sem (sem_top - 3) = size;
    sem (sem_top - 4) = constant;

    /* reset the codeptr */
    codeptr = codesave;
    END template;

    routine (##(217)):
```

Fig. 2-20   Source code for the action routines (cont'd.)

```
      /* production 34 */
      /* production 35 */
      /* array constant to be stored */
      IF (sem (sem_top - 5) < sem (sem_top - 6))
      THEN DO;
             global (sem (sem_top - 5)) = value;
             sem (sem_top - 5) = sem (sem_top - 5) + 1;
      END;
      RETURN;

routine (##(218)):  /* dummy */ RETURN;


      /**************************************/
      /******** procedure declaration ********/

routine (##(221)):
      /* production 02 */
      /* production 08 */
      /* production 09 */
      /* procedure type found */
      codesave = codeptr;
      semsave = sem_top;
      sem_top = sem_top + 1;
      sem (sem_top) = 0;
      RETURN;

routine (##(222)):
      /* production 04 */
      /* procedure type found */
      IF (sem (sem_top - 1) > 0)
      THEN CALL sem_err('proc cannot return array');
      i = sem (sem_top);
      sem_top = sem_top - 6;
      sem (sem_top) = i;
      RETURN;

routine (##(223)):  /* dummy */ RETURN;

routine (##(219)):
      /* production 39 */
      /* beginning of procedure declaration */
      procidptr = idptr;
      IF (symtab (idptr).use = #newident)
      THEN DO;
             symtab (idptr).type = sem (sem_top);
             symtab (idptr).address = procptr;
             procinfo (procptr) = 0;
             procptr = procptr + 1;
      END;
```

Fig. 2-20   Source code for the action routines (cont'd.)

```
        ELSE DO;
                IF (symtab (idptr).type ¬= sem (sem_top))
                THEN CALL sem_err('proc type inconsistent');
                IF (procinfo (symtab (idptr).address) ¬= 0)
                THEN CALL sem_err('proc previously defined');
        END;

        /* prepare to count parameters */
        sem_top = sem_top + 2;
        /* sem (sem_top) is type of parameter */
        sem (sem_top - 1) = 0;  /* dimen of parameter */
        sem (sem_top - 2) = 0;  /* dimen of procedure */
        scope = 'l';  /* internal variables are local */
        RETURN;

routine (##(220)):
        /* production 39 */
        /* parameter list found */
        IF (symtab (procidptr).use = #newident)
        THEN DO;
                symtab (procidptr).dimen = sem (sem_top - 2);
                symtab (procidptr).use = #procident;
                DO i = 1 TO symtab (procidptr).dimen;
                        procinfo (procptr) = symtab (i).type;
                        procinfo (procptr + 1) = symtab (i).dimen;
                        procptr = procptr + 2;
                END;
        END;
        ELSE DO;
                IF (symtab (procidptr).dimen ¬= sem (sem_top - 2))
                THEN DO;
                        CALL sem_err('proc dimension not consistent');
                        IF (sem (sem_top - 2) > symtab(procidptr).dimen)
                        THEN sem(sem_top - 2) = symtab(procidptr).dimen;
                END;
                j = symtab (procidptr).address + 1;
                DO i = 1 TO sem (sem_top - 2);
                        IF (procinfo (j) ¬= symtab (i).type)
                        THEN CALL sem_err('param type not consistent');
                        IF (procinfo (j + 1) ¬= symtab (i).dimen)
                        THEN CALL sem_err('param dimen not consistent');
                        j = j + 2;
                END;
        END;
        procinfo (procptr) = codeptr;
        sem_top = sem_top - 3;
        codeptr = codeptr + 2;
        RETURN;
```

Fig. 2-20   Source code for the action routines (cont'd.)

```
routine (##(224)):
        /* production 49 */
        /* procedure parameter found */
        symtab (idptr).type = sem (sem_top);
        symtab (idptr).dimen = sem ( sem_top - 1);
        IF (symtab (idptr).dimen > 0)
        THEN symtab (idptr).use = #arrayident;
        ELSE symtab (idptr).use = #simpident;
        symtab (idptr).address = localptr;
        localptr = localptr - 1;
        sem (sem_top - 2) = sem (sem_top - 2) + 1;
        sem (sem_top - 1) = 0;
        RETURN;

routine (##(225)):
        /* production 51 */
        /* production 52 */
        /* increment parameter dimension count */
        sem (sem_top - 1 ) = sem (sem_top - 1 ) + 1;
        RETURN;

routine (##(226)):
        /* production 40 */
        /* forward declaration */
        codeptr = codeptr - 2;
        CALL sym_rem;
        scope = 'g';
        RETURN;

routine (##(227)):  /* dummy */ RETURN;

routine (##(228)):
        /* production 42 */
        /* procedure declaration */
        procinfo (symtab (procidptr).address) = procinfo (procptr);
        /* check if space for local variables has been allocated */
        IF (localptr = -(3 + symtab (procidptr).dimen))
        THEN codeptr = codeptr - 2;
        ELSE DO; /* space has been allocated */
                i = procinfo (procptr);
                code (i) = $$incrsp;
                code (i + 1) = -(localptr + 3 +
                        symtab (procidptr).dimen);
        END;
        RETURN;

routine (##(229)):
        /* production 42 */
```

Fig. 2-20   Source code for the action routines (cont'd.)

```
        /* end of procedure */
        IF (symtab (procidptr).type ¬= 0)
        THEN code (codeptr) = $$stop;
        ELSE code (codeptr) = $$return;
        codeptr = codeptr + 1;
        CALL sym_rem;
        scope = 'g';
        RETURN;

/********************** operations **********************/
/**********************************************************/

routine (##(230)):
        /* production 99 */
        CALL relation (#gt,$$sgt,$$igt);
        RETURN;

/**********************************************************/
/*                                                      */
/*                    relation                          */
/*                                                      */
/**********************************************************/

relation: PROCEDURE (tok,stri,inti);

DECLARE
        tok FIXED BIN (15),    /* relation token */
        stri FIXED BIN (15),   /* string instruction */
        inti FIXED BIN (15);   /* integer instruction */

        IF (sem (sem_top) ¬= sem (sem_top - 1))
        THEN DO;
                CALL sem_err (token_str (tok) ||
                        ' between clashing types');
                CALL code_fix(2,1);
        END;
        ELSE
        IF ((tok ¬= #eq | tok ¬= #ne) & sem (sem_top) = #logical)
        THEN CALL sem_err(token_str (tok) || ' between logical types');
        IF (sem (sem_top) = #string)
        THEN code (codeptr) = stri;
        ELSE code (codeptr) = inti;
        codeptr = codeptr + 1;
        sem_top = sem_top - 1;
        sem (sem_top) = #logical;
END relation;
```

Fig. 2-20   Source code for the action routines (cont'd.)

```
/***************************************************************/
/*                                                             */
/*                  code_fix                                   */
/*                                                             */
/***************************************************************/
```

```
/* this procedure generates code to pop and push values on the
run-time stack.  this is done as a run-time response to a
compilation error.  it is hoped that run-time debugging
is improved since as much code as possible is salvaged */

code_fix: PROCEDURE (popcount,pushcount);
      DECLARE (popcount,pushcount) FIXED BIN (15);
      DECLARE i FIXED BIN (15);

      DO i = 1 TO popcount;
             code (codeptr) = $$pop;
             codeptr = codeptr + 1;
      END;
      DO i = 1 TO pushcount;
             code (codeptr) = $$push;
             code (codeptr + 1) = 1;
             codeptr = codeptr + 2;
      END;
END code_fix;

routine (##(231)):
      /* production 100 */
      CALL relation (#lt,$$slt,$$ilt);
      RETURN;

routine (##(232)):
      /* production 101 */
      CALL relation (#eq,$$seq,$$ieq);
      RETURN;

routine (##(233)):
      /* production 102 */
      CALL relation (#ge,$$sge,$$ige);
      RETURN;

routine (##(234)):
      /* production 103 */
      CALL relation (#le,$$sle,$$ile);
      RETURN;

routine (##(235)):
      /* production 104 */
```

Fig. 2-20   Source code for the action routines (cont'd.)

```
        CALL relation (#ne,$$sne,$$ine);
        RETURN;

routine (##(236)):
        /* production 107 */
        CALL bin_op (#integer,$$add);
        RETURN;

/*****************************************************************/
/*                                                        */        */
/*                      bin_op                        */        */
/*                                                        */        */
/*****************************************************************/

bin_op: PROCEDURE (typ,instr);

DECLARE
        typ FIXED BIN (15),    /* type of operation */
        instr FIXED BIN (15);  /* instruction */

        IF (sem (sem_top) ¬= typ
          | sem (sem_top - 1) ¬= typ)
        THEN DO;
                CALL sem_err (instr_str (instr) ||
                        ' operation on non-' ||
                        token_str (typ));
                CALL code_fix(2,1);
                sem (sem_top - 1) = typ;
        END;
        ELSE DO;
                code (codeptr) = instr;
                codeptr = codeptr + 1;
        END;
        sem_top = sem_top - 1;
END bin_op;

routine (##(237)):
        /* production 108 */
        CALL bin_op (#integer,$$subtract);
        RETURN;

routine (##(238)):
        /* production 109 */
        /* logical disjunction */
        CALL split($$or);
        RETURN;
```

Fig. 2-20 · Source code for the action routines (cont'd.)

```
/ * * * * * * * * * * * * * * * * * * * * * * * * * * * * * * * * * * * * * * * * * * * * * * * * * * * * * * * * /
/ *                                                                                              * /
/ *                       split                                                                  * /
/ *                                                                                              * /
/ * * * * * * * * * * * * * * * * * * * * * * * * * * * * * * * * * * * * * * * * * * * * * * * * * * * * * * * * /

split: PROCEDURE (instr);
DECLARE instr FIXED BIN (15);

        IF (sem (sem_top) ¬= #logical)
        THEN DO;
                CALL sem_err (instr_str (instr) ||
                        ' operation on non-logical');
                CALL code_fix (1,1);
        END;
        code (codeptr) = instr;
        sem (sem_top) = codeptr + 1;
        codeptr = codeptr + 2;
END split;


routine (##(262)):
        /* production 109 */
        /* production 115 */
        /* split logical operation */
        IF (sem (sem_top) ¬= #logical)
        THEN DO;
                CALL sem_err ('logical' ||
                        ' operation on non-logical');
                CALL code_fix (1,1);
        END;
        code (sem (sem_top - 1)) = codeptr;
        sem_top = sem_top - 1;
        sem (sem_top) = #logical;
        RETURN;


routine (##(239)):
        /* production 112 */
        CALL bin_op (#integer,$$multiply);
        RETURN;


routine (##(240)):
        /* production 113 */
        CALL bin_op (#integer, $$divide);
        RETURN;


routine (##(241)):
        /* production 114 */
        CALL bin_op (#integer,$$rem);
        RETURN;
```

Fig. 2-20   Source code for the action routines (cont'd.)

```
routine (##(242)):
        /* production 115 */
        /* logical conjunction */
        CALL split($$and);
        RETURN;

routine (##(243)):
        /* production 117 */
        CALL unary_op (#logical,$$not);
        RETURN;

/*****************************************************************/
/*                                                             */
/*                      unary_op                               */
/*.                                                            */
/*****************************************************************/

unary_op: PROCEDURE (typ,instr);
DECLARE
        typ FIXED BIN (15),   /* type of operation */
        instr FIXED BIN (15); /* instruction */

        IF (sem (sem_top) ¬= typ)
        THEN DO;
                CALL sem_err (instr_str (instr) ||
                        ' operation on non-' ||
                        token_str (typ));
                CALL code_fix(1,1);
                sem (sem_top) = typ;
        END;
        ELSE DO;
                code (codeptr) = instr;
                codeptr = codeptr + 1;
        END;
END unary_op;

routine (##(244)):
        /* production 118 */
        CALL unary_op (#integer,$$negate);
        RETURN;

routine (##(245)):
        /* production 120 */
        CALL unary_op (#string,$$length);
        sem (sem_top) = #integer;
        RETURN;
```

Fig. 2-20   Source code for the action routines (cont'd.)

```
routine (##(246)):
      /* production 122 */
      CALL bin_op (#string,$$index);
      sem (sem_top) = #integer;
      RETURN;

routine (##(247)):
      /* production 125 */
      CALL bin_op (#string,$$concat);
      RETURN;

/******************* array elements *******************/
/*************************************************************/

routine (##(253)):
      /* production 69 */
      /* production 83 */
      /* production 94 */
      /* production 131 */
      /* production 132 */
      /* beginning of subscript list */
      sem_top = sem_top + 2;
      sem (sem_top) = -1;
      sem (sem_top - 1) = idptr;
      RETURN;

routine (##(254)):
      /* production 69 */
      /* production 83 */
      /* production 94 */
      /* production 131 */
      /* production 132 */
      /* end of subscript list */
      i = sem_top;
      DO WHILE (sem (sem_top) ¬= -1);
            IF (sem (sem_top) ¬= #integer)
            THEN CALL sem_err('array subscript is non-integer');
            sem_top = sem_top - 1;
      END;
      sem_top = sem_top - 1;
      idptr = sem (sem_top);
      i = symtab (idptr).dimen - (i - sem_top - 1);
      IF (i > 0)
      THEN DO;
            CALL sem_err('missing array subscript(s)');
            CALL code_fix (0,i);
      END;
```

Fig. 2-20 Source code for the action routines (cont'd.)

```
        IF (i < 0)
        THEN DO;
                CALL sem_err('extra array subscript(s)');
                CALL code_fix (-i,0);
        END;

        /* test if identifier is argument */
        IF (idptr <= symtab (procidptr).dimen)
        THEN code (codeptr) = $$derefi;
        ELSE code (codeptr) = $$deref;
        code (codeptr + 1) = symtab (idptr).address;
        codeptr = codeptr + 2;
        RETURN;

routine (##(259)):
        /* production 131 */
        /* production 132 */
        /* reference array element */
        IF (symtab (sem (sem_top)) . type ¬= #string)
        THEN code (codeptr) = $$loada;
        ELSE code (codeptr) = $$loadsa;
        codeptr = codeptr + 1;
        sem (sem_top) = symtab (sem (sem_top)).type;
        RETURN;

/********************** procedures *********************/
/*********************************************************/

routine (##(248)):
        /* production 62 */
        /* production 128 */
        /* procedure name found */
        sem_top = sem_top + 4;
        sem (sem_top) = symtab (idptr).dimen;
        sem (sem_top - 1) = symtab (idptr).address + 1;
        sem (sem_top - 2) = idptr;
        code (codeptr) = $$saveabp;
        code (codeptr + 1) = $$push;
        sem (sem_top - 3) = codeptr + 2;
        codeptr = codeptr + 3;
        RETURN;

routine (##(249)):
        /* production 62 */
        /* production 128 */
        /* procedure argument list complete */
        idptr = sem (sem_top - 2);
        i = sem (sem_top);
```

Fig. 2-20 Source code for the action routines (cont'd.)

```
        IF (i > 0)
        THEN DO;
                CALL sem_err('missing argument(s) in proc');
                CALL code_fix (0,i);
        END;
        IF (i < 0)
        THEN DO;
                CALL sem_err ('extra argument(s) in proc');
                CALL code_fix (-i,0);
        END;
        IF (idptr < 0)
        THEN DO;
                codeptr = sem (sem_top - 3) - 2;
                CALL code_fix (0,1);
                idptr = -idptr;
        END;
        ELSE DO;
                code (codeptr) = $$jump;
                code (codeptr + 1) = jumplink;
                code (codeptr + 2) = idptr;
                jumplink = codeptr + 1;
                codeptr = codeptr + 3;
                code (sem (sem_top - 3)) = codeptr;
        END;
        sem_top = sem_top - 3;
        sem (sem_top) = symtab (idptr).type;
        RETURN;

routine (##(260)):
        /* production 67 */
        /* production 70 */
        /* handle proc argument without subscript list */
        sem (sem_top) = sem (sem_top) - 1;
        IF (sem (sem_top) >= 0)
        THEN DO;
                IF (symtab (idptr).type
                        ¬= procinfo (sem (sem_top - 1)))
                THEN DO;
                        CALL sem_err('proc argument has wrong type');
                        sem (sem_top - 2) = -abs (sem (sem_top - 2));
                END;
                IF (symtab (idptr).dimen
                        ¬= procinfo (sem (sem_top - 1) + 1))
                THEN DO;
                        CALL sem_err('proc argument has wrong dimen');
                        sem (sem_top - 2) = -abs (sem (sem_top - 2));
                END;
                sem (sem_top - 1) = sem (sem_top - 1) + 2;
```

Fig. 2-20 Source code for the action routines (cont'd.)

```
        /* test if identifier is argument */
        IF (idptr <= symtab (procidptr).dimen)
        THEN code (codeptr) = $$load;
        ELSE code (codeptr) = $$absolute;
        code (codeptr + 1) = symtab (idptr).address;
        codeptr = codeptr + 2;
    END;
    RETURN;


routine (##(261)):
    /* production 69 */
    /* handle proc argument with subscript list */
    sem (sem_top) = sem (sem_top) - 1;
    IF (sem (sem_top) >= 0)
    THEN DO;
        IF (symtab (idptr).type
                ¬= procinfo (sem (sem_top - 1)))
        THEN DO;
            CALL sem_err('proc argument has wrong type');
            sem (sem_top - 2) = -abs (sem (sem_top - 2));
        END;
        IF ( 1 ¬= procinfo (sem (sem_top - 1) + 1))
        THEN DO;
            CALL sem_err('proc argument has wrong dimen');
            sem (sem_top - 2) = -abs (sem (sem_top - 2));
        END;
    END;
    RETURN;


/******************** other primaries ********************/
/*************************************************************/


routine (##(250)):
    /* production 129 */
    /* simple identifer */
    /* test if identifier is argument */
    IF (idptr <= symtab (procidptr).dimen)
    THEN IF (symtab (idptr).type ¬= #string)
        THEN code (codeptr) = $$loadi;
        ELSE code (codeptr) = $$loadsi;
    ELSE IF (symtab (idptr).type ¬= #string)
        THEN code (codeptr) = $$load;
        ELSE code (codeptr) = $$loads;

    code (codeptr + 1) = symtab (idptr).address;
    codeptr = codeptr + 2;
    sem_top = sem_top + 1;
    sem (sem_top) = symtab(idptr).type;
    RETURN;
```

Fig. 2-20 Source code for the action routines (cont'd.)

```
routine (##(251)):
        /* production 129 */
        /* production 130 */
        /* production 131 */
        /* production 132 */
        /* handle substring */
        i = sem (sem_top);
        sem_top = sem_top - 1;
        IF (i = 0)
        THEN RETURN;
        sem_top = sem_top - i;
        IF (sem (sem_top) ¬= #string)
        THEN DO;
                CALL sem_err ('substring used on non-string');
                CALL code_fix (i,0);
                RETURN;
        END;
        IF (sem (sem_top + 1) ¬= #integer)
        THEN DO;
                CALL sem_err('start expr is non-integer');
                CALL code_fix (i,0);
                RETURN;
        END;
        IF (i = 1)
        THEN code (codeptr) = $$substring;
        ELSE DO;
                code (codeptr) = $$substringl;
                IF (sem (sem_top + 2) ¬= #integer)
                THEN DO;
                        CALL sem_err ('length expr is non-integer');
                        CALL code_fix (1,1);
                END;
        END;
        codeptr = codeptr + 1;
        RETURN;

routine (##(252)):
        /* production 130 */
        /* simple constant */

        code (codeptr) = $$push;
        code (codeptr + 1) = symtab (idptr).address;
        codeptr = codeptr + 2;
        sem_top = sem_top + 1;
        sem (sem_top) = symtab (idptr).type;
        RETURN;
```

Fig. 2-20   Source code for the action routines (cont'd.)

```
routine (##(255)):
        /* production 133 */
        /* integer constant */
        code (codeptr) = $$push;
        code (codeptr + 1) = value;
        codeptr = codeptr + 2;
        sem_top = sem_top + 1;
        sem (sem_top) = #integer;
        RETURN;

routine (##(256)):
        /* production 134 */
        /* string constant */
        code (codeptr) = $$push;
        code (codeptr + 1) = store_lit;
        codeptr = codeptr + 2;
        sem_top = sem_top + 1;
        sem (sem_top) = #string;
        RETURN;

routine (##(257)):
        /* production 135 */
        /* logical constant true */
        code (codeptr) = $$push;
        code (codeptr + 1) = 1;
        codeptr = codeptr + 2;
        sem_top = sem_top + 1;
        sem (sem_top) = #logical;
        RETURN;

routine (##(258)):
        /* production 136 */
        /* logical constant false */
        code (codeptr) = $$push;
        code (codeptr + 1) = 0;
        codeptr = codeptr + 2;
        sem_top = sem_top + 1;
        sem (sem_top) = #logical;
        RETURN;

routine (##(263)):  /* dummy */ RETURN;

routine (##(264)):  /* dummy */ RETURN;

routine (##(265)):
        /* production 85 */
        /* no substring */
        sem_top = sem_top + 1;
```

Fig. 2-20 Source code for the action routines (cont'd.)

```
        sem (sem_top) = 0;
        RETURN;

routine (##(266)):
        /* production 87 */
        /* substring given length */
        sem_top = sem_top + 1;
        sem (sem_top) = 2;
        RETURN;

routine (##(267)):
        /* production 88 */
        /* substring until end */
        sem_top = sem_top + 1;
        sem (sem_top) = 1;
        RETURN;

routine (##(268)):  /* dummy */ RETURN;

routine (##(269)):  /* dummy */ RETURN;
/*********************** statements ***********************/
/*****************************************************************/

routine (##(270)):
        /* production 62 */
        /* procedure call */
        IF (sem (sem_top) ¬= 0)
        THEN DO;
                CALL sem_err('proc returns value');
                CALL code_fix (1,0);
        END;
        sem_top = sem_top - 1;
        RETURN;

routine (##(271)):
        /* production 74 */
        /* return statement with value */
        IF (symtab (procidptr).type ¬= sem (sem_top))
        THEN DO;
                IF (symtab (procidptr).type = 0)
                THEN DO;
                        CALL sem_err('proc cannot return value');
                        code (codeptr) = $$return;
                        codeptr = codeptr + 1;
                        sem_top = sem_top - 1;
                        RETURN;
                END;
```

Fig. 2-20   Source code for the action routines (cont'd.)

```
                CALL sem_err('proc returns wrong type');
                CALL code_fix(1,1);
        END;
        code (codeptr) = $$returnval;
        codeptr = codeptr + 1;
        sem_top = sem_top - 1;
        RETURN;

routine (##(272)):
        /* production 75 */
        /* return statement without value */
        IF (symtab (procidptr).type ¬= 0)
        THEN DO;
                CALL sem_err('proc does not return value');
                CALL code_fix (0,1);
                code (codeptr) = $$returnval;
        END;
        ELSE code (codeptr) = $$return;
        codeptr = codeptr + 1;
        RETURN;

routine (##(273)):
        /* production 76 */
        /* production 80 */
        /* if or while condition */
        IF (sem (sem_top) ¬= #logical)
        THEN DO;
                CALL sem_err('expecting logical expression');
                CALL code_fix (1,1);
        END;
        code (codeptr) = $$branchf;
        sem (sem_top) = codeptr + 1;
        codeptr = codeptr + 2;
        RETURN;

routine (##(274)):
        /* production 78 */
        /* beginning of else clause */
        code (codeptr) = $$branch;
        i = sem (sem_top);
        sem (sem_top) = codeptr + 1;
        codeptr = codeptr + 2;
        code (i) = codeptr;
        RETURN;

routine (##(275)):
        /* production 76 */
        /* end of else clause */
```

Fig. 2-20   Source code for the action routines (cont'd.)

```
        code (sem (sem_top)) = codeptr;
        sem_top = sem_top - 1;
        RETURN;

routine (##(276)):
        /* production 80 */
        /* beginning of while statement */
        sem_top = sem_top + 1;
        sem (sem_top) = codeptr;
        RETURN;

routine (##(277)):
        /* production 80 */
        /* end of while statement */
        code (codeptr) = $$branch;
        code (codeptr + 1) = sem (sem_top - 1);
        codeptr = codeptr + 2;
        code (sem (sem_top)) = codeptr;
        sem_top = sem_top - 2;
        RETURN;

routine (##(278)):  /* dummy */ RETURN;

routine (##(279)):
        /* production 82 */
        /* production 83 */
        /* automatic string replacement */
        IF (sem (sem_top) ¬= 0) THEN RETURN;
        idptr = sem (sem_top - 1);
        IF (symtab (idptr).type ¬= #string & symtab (idptr).dimen ¬= 0)
        THEN sem_top = sem_top + 2;
        IF (symtab (idptr).type ¬= #string) THEN RETURN;
        sem (sem_top) = 1;
        sem_top = sem_top + 2;      /* setup for routine ##(281) */
        sem (sem_top) = 1;          /* setup for routine ##(281) */
        code (codeptr) = $$push;
        code (codeptr + 1) = 1;
        codeptr = codeptr + 2;
        RETURN;

routine (##(280)):
        /* production 81 */
        /* stop statement */
        code (codeptr) = $$stop;
        codeptr = codeptr + 1;
        RETURN;
```

Fig. 2-20   Source code for the action routines (cont'd.)

```
routine (##(284)):
        /* production 82 */
        /* beginning of assignment to simple identifier */
        sem_top = sem_top + 1;
        sem (sem_top) = idptr;
        codeptr = codeptr + 2;
        RETURN;

routine (##(281)):
        /* production 82 */
        /* middle of assignment to simple identifier */
        i = codesave + 2;
        IF (sem (sem_top) = 0)
        THEN DO;
                codeptr = i;
                RETURN;
        END;
        idptr = sem (sem_top - 3);
        IF (symtab (idptr).type ¬= #string)
        THEN DO;
                CALL sem_err('substring used on non-string');
                sem (sem_top) = 0;
                codeptr = i;
                RETURN;
        END;
        /* test if identifier is parameter */
        IF (idptr <= symtab (procidptr).dimen)
        THEN code (i) = $$load;
        ELSE code (i) = $$absolute;
        code (i + 1) = symtab (idptr).address;
        sem (sem_top - 2) = sem (sem_top);
        sem_top = sem_top - 2;
        RETURN;

routine (##(282)):
        /* production 82 */
        /* end of assignment to simple identifier */
        idptr = sem (sem_top - 2);
        IF (symtab (idptr).type ¬= sem (sem_top))
        THEN DO;
                CALL sem_err('assignment to wrong type');
                CALL code_fix(1,1);
        END;
        IF (sem (sem_top - 1) = 0)
        THEN DO;
                /* test if identifier is parameter */
                IF (idptr <= symtab (procidptr).dimen)
                THEN code (codeptr) = $$storei;
```

Fig. 2-20   Source code for the action routines (cont'd.)

```
            ELSE code (codeptr) = $$store;
            code (codeptr + 1) = symtab (idptr).address;
            codeptr = codeptr + 2;
        END;
        ELSE DO;
            IF (sem (sem_top - 1) = 1)
            THEN code (codeptr) = $$replace;
            ELSE code (codeptr) = $$replacel;
            codeptr = codeptr + 1;
        END;
        sem_top = sem_top - 3;
        RETURN;

routine (##(283)):
        /* production 83 */
        /* assignment to array element */
        idptr = sem (sem_top - 4);
        IF (symtab (idptr).type ¬= sem (sem_top))
        THEN DO;
            CALL sem_err('assignment to wrong type');
            CALL code_fix(1,1);
        END;
        IF (sem (sem_top - 3) = 0)
        THEN code (codeptr) = $$storea;
        ELSE IF (sem (sem_top - 3) = 1)
            THEN code (codeptr) = $$replace;
            ELSE code (codeptr) = $$replacel;
        codeptr = codeptr + 1;
        sem_top =sem_top - 5;
        RETURN;

routine (##(285)):
        /* production 93 */
        /* read simple identifier */
        /* test if identifier is parameter */
        IF (idptr <= symtab (procidptr).dimen)
        THEN code (codeptr) =  $$load;
        ELSE code (codeptr) = $$absolute;
        code (codeptr + 1) = symtab (idptr).address;
        codeptr = codeptr + 2;
        IF (symtab (idptr).type = #integer)
        THEN code (codeptr) = $$readint;
        ELSE
        IF (symtab (idptr).type = #string)
        THEN code (codeptr) = $$readstr;
        ELSE code (codeptr) = $$readlog;
        codeptr = codeptr + 1;
        RETURN;
```

Fig. 2-20 Source code for the action routines (cont'd.)

```
routine (##(286)):
        /* production 94 */
        /* read array element */
        idptr = sem (sem_top);
        sem_top = sem_top - 1;
        IF (symtab (idptr).type = #integer)
        THEN code (codeptr) = $$readint;
        ELSE
        IF (symtab (idptr).type = #string)
        THEN code (codeptr) = $$readstr;
        ELSE code (codeptr) = $$readlog;
        codeptr = codeptr + 1;
        RETURN;

routine (##(287)):
        /* production 93 */
        /* write statement beginning */
        sem_top = sem_top + 1;
        sem (sem_top) = -1;
        RETURN;

routine (##(288)):
        /* production 93 */
        /* write statement end */
        CALL format_lit;
        RETURN;

/*****************************************************************/
/*                                                               */
/*                      format_lit                               */
/*                                                               */
/*****************************************************************/

format_lit:  PROCEDURE;
        DECLARE (t, len) FIXED BIN (15);
        DECLARE (top, bottom) FIXED BIN (15);
        DECLARE (fchar, nchar) CHAR (1);
        DECLARE int BIT (1);
        DECLARE (digit, value) FIXED BIN (15);

        /* locate the arguments */
        top = sem_top;
        DO WHILE (sem (sem_top) ¬= -1);
                sem_top = sem_top - 1;
        END;
        code (codeptr) = $$write;
        code (codeptr + 1) = top - sem_top;
        codeptr = codeptr + 2;
```

Fig. 2-20 Source code for the action routines (cont'd.)

```
bottom = sem_top + 1;
sem_top = sem_top - 1;

/* examine the using literal */
t = 0;
len = LENGTH (strbuf);
DO WHILE (t < len);

        /* get format character */
        fchar = ' ';
        DO WHILE (fchar = ' ');
                t = t + 1;
                IF (t > len)
                THEN fchar = ',';
                ELSE DO;
                        fchar = SUBSTR (strbuf,t,1);
                        IF (fchar = ',')
                        THEN DO;
                                CALL sem_err
                                ('extra format comma');
                                fchar = ' ';
                        END;
                END;
        END;

        /* removes trailing blanks */
        nchar = ' ';
        DO WHILE (nchar = ' ');
                t = t + 1;
                IF (t > len)
                THEN nchar = ',';
                ELSE nchar = SUBSTR (strbuf,t,1);
        END;

        /* check for integer */
        int = '0'B;
        value = 0;
        DO WHILE ('0' <= nchar & nchar <= '9');
                int = '1'B;
                GET STRING (nchar) EDIT (digit) (F(1));
                value = value * 10 + digit;
                t = t + 1;
                IF (t > len)
                THEN nchar = ',';
                ELSE nchar = SUBSTR (strbuf,t,1);
        END;
```

Fig. 2-20   Source code for the action routines (cont'd.)

```
/* remove blanks */
DO WHILE (nchar = ' ');
        t = t + 1;
        IF (t > len)
        THEN nchar = ',';
        ELSE nchar = SUBSTR (strbuf,t,1);
END;

/* check for comma */
IF (nchar ¬= ',')
THEN DO;
        CALL sem_err('missing format comma');
        t = t - 1;
END;

case_in:

/* integer item */
IF (fchar = 'i')
THEN DO;
        IF (bottom > top)
        THEN DO;
                CALL sem_err('extra format item(s)');
                RETURN;
        END;
        IF (sem (bottom) ¬= #integer)
        THEN DO;
                CALL sem_err ('wrong format item');
                IF (sem(bottom) = #string)
                THEN fchar = 's';
                ELSE fchar = 'I';
                GO TO case_in;
        END;
        code (codeptr) = $$writeint;
        code (codeptr + 1) = value;
        codeptr = codeptr + 2;
        bottom = bottom + 1;
        GO TO case_out;
END;

/* string item */
IF (fchar = 's')
THEN DO;
        IF (bottom > top)
        THEN DO;
                CALL sem_err('extra format item(s)');
                RETURN;
        END;
```

Fig. 2-20   Source code for the action routines (cont'd.)

```
              IF (sem (bottom) ¬= #string)
              THEN DO;
                      CALL sem_err ('wrong format item');
                      IF (sem (bottom) = #integer)
                      THEN fchar = 'i';
                      ELSE fchar = 'l';
                      GO TO case_in;
              END;
              code (codeptr) = $$writestr;
              code (codeptr + 1) = value;
              codeptr = codeptr + 2;
              bottom = bottom + 1;
              GO TO case_out;
      END;

      /* logical item */
      IF (fchar = 'l')
      THEN DO;
              IF (bottom > top)
              THEN DO;
                      CALL sem_err('extra format item(s)');
                      RETURN;
              END;
              IF (sem (bottom) ¬= #logical)
              THEN DO;
                      CALL sem_err ('wrong format item');
                      IF (sem (bottom) = #integer)
                      THEN fchar = 'i';
                      ELSE fchar = 's';
                      GO TO case_in;
              END;
              code (codeptr) = $$writelog;
              codeptr = codeptr + 1;
              IF (int)
              THEN CALL sem_err('unexpected format integer');
              bottom = bottom + 1;
              GO TO case_out;
      END;

      /* space item */
      IF (fchar = 'x')
      THEN DO;
              code (codeptr) = $$space;
              IF (int)
              THEN code (codeptr + 1) = value;
              ELSE DO;
                      CALL sem_err('missing format integer');
                      code (codeptr + 1) = 1;
              END;
```

Fig. 2-20   Source code for the action routines (cont'd.)

```
                    codeptr = codeptr + 2;
                    GO TO case_out;
            END;

            /* tab item */
            IF (fchar = 't')
            THEN DO;
                    code (codeptr) = $$tab;
                    IF (int)
                    THEN code (codeptr + 1) = value;
                    ELSE DO;
                            CALL sem_err('missing format integer');
                            code (codeptr + 1) = 1;
                    END;
                    codeptr = codeptr + 2;
                    GO TO case_out;
            END;

            /* newline item */
            IF (fchar = 'n')
            THEN DO;
                    code (codeptr) = $$newline;
                    codeptr = codeptr + 1;
                    IF (int)
                    THEN CALL sem_err('extra format integer');
                    GO TO case_out;
            END;

            /* default item */
            IF (fchar = ',')
            THEN CALL sem_err('illegal format item');

            case_out:
    END;

    IF (bottom <= top)
    THEN DO;
            CALL sem_err ('missing format item(s)');
            code (codeptr) = $$space;
            code (codeptr + 1) = 1;
            codeptr = codeptr + 2;
            DO WHILE (bottom < top);
                    IF (sem (bottom) = #integer)
                    THEN DO;
                            code (codeptr) = $$writeint;
                            code (codeptr + 1) = 0;
                            codeptr = codeptr + 2;
                    END;
```

Fig. 2-20   Source code for the action routines (cont'd.)

```
                    ELSE
                    IF (sem (bottom) = #string)
                    THEN DO;
                            code (codeptr) = $$writestr;
                            code (codeptr + 1) = 0;
                            codeptr = codeptr + 2;
                    END;
                    ELSE DO;
                            code (codeptr) = $$writelog;
                            codeptr = codeptr + 1;
                    END;
              code (codeptr) = $$space;
              code (codeptr + 1) = 1;
              codeptr = codeptr + 2;
              bottom = bottom + 1;
        END;
END format_lit;

routine (##(289)):
        /* production 42 */
        /* production 43 */
        /* production 77 */
        /* production 78 */
        /* beginning of a new statement */
        codesave = codeptr;
        semsave = sem_top;
        code (codeptr) = $$line;
        code (codeptr + 1) = line_num;
        codeptr = codeptr + 2;
        RETURN;

END action;

        /********************************************/
        /*                                          */
        /*            sem_err                       */
        /*                                          */
        /********************************************/

sem_err: PROCEDURE ( message );

/* sem_err is the error message routine for semantic errors. */

        DECLARE
              message CHARACTER (*);
        PUT SKIP EDIT ( line_num, ' **** error **** ', message )
              (F(4),A,A);
END sem_err;
```

Fig. 2-20   Source code for the action routines (cont'd.)

2-5.13   Compilation Errors

Compilation errors can arise in the scanner, table handler, parser, or code generation routines. This section provides a listing of compilation errors.

There are two types of compilation errors reported by GAUSS. The code generation routines report semantic errors using the *sem_err* procedure. The scanner, table handler, and parser report all other errors using the *error* and *list_err* procedures.

An example invocation of the *sem_err* procedure is as follows:

sem_err ('array subscript is non-integer').

The effect of the *sem_err* procedure is to display the error message with the following format:

DDDD **** error **** array subscript is non-integer

where DDDD denotes the line number at the place of the error.

A listing of all semantic error messages in GAUSS is now given:

'dimen bound not known'
'dimen bound not integer'
'array constant expected'
'simple constant expected'
'constant count wrong'
'wrong constant type'
'lower bound exceeds upper bound'
'proc cannot return array'
'proc type inconsistent'
'proc previously defined'
'proc dimension not consistent'
'param type not consistent'
'param dimen not consistent'
'array subscript is non-integer'
'missing array subscript(s)'
'extra array subscript(s)'
'missing argument(s) in proc'
'extra argument(s) in proc'
'proc argument has wrong type'
'proc argument has wrong dimen'
'substring used on non-string'
'start expr is non-integer'
'length expr is non-integer'
'proc returns value'
'proc cannot return value'
'proc returns wrong type'
'proc does not return value'
'expecting logical expression'
'assignment to wrong type'
'missing format comma'
'extra format comma'

'extra format item(s)'
'wrong format item'
'unexpected format integer'
'missing format integer'
'extra format integer'
'illegal format item'
'missing format item(s)'
'logical operation on non-logical'
token_str (tok) || ' between clashing types'
token_str (tok) || ' between logical types'
instr_str (instr) || ' operation on non-' || token_str (typ)
instr_str (instr) || ' operation on non-logical'
symtab (idptr).name || ' procedure undefined'

Note that an expression which evaluates to a string can be passed to the *sem_err* procedure. Therefore, explicit reference to variable names or token names can be made.

The *error* procedure is used to report all other error messages in GAUSS. An example invocation of the *error* procedure is as follows:

error (1, 0, 0, 0)

where the first argument is the error message number and the remaining three arguments are parameters of the error message. The effect of the *error* procedure is to insert the error message number and parameters in an error buffer. In addition, it marks the location within a line of each error.

No error messages are displayed until the *list_err* procedure is called. Then all error messages in the buffer are displayed. If the the *list_flag* is *true*, then the offending line has just been displayed by the scanner. Therefore, if the *list_flag* is *false*, then the *list_err* procedure displays the line using the following format:

DDDD: LINE

where DDDD is the line number. The location of errors within a line are marked by printing a line of blanks and digits in such a way that 1 is displayed immediately below the location of the first error, 2 is displayed immediately below the location of the second error, and so on for up to nine errors. Then, the error messages in the error buffer are displayed according to the following format:

**** error(D): unknown character

where D is the number of the error within the line.

Clearly, there must exist some way to translate an error message number into an error message. The approach used in GAUSS is to build a dictionary of words used in error messages and then replace the words in an error message by the corresponding index into the dictionary. An error message table is used to point to a pattern space table. The entries in the pattern space table are indices into the dictionary.

The rationale behind the use of such tables is to minimize the amount of storage required for error messages. Presumably, the number of words in the dictionary grows at a slower rate then the number of error messages.

A listing of the error messages handled through the *error* procedure follows:

'unknown character'
'illegal comment syntax'
'string constant too long'
'nonterminated string'
'numeric constant too large'
'compiler error - sentential stack overflow'
'compiler error - sentential stack underflow'
'missing option name on ?option command'
'invalid option name on ?option command'
'missing ?program command'
'compiler error - symbol table overflow symbol not inserted'
'compiler error - xr (cross reference) table overflow'
'compiler error - in prefix table'
'expecting' <terminal list> 'but found' <terminal>

For such a small number of error messages, it is doubtful that the use of a dictionary resulted in any significant savings in storage. If semantic errors in GAUSS were reported using the same procedure, then the use of a dictionary would be more feasible. Unfortunately, the code for the GAUSS compiler would be less clear with statements of the form "error (97,0,0,0)" as opposed to "sem_err ('missing format item')." Consequently, the trade-off has been resolved in favor of perspicuity over space efficiency. We have, however, illustrated a method in which space efficiency can be achieved.

2-6 GAUSS SOURCE LISTING

The source code for the main module of the GAUSS compiler is given in Fig. 2-21.

```
/* The following are some useful macros, which define the
   sizes of certain tables, etc. */
*MACRO
    strlen = 255 %;
    idlen = 16 %;
    #_of_symbols = 122 %;
    #_of_terminals = 57 %;
    #_of_keywords = 26 %;
    #_of_instructions = 65 %;
    forever = while ('1'b) %;
    parse_limit = 250 %;
    nhash = 53 %;
    nsymtab = 200 %;
    ncode = 600 %;
```

Fig. 2-21   Source code for the main module

```
      nglobal = 400 %;
      npinfo = 100 %;
      nsem = 100 %;
      nxr = 200 %;
      xrnode = 5 %;
      null = 0 %;
      nrun = 100 %;
      strsize = 200 %;
      nsize = 200 %;
*MEND
      /* The following macros are used to defined the table entries
      for the LL(1) parser. */
*MACRO
      @pop = 159 %;
      @accept = 160 %;
      @error = 161 %;
*MEND
      /* the following macros are used to define token names to be
      used in the compiler, instead of using integer constants
      for tokens. when inserting another token definition, a
      corresponding entry must also be made in the 'token_str'
      vector defined in the init procedure.
      all tokens begin with the '#' character so that they are
      easily distinguishable from identifiers in the compiler
      source listings. */
*MACRO

      #and = 1 %;
      #array = 2 %;
      #const = 3 %;
      #else = 4 %;
      #endif = 5 %;
      #endloop = 6 %;
      #endproc = 7 %;
      #false = 8 %;
      #forward = 9 %;
      #if = 10 %;
      #integer = 11 %;
      #logical = 12 %;
      #loop = 13 %;
      #not = 14 %;
      #of = 15 %;
      #or = 16 %;
      #proc = 17 %;
      #read = 18 %;
      #return = 19 %;
      #string = 20 %;
      #stop = 21 %;
```

Fig. 2-21   Source code for the main module (cont'd.)

```
#then = 22 %;
#true = 23 %;
#using = 24 %;
#while = 25 %;
#write = 26 %;

#arrayident = 27 %;
#arrayconident = 28 %;
#assign = 29 %;
#colon = 30 %;
#comma = 31 %;
#concat = 32 %;
#div = 33 %;
#eof = 34 %;
#eq = 35 %;
#ge = 36 %;
#gt = 37 %;
#index = 38 %;
#le = 39 %;
#length = 40 %;
#literal = 41 %;
#lparen = 42 %;
#lt = 43 %;
#minus = 44 %;
#mult = 45 %;
#mod = 46 %;
#ne = 47 %;
#newident = 48 %;
#number = 49 %;
#plus = 50 %;
#procident = 51 %;
#rparen = 52 %;
#semi = 53 %;
#simpident = 54 %;
#simpconident = 55 %;
#substr = 56 %;
#uminus = 57 %;
*MEND
    /* The next set of macro definitions are for the non-terminal
    symbols used in the LL(1) grammar for GAUSS.  They all begin
    with a $ so that they can be easily distinguished in the
    source code.  */
*MACRO
    $program = 58 %;
    $global = 59 %;
    $core = 60 %;
    $declaration_list = 61 %;
    $procedure_list = 62 %;
```

Fig. 2-21   Source code for the main module (cont'd.)

```
$declaration = 63 %;
$entity_list = 64 %;
$constant_list = 65 %;
$type_specifier = 66 %;
$simple_type = 67 %;
$array = 68 %;
$bound_pair_list = 69 %;
$bound_pair = 70 %;
$second_bound = 71 %;
$constant = 72 %;
$simple_constant = 73 %;
$array_constant = 74 %;
$simple_constant_list = 75 %;
$ident_list = 76 %;
$procedure = 77 %;
$procedure_tail = 78 %;
$procedure_body = 79 %;
$statement_list = 80 %;
$parameter_list = 81 %;
$parameters = 82 %;
$parameter = 83 %;
$parameter_type = 84 %;
$comma_list = 85 %;
$statement = 86 %;
$procedure_call = 87 %;
$argument_list = 88 %;
$arguments = 89 %;
$argument = 90 %;
$sublist = 91 %;
$return_stmt = 92 %;
$ret_expression = 93 %;
$if_stmt = 94 %;
$then_clause = 95 %;
$else_clause = 96 %;
$while_stmt = 97 %;
$stop_stmt = 98 %;
$assignment_stmt = 99 %;
$substring = 100 %;
$start = 101 %;
$length = 102 %;
$read_stmt = 103 %;
$input_goal_list = 104 %;
$input_goals = 105 %;
$input_goal = 106 %;
$write_stmt = 107 %;
$expression_list = 108 %;
$expressions = 109 %;
$expression = 110 %;
```

Fig. 2-21 Source code for the main module (cont'd.)

```
        $etail = 111 %;
        $part = 112 %;
        $ptail = 113 %;
        $term = 114 %;
        $ttail = 115 %;
        $factor = 116 %;
        $index = 117 %;
        $itail = 118 %;
        $catena = 119 %;
        $ctail = 120 %;
        $primary = 121 %;
        $proc_name = 122 %;
*MEND
        /* The following macros are used to define instructions used
        in code generation. */
*MACRO
        $$absolute = 1 %;
        $$add = 2 %;
        $$allocate = 3 %;
        $$concat = 4 %;
        $$deref = 5 %;
        $$derefi = 6 %;
        $$divide = 7 %;
        $$dump = 8 %;
        $$ieq = 9 %;
        $$ige = 10 %;
        $$igt = 11 %;
        $$ile = 12 %;
        $$ilt = 13 %;
        $$ine = 14 %;
        $$index = 15 %;
        $$newline = 16 %;
        $$jump = 17 %;
        $$readlog = 18 %;
        $$load = 19 %;
        $$loadi = 20 %;
        $$line = 21 %;
        $$multiply = 22 %;
        $$negate = 23 %;
        $$push = 24 %;
        $$loada = 25 %;
        $$rem = 26 %;
        $$seq = 27 %;
        $$sge = 28 %;
        $$sgt = 29 %;
        $$sle = 30 %;
        $$slt = 31 %;
        $$sne = 32 %;
```

Fig. 2-21   Source code for the main module (cont'd.)

```
            $$store = 33 %;
            $$storei = 34 %;
            $$subtract = 35 %;
            $$substring = 36 %;
            $$substringl = 37 %;
            $$template = 38 %;
            $$return = 39 %;
            $$returnval = 40 %;
            $$saveabp = 41 %;
            $$incrsp = 42 %;
            $$and = 43 %;
            $$not = 44 %;
            $$or = 45 %;
            $$branch = 46 %;
            $$branchf = 47 %;
            $$pop = 48 %;
            $$replace = 49 %;
            $$replacel = 50 %;
            $$stop = 51 %;
            $$storea = 52 %;
            $$readint = 53 %;
            $$readstr = 54 %;
            $$write = 55 %;
            $$writeint = 56 %;
            $$writelog = 57 %;
            $$writestr = 58 %;
            $$space = 59 %;
            $$tab = 60 %;
            $$end_of_file = 61 %;
            $$loads = 62 %;
            $$loadsi = 63 %;
            $$loadsa = 64 %;
            $$length = 65 %;
*MEND
       /* the following macro is a signal for an action routine */
*MACRO
       ##(n) = n %;
*MEND
            /*****************************************/
            /*                                       */
            /*            compile                    */
            /*                                       */
            /*****************************************/

compile: PROCEDURE OPTIONS (MAIN);
       DECLARE real_eof BIT(1);

       real_eof = '0'B;
```

Fig. 2-21   Source code for the main module (cont'd.)

```
        DO WHILE (real_eof);
                CALL init;
                IF (real_eof)
                THEN PUT PAGE;
        END;
                /*******************************************/
                /*                                         */
                /*              init                       */
                /*                                         */
                /*******************************************/
```

/* This procedure is used to initialize all of the global variables
that are required in order for the compiler to work. Note that
the scope of this procedure covers the whole of the compiler. */

```
init: PROCEDURE;
        DECLARE
                scanner ENTRY RETURNS (FIXED BIN (15)),
                error ENTRY (FIXED BIN (15), FIXED BIN (15), FIXED BIN (15),
                        FIXED BIN (15)),
                llparse ENTRY RETURNS (BIT (1)),
                action ENTRY (FIXED BIN (15)),
                token_pr ENTRY (FIXED BIN (15)) RETURNS (CHAR (26) VARYING),
                execution_phase ENTRY,
                list_err ENTRY;


        DECLARE
                begin_tok FIXED BIN (15),       /* beginning pos. of token   */
                line_buf CHAR (81),             /* input line buffer         */
                line_ptr FIXED BIN (15),        /* index into line_buf       */
                code_debug BIT (1),             /* to debug code generator   */
                codesave FIXED BIN (15),        /* saves codeptr             */
                eof BIT (1),                    /* signals end of program    */
                error_mark CHAR (80),           /* errors in current line    */
                error_num FIXED BIN (15),       /* # of errors detected      */
                idptr FIXED BIN (15),           /* pointer into symbol table */
                int_debug BIT (1),              /* trace of interpreter      */
                jumplink FIXED BIN (15),        /* list head of jump fixups  */
                line_errors FIXED BIN (15),     /* # of errors in this line  */
                line_num FIXED BIN (15),        /* current line number       */
                list_flag BIT (1),              /* requests a listing        */
                ll1_debug BIT (1),              /* to debug the ll(1) parser */
                new_line BIT (1),               /* new line read by scanner? */
                next_token FIXED BIN (15),      /* next input token          */
                no_code BIT (1),                /* do not generate code if '1'*/
                next_char CHAR (1),             /* scanner's next character  */
                procidptr FIXED BIN (15),       /* idptr for last procedure  */
                scanner_debug BIT (1),          /* for printing tokens       */
```

Fig. 2-21   Source code for the main module (cont'd.)

```
        scope CHAR (1),                     /* scope of identifier    */
        semsave FIXED BIN (15),                /* saves sem_top        */
        strbuf CHAR (strlen) VAR,        /* to hold literals        */
        sym_debug BIT (1),              /* to print symbol table    */
        value FIXED BIN (15),           /* value of constant       */
        xref_flag BIT (1);              /* requests cross reference  */

DECLARE
        1 symtab (nsymtab),   /* symbol table */
                2 name CHAR (idlen) VARYING,      /* identifier name */
                2 type FIXED BIN (15),            /* type of ident */
                2 dimen FIXED BIN (15),           /* dimen of ident */
                2 use FIXED BIN (15),             /* how ident is used */
                2 address FIXED BIN (15),   /* memory location */
                2 xrhead FIXED BIN (15),    /* head of xr list */
                2 xrtail FIXED BIN (15),    /* tail of xr list */
                2 link FIXED BIN (15);            /* link to next ident  */

DECLARE code(ncode) FIXED BIN (15),     /* program area */
        codeptr FIXED BIN (15),
        ghashtab (nhash) FIXED BIN (15) INIT ((nhash) null),
        global (0: nglobal) FIXED BIN (15) INIT (0, (nglobal) 0),
        globalptr FIXED BIN (15),
        gsymfree FIXED BIN (15),
        gxrptr FIXED BIN (15),
        lhashtab (nhash) FIXED BIN (15) INIT ((nhash) null),
        localptr FIXED BIN (15),
        lsymfree FIXED BIN (15),
        lxrptr FIXED BIN (15),
        procinfo (npinfo) FIXED BIN (15),
        procptr FIXED BIN (15),
        sem (nsem) FIXED BIN (15),  /* semantic stack */
        sem_top FIXED BIN (15),
        xr (nxr) FIXED BIN (15);       /* cross reference list */
```

```
/* The following table is used to associate tokens with
their values. When the value of the token is used as an
index into this table, the corresponding entry is the
string representation of the token. Thus, this table is
closely linked to the macro definitions for the token
values. The key-words of the gauss language appear at the
beginning of the table. After these come the symbol tokens.
If the language is to be expanded, the following must be
kept in mind when adding entries to this table.
1.  Key-words appear at the beginning of the table, with
    symbols appearing after all keywords.
2.  The macro definitions for the new entries must be created,
    and the old definitions may have to be change so that
```

Fig. 2-21   Source code for the main module (cont'd.)

the defined value of each token is the same as the index
of that token in this vector.

3. If the size of this vector is changed, the macro definition
   of '#_of_symbols', '#_of_keywords' and '#_of_terminals' may
   have to be changed, depending on the changes made to the
   compiler. */

DECLARE token_str (0 : #_of_symbols) CHAR (26) VARYING STATIC INIT
      ('', 'and', 'array', 'const', 'else',
      'endif', 'endloop', 'endproc', 'false',
      'forward', 'if', 'integer', 'logical',
      'loop', 'not', 'of', 'or', 'proc',
      'read', 'return', 'string', 'stop',
      'then', 'true', 'using', 'while', 'write',
      'array identifier', 'array constant identifier', ':=',
      ':', ',', '&', '/', 'end-of-file', '=',
      '>=', '>', '@', '<=', '#', 'literal',
      '(', '<', '-', '*', '%', '<>',
      'new identifier', 'number', '+', 'procedure identifier',
      ')', ';', 'simple identifier',
      'simple constant identifier', '|', '-',
      'program', 'global', 'core', 'declaration list',
      'procedure list', 'declaration', 'entity list', 'const list',
      'type specifier', 'simple type', 'array', 'bound pair list',
      'bound pair', 'second bound', 'constant', 'simple constant',
      'array constant', 'simple constant list', 'ident list',
      'procedure','procedure tail','procedure body', 'statement list',
      'parameter list', 'parameters', 'parameter', 'parameter type',
      'comma list', 'statement', 'procedure call', 'argument list',
      'arguments', 'argument', 'sublist',
      'return stmt', 'ret expression', 'if stmt', 'then clause',
      'else clause', 'while stmt', 'stop stmt', 'assignment stmt',
      'substring', 'start', 'length', 'read stmt', 'input goal list',
      'input goals', 'input goal', 'write stmt', 'expression list',
      'expressions', 'expression', 'etail', 'part', 'ptail',
      'term', 'ttail', 'factor', 'index', 'itail', 'catena',
      'ctail', 'primary', 'procedure name');

/* instr_str contains the mnemonic names of the code instructions */

DECLARE instr_str (1:#_of_instructions)
      character (25) VARYING STATIC INITIAL
      ('absolute','add','allocate','concatenate','dereference',
      'dereference indirect','divide','dump', 'int =','int >=',
      'int >','int <=','int <','int <>','index','newline','jump',
      'read logical','load','load indirect','line number','multiply',
      'negate','push','load absolute','remainder','string =',
      'string >=','string >','string <=','string <','string <>',

Fig. 2-21   Source code for the main module (cont'd.)

'store','store indirect','subtract','substring until end',
'substring given length','template','return',
'return value','save act base ptr','incr stack ptr',
'and','not','or','branch','branch on false','pop',
'replace until end','replace given length','stop',
'store absolute','read integer','read string','start write',
'write integer','write logical','write string',
'space','tab','end of file','load string','load string indirect',
'load string absolute','store string','store string indirect',
'store string absolute','length');

/* num_ops gives number of operands associated with each instruction */

DECLARE num_ops (1:#_of_instructions)
    FIXED BINARY (15) STATIC INITIAL
    (1,0,2,0,1,1,0,1,0,0,
    0,0,0,0,0,0,2,0,1,1,
    1,0,0,1,0,0,0,0,0,0,
    0,0,1,1,0,0,0,2,0,0,
    0,1,1,0,1,1,1,0,0,0,
    0,0,0,0,1,1,0,1,1,1,
    0,1,1,0,1,1,0,0);

/* The err_mesg_tab contains indices into the pat_space table, which
will give the indices into dict for the corresponding error number.
For example, for error number 3, err_mesg_tab (3) will give
an index into pat_space where the indices into dict can be found
to generate the error message for error number 3. */

DECLARE
    err_mesg_tab (15) FIXED BIN (15) STATIC INIT
    (1, 3, 6, 10, 12, 16, 21, 26, 26, 32, 38, 41, 49, 54, 59);

/* The pat_space table contains indices into the dict table, which will
generate the appropriate error messages. The err_mesg_tab is used to
find the indices for any given error number. */

DECLARE
    pat_space (58) FIXED BIN (15) STATIC INITIAL
    (1, 2, 3, 4, 5, 6, 7, 8, 9, 10, 6, 11, 7, 8, 12, 19, 20,
    15, 16, 17, 19, 20, 15, 16, 18, 21, 22, 23, 24, 25, 26,
    27, 22, 23, 24, 25, 26, 21, 28, 26, 19, 20, 29, 30, 17, 29,
    31, 32, 19, 20, 34, 30, 17, 19, 20, 36, 37, 30);

/* The dict table contains the words that appear in the error messages
generated by the error procedure. */

Fig. 2-21 Source code for the main module (cont'd.)

```
DECLARE
        dict (37) CHAR (15) VARYING STATIC INITIAL
        ('unknown', 'character', 'illegal', 'comment', 'syntax',
        'string', 'constant', 'too', 'long', 'nonterminated', 'numeric',
        'large', '32,767', 'used', 'sentential', 'stack',
        'overflow', 'underflow', 'compiler', 'error -', 'missing',
        'option', 'name', 'on', '?OPTION', 'line', 'invalid',
        '?PROGRAM', 'symbol', 'table', 'not', 'inserted', 'into',
        'xr (cross reference)', 'initialize', 'in', 'prefix');

DECLARE error_buf (0 : 9, 4) FIXED BIN (15);  /* where error numbers a
                                        parameters are stored
                                        while a line is being
                                        processed. */

DECLARE
        temp BIT (1),
        ptr FIXED BIN (15),
        (i, j, k) FIXED BIN (15),
        lowname CHAR (1);

/* The following macro definition is used in several places to read
   in the next line of input, list it if necessary, and set the
   appropriate flags and pointers. */
*MACRO
        get_line =
DO;
        GET EDIT (line_buf) (A(80));
        IF (SUBSTR (line_buf,1, 8) = '?PROGRAM')
        THEN DO;
                line_num = line_num + 1;
                IF (list_flag)
                THEN
                        PUT SKIP EDIT (line_num, ':', line_buf)
                                (F(4), A, X(2), A(80));
        END;
        new_line = '0'B;
        line_ptr = 0;
END %;
*MEND

/* now do the initializations for the variables */

code_debug = '0'B;
eof = '0'B;
error_mark = '';
error_num = 0;
globalptr = 1;
```

Fig. 2-21 Source code for the main module (cont'd.)

```
        gsymfree = nhash;
        gxrptr = nxr - xrnode + 1;
        int_debug = '0'B;
        line_errors = 0;
        line_num = 0;
        list_flag = '1'B;
        ll1_debug = '0'B;
        localptr = -3;
        lsymfree = 1;
        lxrptr = 1;
        next_char = ' ';
        next_token = 0;
        no_code = '0'B;
        scanner_debug = '0'B;
        scope = 'g';
        sem_top = 0;
        sym_debug = '0'B;
        xref_flag = '0'B;

        /* insert 'main' procedure into symbol table */
        ptr = lookup ('main');
        symtab (ptr).type = 0;
        symtab (ptr).use = #procident;
        symtab (ptr).dimen = 0;
        symtab (ptr).address = 1;
        procinfo (1) = 0;

        code (1) = $$saveabp;
        code (2) = $$push;
        code (3) = 7;
        code (4) = $$jump;
        code (5) = 0;
        code (6) = ptr;
        code (7) = $$stop;
        code (8) = $$end_of_file;
        code (9) = $$returnval;
        jumplink = 5;
        codeptr = 10;
        codesave= 10;
        semsave= 0;

        /* insert 'end_of_file' procedure into symbol table */
        ptr = lookup ('end_of_file');
        symtab (ptr).type = #logical;
        symtab (ptr).use = #procident;
        symtab (ptr).dimen = 0;
        symtab (ptr).address = 2;
        procinfo (2) = 8;
        procptr = 3;
```

Fig. 2-21   Source code for the main module (cont'd.)

```
get_line;
IF (SUBSTR (line_buf, 1, 8) = '?PROGRAM')
THEN get_line;
temp = llparse;

/* fixup jumps */
DO WHILE (jumplink ¬= 0);
        i = jumplink;
        jumplink = code (i);
        idptr = code (i + 1);
        code (i) = procinfo (symtab (idptr).address);
        code (i + 1) = symtab (idptr).dimen;
        IF (code (i) = 0)
        THEN DO;
                CALL sem_err (symtab (idptr).name ||
                        ' procedure undefined');
                code (i) = $$stop;
        END;
END;

IF (sym_debug)
THEN DO;
        PUT SKIP (2) LIST ('Global symbol table debug:');
        PUT SKIP (2) EDIT ('name','hash loc.','link','address')
                (A, COL(18), A, COL(31), A, COL(39), A);
        PUT SKIP;

        DO i = 1 TO nhash;
                ptr = ghashtab (i);
                DO WHILE (ptr ¬= null);
                        PUT SKIP EDIT (symtab (ptr).name,
                                i, symtab (ptr).link,
                                symtab (ptr).address)
                                (A(16), COL(18), F(3),
                                COL(31), F(3), COL(39), F(4));
                        ptr = symtab (ptr).link;
                END;
        END;
        PUT SKIP;
END;

IF (xref_flag)
THEN DO;
        PUT SKIP (2) LIST ('Global cross reference:');
        PUT SKIP (2) EDIT ('name', 'type', 'use', 'dimen',
                'references') (A, COL(18), A, COL(32), A,
                COL(63), A, COL(70), A);
        PUT SKIP;
```

Fig. 2-21   Source code for the main module (cont'd.)

```
          DO i = gsymfree + 1 TO nhash;
                lowname = '0';
                DO j = gsymfree + 1 TO nhash;
                        IF (symtab (j).name < lowname)
                        THEN DO;
                                ptr = j;
                                lowname = symtab (j).name;
                        END;
                END;
                PUT SKIP EDIT (symtab (ptr).name,
                        token_str (symtab (ptr).type),
                        token_str (symtab (ptr).use),
                        symtab(ptr).dimen)
                        (A(16), COL(18), A(9),
                        COL(32), A(26), COL(63), F(4));
                j = symtab (ptr).xrhead;
                PUT EDIT (xr(j)) (COL(70), F(3));
                j = j + 1;
                k = 1;
                DO WHILE (j ¬= symtab (ptr).xrtail + 1);
                        IF (mod(j,xrnode) = 0)
                        THEN j = xr(j);
                        IF (k = 10)
                        THEN DO;
                                PUT EDIT (',', xr(j))
                                (A, COL(70), F(3));
                                k = 1;
                        END;
                        ELSE DO;
                                PUT EDIT (',', xr(j))
                                (A, X(1), F(3));
                                k = k + 1;
                        END;
                        j = j + 1;
                END;
                symtab (ptr).name = '0';
        END;
        PUT SKIP;
END;

IF (code_debug)
THEN DO;

        PUT SKIP (2) LIST ('code area is:');
        i = 1;
        DO WHILE (i < codeptr);
                PUT SKIP EDIT (i, instr_str (code (i)))
                (F(5),COL(10),A);
```

Fig. 2-21   Source code for the main module (cont'd.)

```
              DO j = i + 1 TO i + num_ops (code (i));
                    PUT EDIT (code (j)) (X(5),F(5));
              END;
              i = j;
        END;

        PUT SKIP (2) LIST ('global area is:');
        DO i = 1 TO globalptr - 1;
              PUT SKIP EDIT (i,global (i))
              (F(5),COL(10),F(6));
        END;

        PUT SKIP (2) LIST ('procinfo area is:');
        DO i = 1 TO procptr - 1;
              PUT SKIP EDIT (i,procinfo(i))
              (F(5),COL(10),F(7));
        END;
END;

/* execute the object code */
IF (no_code)
THEN CALL execution_phase;
```

Fig. 2-21   Source code for the main module (cont'd.)

Refer back to section 2-2.6 for scanner source.

Refer back to section 2-3.7 for parser source.

Refer to back to section 2-4.6 for table handler source.

Refer back to section 2-5.12 for code generator source.

BIBLIOGRAPHY

FISHER, C.N., MILTON, D.R., and S.B. QUIRING, "An Efficient Insertion-Only Error-Corrector For LL(1) Parser," Fourth ACM Symposium on the Principles of Programming Languages, 1977, pp. 97-103.

TREMBLAY, J.P., and P.G. Sorenson, "An Introduction to Data Structures With Applications," McGraw-Hill Book Co., New York, 1976.

TREMBLAY, J.P., and P.G. Sorenson, "The Theory And Practice of Compiler Writing," McGraw-Hill Book Co., New York, 1982.

Chapter 3

THE RUN-TIME

ENVIRONMENT

3-1 INTRODUCTION

The GAUSS compiler presented in Chap. 2 generates code that executes on a hypothetical machine. The structure of the machine was established with two purposes in mind: first, to simplify the code-generation phase of the GAUSS compiler so that the emphasis would be directed toward the basic problems of implementing a compiler, and second, to simplify the implementation of an interpreter that executes the generated machine code.

This chapter describes an interpreter for the code generated by the GAUSS compiler and, in particular, the run-time environment in which the machine code is executed. The hypothetical machine is stack-oriented; the code it executes is designed specifically for GAUSS programs. Because this chapter concentrates on the run-time environment, the reader is referred to the appendix for specifics concerning the machine-code instructions and their meanings.

Chapter 3 is organized into two major sections. The next section, Sec. 3-2, examines the implementation of the interpreter to execute code for the hypothetical machine. Thus, the simulated run-time environment of the hypothetical machine is outlined. This includes descriptions on the storage and retrieval of values for both local and global variables and a detailed examination of the string-space organization. Sec. 3-3 describes the run-time errors that may be reported by the machine-code interpreter as it executes a GAUSS program.

3-2 THE IMPLEMENTATION OF THE HYPOTHETICAL MACHINE INTERPRETER

The machine for which the GAUSS compiler generates code exists only on paper. An interpreter is required that simulates the behavior of the machine. This section is concerned with the implementation of such an interpreter. First, Sec. 3-2.1 examines the run-time environment, including the storage and handling of both local and global variables. Then, Sec. 3-2.2 describes the string-space organization. Because string lengths are not defined at compile time, their dynamic storage requirements necessitate that they be handled differently from other data types. Next, Sec. 3-2.3 outlines the garbage collection approach for strings. Finally, Sec. 3-2.4 gives the software which implements the interpreter, and Sec. 3-2.5 discusses some example GAUSS programs, including the machine code generated by the compiler and the output generated when the code is executed by the interpreter.

3-2.1 The Run-Time Environment

This subsection describes the environment in which the intermediate code generated by the GAUSS compiler is executed. Because an interpreter is used to simulate the hypothetical machine, "run-time environment" refers to the time at which the code is interpreted.

The storage structure of the hypothetical machine is divided into two major components: a code area and a data area. The data area is further subdivided into local, global, and string storage areas. The memory within each area is contiguous, although all three areas need not be contiguous.

The intermediate language instructions generated during compilation are stored linearly in the code area. Each instruction occupies one or more contiguous memory locations. For example, the first location stores the first instruction, and any immediately succeeding locations store the operands of the instruction if the instruction requires one or more operands. Thus, an instruction with one operand occupies two locations, with the second location reserved for the operand. The size of the code area is determined at compile time and, therefore, it is fixed at run time. The code is stored in the linear array called *code*. The size of this array is set by the constant *ncode*.

As each machine-code instruction is being executed, a register in the hypothetical machine, called the *address counter*, determines the location of the current instruction. A pointer into the *code* array in the GAUSS interpreter simulates this register. The interpreter accesses the location indicated by the pointer and any immediately following locations to determine the operator and its operands. Once an instruction has been executed, the address counter is reset to point to the location immediately following the locations occupied by the current instruction unless a branch instruction has been executed. In the case of a branch instruction, the address counter is set to the location indicated by the operand of that instruction. The initial instruction to be executed by the interpreter once a GAUSS program has been compiled is found in the first location of the code area.

The data area contains the storage allocated for the variables and constants of a GAUSS program and all temporary variables required for execution. The structure of the data area is more complex than that of the code area and is illustrated in Fig. 3-1. The data area is broken into three separate sections. This structure was created for simplifying the implementation of the intepreter, and it can be wasteful of storage. The cross-hatched areas in the figure indicate locations allocated for storage, and the arrows designate the way memory is allocated if more storage space is required. The sizes of the storage areas are determined externally by adjusting the values of their corresponding system parameters. The parameters *nsize, nglobal,* and *strsize* define the size of the local area, global area, and string area, respectively. The string area shrinks toward the middle because of the way strings are stored. The string-space organization is discussed in Sec. 3-2.2.

Global variables, constant arrays, and string constants are stored in the global area. Global string variables are stored partially in the global area and partially in the string area. The manner in which strings are saved is detailed in Sec. 3-2.2. The size of the global area is determined at compile time and fixed at interpretation time.

The local area saves all local integer and logical variables and temporary variables. Like global string variables, local string variables are saved partially in the local area and partially in the string area. The local area is structured by using activation records. Activation records are described later in this subsection.

A separate string area is required to store the strings created at run time. The string length is dynamic, and it is impossible to create a fixed-size storage area for a given string variable or array element until a value is defined for a string. The local and global areas may store pointers that indicate the locations of strings and their descriptors in the string area.

Registers in the hypothetical machine are used to determine storage spaces allocated for the local and string areas. The allocated space varies dynamically while a GAUSS program is being interpreted. Another register saves the line number in the source listing to which the set of intermediate instructions being executed corresponds. A register called the "write pointer" is used when output is being generated.

The values of global constants and the storage requirements of most global variables can be determined at compile time. Space is allocated in the global area by the compiler for each global variable or array and each constant. In the case of constants, including string constants, the values of the constants are saved in the global area at compile time.

The allocated space in the local area is not of a fixed size. The storage requirements of an executing procedure are organized into a single contiguous area called an *activation record* that is similar in organization to the one illustrated in Fig. 2-13. New space must be allocated whenever a new executing procedure is invoked (that is, a new activation record is created), and the space for an activation record is freed at the time the procedure has returned or its execution is terminated. Each activation record stores the return address, the parameters of the procedure, the local variables, and any required temporary storage locations. The number of temporary locations varies as a procedure is being executed and is called the "variable portion" of the activation record. Temporary locations are used to save temporary values while a GAUSS program statement is being executed. Because of the way space is allocated and deallocated in the local area, it is sometimes referred to as the *run-time stack*.

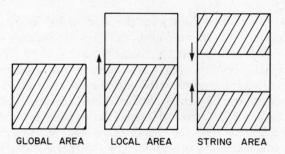

GLOBAL AREA   LOCAL AREA   STRING AREA

Fig. 3-1   Structure of data area in interpreter

A special register, called the *activation base pointer (abp)*, contains the base address of the activation record for the currently executing procedure. Addressing other locations in the current activation record is done relative to this base address. When an executing procedure returns to its calling procedure, the space for its activation record is freed. The *abp* is reset to its previous value. The previous *abp* is saved in a new activation record whenever it is created.

The construction of an activation record is handled in two steps. The first step saves the implicit parameters, the return address, the current value of the *abp*, and the explicit parameters. The machine-code instructions generated by the GAUSS compiler push the *abp*, the return address, and finally the explicit parameters onto the run-time stack. When a procedure is invoked, a "jump" instruction is executed. It sets the *abp* to the base of the new activation record and changes the address given by the instruction counter and thereby transferring control to the called procedure.

The second step occurs when the local variable declarations are handled. Space is allocated in the activation record for the local variables. The machine instruction "incsp" allocates storage for simple variables. Arrays are handled somewhat diffently. First, a template outlining the dimensions of the array and the bounds of each dimension is created. The instruction "template" performs this. Finally, the instruction "allocate" allocates the space for the array.

The activation records are stacked on top of each other, reflecting the calling sequence. If procedure A calls procedure B, B calls C, and C calls D, then the activation records are ordered DCBA from top to bottom. If procedure D returns, C returns, and B calls E, then the order is EBA.

While the code for a GAUSS program is being interpreted, simple variables, array elements, and procedure parameters must be accessed, allowing both the retrieval and storage of values. Two modes of addressing are used to access a location: relative and absolute. The *absolute address of a location in the local area* is its position number from the bottom of the run-time stack. The *relative address of a location in the global area and in the string area* is its absolute address as measured from the bottom of the area. The *relative address of a location in the local area* is the negation of the offset from the activation base pointer. Therefore, when the relative address is positive, it refers to the global area. If it is negative and not a string, it refers to the local area, and if it is a string, it refers to the string area.

In general, addressing is done directly. However, because procedure arguments are passed by reference, they must be accessed indirectly. Many machine instructions, such as those for loading strings and nonstring values and for storing values, use either direct addressing or indirect addressing. For example, the instruction "store" saves a value given the location of the variable, while the instruction "storei" is given the location of a parameter. The parameter's location gives the absolute location of the variable being referenced, and so, in this case, indirect addressing is used. It should be noted that whether addressing is done directly or indirectly, the sign of the address (that is, positive or negative) determines whether the address is an absolute address or a relative address.

Before an array element can be accessed, its location must be determined. The machine instructions "deref" and "derefi" are used to dereference array elements directly and indirectly, respectively. In other words, given values for the subscripts and given the base address of the array, these instructions determine the absolute address of the array element.

The variable portion of an activation record can only be accessed if the activation record is the current one. The variable portion contains the intermediate values of a GAUSS program statement while it is being interpreted. The size of the variable portion of the activation record remains constant between statements of a GAUSS program and varies as a statement is being executed.

Temporary values are pushed, accessed, and popped from the top of the local area (that is, the top of the local area is treated as an operand stack). Only the temporary values of the current activation record can be retrieved. The use of the variable portion of an activation record can be described as follows. Each intermediate code instruction accesses the topmost 0 or more temporary locations, deletes them from the stack, and finally pushes 0 or more values onto the stack.

3-2.2 String-Space Organization

Strings are stored differently from integer and logical variables because of their dynamic storage requirements. The space required to store a string in a string variable cannot be determined until the string variable is assigned a value. A string is saved as a sequence of characters, with the amount of space required being determined by the length of the string. A string descriptor of fixed size is defined for each string and describes the length of the string and its location in memory. This choice of representation permits strings to be handled by using fixed-length descriptors rather than by allocating a fixed-size memory space into which all values to be stored must fit.

Each simple string variable and string array element is allocated one memory location in the local area if the variable is a local variable. A similar arrangement is made for global strings in the global area. Each memory location allocated for a string is a pointer that gives the location of the string descriptor in the global area or the string area. When memory for the pointer to a string descriptor is being allocated, the pointer is initialized to 0. This value indicates that no string has yet been assigned to the simple variable or array element. This is unlike logical and integer variables and arrays, where each location stores the value. Global variables and arrays are allocated space for the string pointer in the global area and local variables and arrays are given space in the fixed portion of the activation record in the local area. It should be noted that because string constants and string array constants are defined at compile time, the location of the string descriptor and the size and composition of the string are known at compile time, and a string pointer is not required. However, to make the access to string variables and arrays and string constants consistent, a string pointer is given for each string constant or string array element constant. The pointer gives the location of the string descriptor in the global area.

The structure of a string descriptor is illustrated in Fig. 3-2. The first location of the string descriptor describes the length of the string. The next two positions together describe the location in the string area or the global area that the string is found. The fourth position is a pointer that is used for garbage collection. Garbage collection will be discussed later in this subsection.

Access to strings is handled in two ways. For local variables and arrays, the string descriptor is in the string area and is pointed to by the string pointer in the local area. The string pointer has a positive value as an address. For global variables and array elements, the relative address of the string pointer in the global area is known. The absolute value of this value gives the location of the string pointer in the global area. For global variables and arrays, the pointer is negative and its address gives the location of the string descriptor in the string area. String constants and string array constants have the string stored in the global area. The string pointer for constants has a positive value, indicating that the location of the string descriptor is in the global area. This design makes accessing string constants and global string variables and arrays consistent. Note that the string descriptor and the string are always found in the same storage area. Illustrated in Fig. 3-3 is an example of the storage for the string "ABCDEFG". Each location storing the string characters contains two characters of the string. If the string is of odd length, the second character of the last location is unused.

The string area is organized with string descriptors at one end of the memory space and with strings at the other end. This organization is illustrated in Fig. 3-4. As new values for strings are created and saved, memory is allocated for string descriptors and the actual string. Memory that was used for storing a previous string value is not freed until garbage collection is performed. Memory is allocated at each end of the string area for strings and their descriptors until there is insufficient memory left in which to store a new string. At this point, garbage collection occurs.

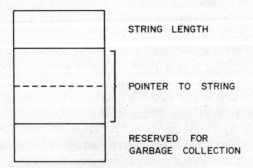

Fig. 3-2   Structure of a string descriptor

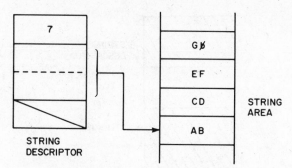

Fig. 3-3   Storage representation of a sample string

3-2.3   Garbage Collection of String Space

During garbage collection, strings are compacted at one end of the string area. The garbage collection algorithm can determine when strings can be freed, because the length of a string pointed to by a string descriptor is negated whenever a string variable or array element is assigned a new value and the old value can be discarded. Once the space for a string has been reclaimed, the string descriptors that pointed to the unused strings are freed by negating the pointer to the actual string. String descriptors cannot be compacted because the garbage collection algorithm cannot trace back to the string pointers in the local and global areas. By negating the value of the pointer in a string descriptor, it can be determined whether a string descriptor is currently being used. Thus, whenever a new string is to be stored, a search is first made for a freed string descriptor, and if none is available, then space is allocated from the center portion of the string area for a new descriptor.

The fourth location in the string descriptor is used by the garbage collection algorithm to order the string descriptors. The order in which the strings and string descriptors occur in memory do not necessarily correspond. This is because a new string is stored in the space immediately following the space which currently stores all strings created and because string descriptors are saved at unused string descriptor locations, if possible, before allocating more memory for a new location. The strings are stored in the order in which they are created, while string descriptors are not. The fourth location is used by the garbage collection algorithm to create a linked list of string descriptors in which the ordering of the descriptors reflects the order in which the strings were allocated. This simplifies string compaction because once a string has been moved and the pointer for the string descriptor has been negated, the string descriptor for the next string to be moved or freed is easily found.

3-2.4   Software Organization

This subsection outlines the implementation of the interpreter, including a source listing. The hierarchy of the procedures comprising the interpreter is illustrated in Fig. 3-5. The interpreter is invoked by calling the procedure *execution_phase*. This procedure first allocates the storage for the local area and the string area. Two global arrays, *global* and *code*, are the global area and the

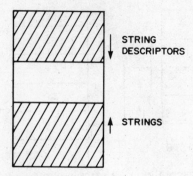

Fig. 3-4   Organization of the string area

code area, respectively. The procedure then initializes the input data buffer if there is any data. The input data is exhausted when the next control command indicating a new GAUSS program is reached or when the end of the input is reached. Then the procedure calls another procedure, *next_instruction*, to execute the instructions. This procedure is repetitively called until some condition occurs that requires execution to terminate. Execution stops when the program has been completely run or when an unrecoverable error condition occurs.

The procedure *next_instruction* executes the instruction in the code area whose address is given by the instruction counter. It then resets the instruction counter to the address of the next instruction to be executed and returns. The procedure behaves as follows. First, a number of error conditions are checked. A run-time error is reported if an error condition exists. If no errors are discovered, a segment of the code which performs the operations of the instruction to be interpreted is executed. A GOTO statement and the *op* label array simulate a case construct. Each segment of the simulated case statement contains the code which performs the operation that defines the corresponding instruction. The numerical representation of an intermediate instruction is used to determine which segment of the code is executed. Once at the appropriate location, the interpreter executes the operation that an instruction is to perform. The operations for the instructions are defined in the appendix. After the operation is performed, the procedure returns. Executing the operations of an instruction may be terminated prematurely if a run-time error is detected. For example, if the division operator is being interpreted and the divisor is zero, the interpreter reports the error and returns without performing the division.

A number of procedures are called by the procedure *next_instruction*. The procedures *run_stack, assign_rs,* and *globall* check the bounds of the local area and global area before access to the area is attempted. If the index to the location is out of bounds, an error is reported. The procedure *find* computes the location of a variable in the local area given its absolute address or its relative address. The procedures *string* and *find_string* return the string given its descriptor. The procedure *descriptor* saves the string that is its argument and returns the string descriptor. The procedure *garbage_collect* performs garbage collection in the string area whenever the free space in the string area is consumed. The procedure *scan_over* scans the input stream, stopping at the next valid data type. The

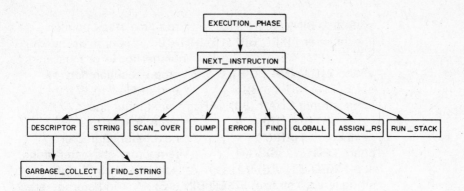

Fig. 3-5   Top-down description chart of the interpreter

procedure *error* handles the printing of error messages, while the procedure *dump* prints a dump of the local area and some register values.

To allow debugging of the interpreter, the flag *int_debug* can be turned on using the ?OPTION control command. With the flag turned on, a trace of the execution of the interpreter is printed (namely, the instructions executed), and a dump of the local area is printed whether execution is terminated normally or abnormally. This is especially useful for debugging the code generated by the compiler.

The remainder of this subsection gives the source code for the interpreter. (See Fig. 3-6.)

```
/***************************************************/
/*                                                 */
/*              execution_phase                    */
/*                                                 */
/***************************************************/
```

```
        /* this procedure and all called procedures comprise the interpreter
        that executes the object code generated by the action routines.
        Note that the object code is saved in the global array 'code'.  */

execution_phase: PROCEDURE;

        DECLARE
                next_instruction ENTRY,
                dump ENTRY;

        DECLARE
                rs(0: nsize) FIXED BIN (15) INIT (0, (nsize) 0),
                                        /* run-time stack     */
```

Fig. 3-6   Source code for the interpreter

```
        sp FIXED BIN (15) INIT (0),   /* run-time stack pointer    */
        line_number FIXED BIN (15) INIT (0), /* source-listing line
                                  number for error messages */
        abend BIT(1) INIT ('0'B),    /* stop execution flag */
        eof BIT (1) INIT ('0'B),     /* end-of-file flag */
        input_stream CHAR (80) VAR, /* next input line */
        wp FIXED BIN (15),           /* write pointer */
        next_char CHAR (1),          /* next input character */
        chars CHAR (256) VAR,        /* temporary character string */
        abp FIXED BIN (15) INIT (1), /* activation base pointer    */
        string_area(0:strsize) FIXED BIN (15) /* string storage area */
               INIT (0, (strsize) 0),
        str_ptr FIXED BIN (15) INIT (strsize),
                              /* string storage stack pointer */
        descr_ptr FIXED BIN (15) INIT (1),   /* pointer to descriptior stack */
        prev_descr FIXED BIN (15) INIT (0), /* pointer to last descriptor  */
        ic FIXED BIN (15) INIT (1);   /* instruction counter */


IF (real_eof)
THEN eof = '1'B;
ON ENDFILE (SYSIN) BEGIN;
        real_eof, eof = '1'B;
        line_buf = '?PROGRAM';
END;

/* check if there is some input data */
IF (SUBSTR (line_buf, 1, 5) = '?DATA')
THEN DO;
        GET EDIT (input_stream) (A(80));
        IF (real_eof)
        THEN IF (SUBSTR (input_stream, 1, 8) = '?PROGRAM' |
                SUBSTR (input_stream, 1, 8) = '?OPTION')
            THEN DO;
                    eof = '1'B;
                    line_buf = input_stream;
            END;
END;

PUT SKIP EDIT ('output -->') (A);
PUT SKIP;
DO WHILE (abend & no_code);
        CALL next_instruction;
END;
IF (int_debug)
THEN CALL dump;

/* scan input until end-of-file */
IF (LENGTH (input_stream) = 80)
```

Fig. 3-6 Source code for the interpreter (cont'd.)

```
       THEN IF (SUBSTR (input_stream, 1, 8) = '?PROGRAM' |
                  SUBSTR (input_stream, 1, 7) = '?OPTION')
          THEN DO;
                  line_buf = input_stream;
                  eof = '1'B;
          END;
       DO WHILE (eof & real_eof);
          GET EDIT (line_buf) (A(80));
          IF (real_eof)
          THEN RETURN;
          IF (SUBSTR (line_buf, 1, 8) = '?PROGRAM' |
             SUBSTR (line_buf, 1, 7) = '?OPTION')
          THEN eof = '1'B;
       END;


       /*******************************************************/
       /*                                                     */
       /*                 next_instruction                    */
       /*                                                     */
       /*******************************************************/
```

/* this procedure interprets the instructions in the array 'code'.
The global variable 'codeptr' gives
the number of elements in the array 'code'. */

```
next_instruction: PROCEDURE;
    DECLARE
            run_stack ENTRY (FIXED BIN (15)) RETURNS (FIXED BIN (15)),
            assign_rs ENTRY (FIXED BIN (15)) RETURNS (FIXED BIN (15)),
            error ENTRY (CHAR (*) VAR, FIXED BIN (15)),
            find ENTRY (FIXED BIN (15)) RETURNS (FIXED BIN (15)),
            scan_over ENTRY,
            string ENTRY (FIXED BIN (15)) RETURNS (CHAR (256) VAR),
            descriptor ENTRY (CHAR (*) VAR) RETURNS (FIXED BIN (15));

    DECLARE
            scope CHAR (1),                 /* local or global variable   */
            (str, chars) CHAR (256) VAR,    /* temporary string variables*/
            (t, i, n, ctr, size, p)
                    FIXED BIN (15),         /* temporary variables */
            (number, digit) FIXED BIN (15), /* used to convert strings to
                                                            integers */
            (neg, not_done, flag, warning) BIT (1);
                                      /* temporary boolean variables */

    DECLARE
            op (#_of_instructions) LABEL;
```

Fig. 3-6   Source code for the interpreter (cont'd.)

```
        ON FIXEDOVERFLOW BEGIN;
                CALL error ('integer over(under)flow', 1);
        END;

        IF (int_debug)
        THEN PUT SKIP (2) EDIT ('Next instruction location: ', ic) (a, f(3));
        /* check if next instruction cannot be exectuted */
        IF (ic >= codeptr | ic < 1)
        THEN DO;
                CALL error ('out of code area', 1);
                RETURN;
        END;
        IF (ic + num_ops(code(ic)) >= codeptr)
        THEN DO;
                CALL error ('out of code area', 1);
                RETURN;
        END;
        IF (code(ic) < 1 | code(ic) > #_of_instructions)
        THEN DO;
                CALL error ('illegal instruction', 1);
                RETURN;
        END;
        IF (int_debug)
        THEN DO;
                PUT SKIP EDIT ('Instruction is: ', instr_str(code(ic))) (a, a);
                DO i = ic + 1 TO ic + num_ops(code(ic));
                        PUT EDIT (code(i)) (F(8));
                END;
                PUT SKIP EDIT ('Stack pointer: ', sp) (A, F(5));
        END;
        IF (sp < 0 | sp + 5 > nsize)
        THEN DO;
                CALL error ('run-time stack area over(under)flow', 1);
                RETURN;
        END;



        GO TO op(code(ic));

/************************** instructions *****************/
/*****************************************************************/

op(1): /* absolute - place the absolute address of the identifier
        on top of the stack */
        sp = sp + 1;
        rs(assign_rs(sp)) = find (code(ic + 1));
        IF (scope = 'g')
        THEN rs(assign_rs(sp)) = - rs(assign_rs(sp));
```

Fig. 3-6   Source code for the interpreter (cont'd.)

```
      ic = ic + 2;
      RETURN;


op(2): /* add - the sum of the two top elements of the run-time stack
          is placed on the stack */
      rs(assign_rs(sp - 1)) = run_stack(sp - 1) + run_stack(sp);
      sp = sp - 1;
      ic = ic + 1;
      RETURN;


op(3): /* allocate - space is allocated for a dynamic array */
      rs(assign_rs(find (code(ic + 1)))) = find (code(ic + 2));
      rs(assign_rs(find (code(ic + 1)) + 1)) =
              run_stack(find (code(ic + 2))) + sp + 1;
      n = run_stack(find (code(ic + 2)) + 2 +
              3 * (run_stack(find (code(ic + 2)) + 1) - 1));
      DO i = sp + 1 TO sp + n;
              rs(i) = 0;
      END;
      sp = sp + n;
      ic = ic + 3;
      RETURN;


op(4): /* concat - a descriptor of the concatenated strings is placed on top
          of the stack */
      str = string (run_stack(sp - 1)) || string (run_stack(sp));

      /* free operands */
      IF (run_stack(sp - 1) > 0)
      THEN string_area(run_stack(sp - 1)) = -string_area(run_stack(sp - 1));
      IF (run_stack(sp) > 0)
      THEN string_area(run_stack(sp)) = -string_area(run_stack(sp));
      rs(assign_rs(sp - 1)) = descriptor (str);
      sp = sp - 1;
      ic = ic + 1;
      RETURN;


op(5): /* deref - the absolute address of the array element is placed on
          top of the stack */
      p = find (code(ic + 1));
      IF (scope = 'l')
      THEN DO;
              t = run_stack(find (code(ic + 1)));
              n = run_stack(t + 1);
              ctr = run_stack(find (code(ic + 1)) + 1);
              DO i = 1 TO n;
                      IF (run_stack(sp - n + i) < run_stack(t + 3 * (i - 1) + 3) |
                          run_stack(sp - n + i) > run_stack(t + 3 * (i - 1) + 4))
```

Fig. 3-6   Source code for the interpreter (cont'd.)

```
                                        THEN DO;
                                                CALL error ('dimension for array is out-of-bounds', 1);
                                                RETURN;
                                        END;
                                        ELSE IF (i¬= 1)
                                                THEN ctr = ctr + run_stack(sp - n + i) *
                                                        run_stack(t + 3 * (i - 2) + 2);
                                                ELSE ctr = ctr + run_stack(sp - n + i);
                                END;
                                sp = sp - (n - 1);
                                rs(assign_rs(sp)) = ctr;
                        END;
                        ELSE DO;
                                t = global(globall(find (code(ic + 1))));
                                n = global(globall(t + 1));
                                ctr = global(globall(find (code(ic + 1)) + 1));
                                DO i = 1 TO n;
                                        IF (run_stack(sp - n + i) < global(globall(t + 3 * (i - 1) + 3)) |
                                                run_stack(sp - n + i) > global(globall(t + 3 *
                                                                        (i - 1) + 4)))
                                        THEN DO;
                                                CALL error ('dimension for array is out-of-bounds', 1);
                                                RETURN;
                                        END;
                                        ELSE IF (i¬= 1)
                                                THEN ctr = ctr + run_stack(sp - n + i) *
                                                        global(globall(t + 3 * (i - 2) + 2));
                                                ELSE ctr = ctr + run_stack(sp - n + i);
                                END;
                                sp = sp - (n - 1);
                                rs(assign_rs(sp)) = - ctr;
                        END;
                        ic = ic + 2;
                        RETURN;

op(6):  /* derefi (indirect dereference) - the absolute address of the array
            element is placed on top of the stack */
        IF (run_stack(find (code(ic + 1))) > 0)
        THEN DO;
                        t = run_stack(run_stack(find (code(ic + 1))));
                        n = run_stack(t + 1);
                        ctr = run_stack(run_stack(find (code(ic + 1))) + 1);
                        DO i = 1 TO n;
                                IF (run_stack(sp - n + i) < run_stack(t + 3 * (i - 1) + 3) |
                                        run_stack(sp - n + i) > run_stack(t + 3 * (i - 1) + 4))
                                THEN DO;
                                        CALL error ('dimension for array is out-of-bounds', 1);
                                        RETURN;
                                END;
```

Fig. 3-6   Source code for the interpreter (cont'd.)

```
                    ELSE IF (i ¬= 1)
                        THEN ctr = ctr + run_stack(sp - n + i) *
                                    run_stack(t + 3 * (i - 2) + 2);
                        ELSE ctr = ctr + run_stack(sp - n + i);
                END;
                sp = sp - (n - 1);
                rs(assign_rs(sp)) = ctr;
        END;
        ELSE DO;
                t = global(globall(-run_stack(find (code(ic + 1)))));
                n = global(globall(t + 1));
                ctr = global(globall(-run_stack(find (code(ic + 1))) + 1));
                DO i = 1 TO n;
                        IF (run_stack(sp - n + i) < global(globall(t + 3 *
                                                (i - 1) + 3)) |
                            run_stack(sp - n + i) > global(globall(t + 3 *
                                                (i - 1) + 4)))
                        THEN DO;
                                CALL error ('dimension for array is out-of-bounds', 1);
                                RETURN;
                        END;
                        ELSE IF (i ¬= 1)
                                THEN ctr = ctr + run_stack(sp - n + i) *
                                        global(globall(t + 3 * (i - 2) + 2));
                                ELSE ctr = ctr + run_stack(sp - n + i);
                END;
                sp = sp - (n - 1);
                rs(assign_rs(sp)) = - ctr;
        END;
        ic = ic + 2;
        RETURN;

op(7): /* divide - the quotient is placed on top of the stack */
        IF (run_stack(sp) = 0)
        THEN DO;
                CALL error ('attempt to divide by zero', 1);
                RETURN;
        END;
        rs(assign_rs(sp - 1)) = run_stack(sp - 1) / run_stack(sp);
        ic = ic + 1;
        sp = sp - 1;

op(8): /* dump - dump the contents of the appropriate memory locations */
        CALL dump;
        ic = ic + 1;
        RETURN;
```

Fig. 3-6   Source code for the interpreter (cont'd.)

```
op(9): /* ieq - the truth value of the integer relation = is placed on
        top of the stack */
     IF (run_stack(sp - 1) = run_stack(sp))
     THEN rs(assign_rs(sp - 1)) = 1;
     ELSE rs(assign_rs(sp - 1)) = 0;
     sp = sp - 1;
     ic = ic + 1;
     RETURN;

op(10): /* ige - the truth value of the integer relation >= is placed on
        top of the stack */
     IF (run_stack(sp - 1) >= run_stack(sp))
     THEN rs(assign_rs(sp - 1)) = 1;
     ELSE rs(assign_rs(sp - 1)) = 0;
     sp = sp - 1;
     ic = ic + 1;
     RETURN;

op(11): /* igt - the truth value of the integer relation > is placed on
        top of the stack */
     IF (run_stack(sp - 1) > run_stack(sp))
     THEN rs(assign_rs(sp - 1)) = 1;
     ELSE rs(assign_rs(sp - 1)) = 0;
     sp = sp - 1;
     ic = ic + 1;
     RETURN;

op(12): /* ile - the truth value of the integer relation <= is placed on
        top of the stack */
     IF (run_stack(sp - 1) <= run_stack(sp))
     THEN rs(assign_rs(sp - 1)) = 1;
     ELSE rs(assign_rs(sp - 1)) = 0;
     sp = sp - 1;
     ic = ic + 1;
     RETURN;

op(13): /* ilt - the truth value of the integer relation < is placed on
        top of the stack */
     IF (run_stack(sp - 1) < run_stack(sp))
     THEN rs(assign_rs(sp - 1)) = 1;
     ELSE rs(assign_rs(sp - 1)) = 0;
     sp = sp - 1;
     ic = ic + 1;
     RETURN;

op(14): /* ine - the truth value of the integer relation ¬= is placed on
        top of the stack */
     IF (run_stack(sp - 1) ¬= run_stack(sp))
```

Fig. 3-6 Source code for the interpreter (cont'd.)

```
           THEN rs(assign_rs(sp - 1)) = 1;
           ELSE rs(assign_rs(sp - 1)) = 0;
           sp = sp - 1;
           ic = ic + 1;
           RETURN;

op(15):  /* index - the index of the configuration in the host string
             is placed on top of the stack */
           t = INDEX (string (run_stack(sp - 1)), string (run_stack(sp)));
           IF (run_stack(sp) > 0)
           THEN string_area(run_stack(sp)) = -string_area(run_stack(sp));
           IF (run_stack(sp - 1) > 0)
           THEN string_area(run_stack(sp - 1)) = -string_area(run_stack(sp - 1));
           rs(assign_rs(sp - 1)) = t;
           sp = sp - 1;
           ic = ic + 1;
           RETURN;

op(16): /* newline - the output device advances to a new line */
           PUT SKIP;
           ic = ic + 1;
           RETURN;

op(17): /* jump - control is transferred to another procedure:
             the activation base pointer and the instruction pointer are reset */
           abp = sp - code(ic + 2) - 1;
           IF (abp < 1 | abp > sp)
           THEN CALL error ('activation base pointer out of stack area', 1);
           ic = code(ic + 1);
           RETURN;

op(18): /* readlog - a value is read into the Boolean variable */
           CALL scan_over;
           IF (eof | real_eof)
           THEN DO;
                   CALL error ('attempt to read past end of file', 1);
                   RETURN;
           END;
           IF (LENGTH (input_stream) >= 5)
           THEN IF (SUBSTR (input_stream, 1, 4) ¬= 'TRUE' &
                   SUBSTR (input_stream, 1, 5) ¬= 'FALSE')
               THEN DO;
                       CALL error ('invalid data type in input, boolean' ||
                               ' constant expected', 1);
                       RETURN;
               END;
           ELSE;
```

Fig. 3-6   Source code for the interpreter (cont'd.)

```
            ELSE IF (LENGTH (input_stream) >= 4)
                THEN IF (SUBSTR (input_stream, 1, 4) ¬= 'TRUE')
                    THEN DO;
                            CALL error ('invalid data type in input, ' ||
                                'boolean constant expected', 1);
                            RETURN;
                    END;
            IF (SUBSTR (input_stream, 1, 4) = 'TRUE')
            THEN DO;
                    IF (run_stack(sp) > 0)
                    THEN rs(assign_rs(run_stack(sp))) = 1;
                    ELSE global(globall(-run_stack(sp))) = 1;
                    IF (LENGTH (input_stream) > 4)
                    THEN input_stream = SUBSTR (input_stream, 5);
                    ELSE input_stream = '';
            END;
            ELSE DO;
                    IF (run_stack(sp) > 0)
                    THEN rs(assign_rs(run_stack(sp))) = 0;
                    ELSE global(globall(-run_stack(sp))) = 0;
                    IF (LENGTH (input_stream) > 5)
                    THEN input_stream = SUBSTR (input_stream, 6);
                    ELSE input_stream = '';
            END;
            IF (SUBSTR (input_stream, 1, 4) = 'TRUE')
            THEN IF (LENGTH (input_stream) > 4)
                    THEN input_stream = SUBSTR (input_stream, 5);
                    ELSE GET EDIT (input_stream) (A(80));
            ELSE IF (LENGTH (input_stream) > 5)
                    THEN input_stream = SUBSTR (input_stream, 6);
                    ELSE GET EDIT (input_stream) (A(80));
            sp = sp - 1;
            ic = ic + 1;
            RETURN;

op(19): /* load - the value of the variable is placed on the stack */
        sp = sp + 1;
        t = find (code(ic + 1));
        IF (scope = 'g')
        THEN rs(assign_rs(sp)) = global(globall (t));
        ELSE rs(assign_rs(sp)) = run_stack(t);
        ic = ic + 2;
        RETURN;

op(20): /* loadi (load indirect) - the value of the variable is placed
            on the stack */
        sp = sp + 1;
        t = find (code(ic + 1));
```

Fig. 3-6   Source code for the interpreter (cont'd.)

```
        IF (run_stack(t) > 0)
        THEN rs(assign_rs(sp)) = run_stack(run_stack(t));
        ELSE rs(assign_rs(sp)) = global(globall(-run_stack(t)));
        ic = ic + 2;
        RETURN;

op(21): /* line - the line number is saved in the line number counter */
        line_number = code(ic + 1);
        ic = ic + 2;
        RETURN;

op(22): /* multiply - the product is placed on top of the stack */
        rs(assign_rs(sp - 1)) = run_stack(sp - 1) * run_stack(sp);
        ic = ic + 1;
        sp = sp - 1;
        RETURN;

op(23): /* negate - the arithmetic negation is placed on top of the stack */
        rs(assign_rs(sp)) = - run_stack(sp);
        ic = ic + 1;
        RETURN;

op(24): /* push - the value is placed on top of the stack */
        sp = sp + 1;
        rs(assign_rs(sp)) = code(ic + 1);
        ic = ic + 2;
        RETURN;

op(25): /* loada (load absolute) - the value of the variable is placed
            on the stack */
        IF (run_stack(sp) > 0)
        THEN rs(assign_rs(sp)) = run_stack(run_stack(sp));
        ELSE rs(assign_rs(sp)) = global(globall(-run_stack(sp)));
        ic = ic + 1;
        RETURN;

op(26): /* rem (remainder on division) - the remainder of the division
            is placed on top of the stack */
        IF (run_stack(sp) = 0)
        THEN DO;
                CALL error ('division by zero', 1);
                RETURN;
        END;
        rs(assign_rs(sp - 1)) = MOD (run_stack(sp - 1), run_stack(sp));
        sp = sp - 1;
        ic = ic + 1;
        RETURN;
```

Fig. 3-6   Source code for the interpreter (cont'd.)

```
op(27): /* seq (string relation) - the truth value of the string relation
          = is placed on top of the stack */
     IF (string (run_stack(sp - 1)) = string (run_stack(sp)))
     THEN i = 1;
     ELSE i = 0;

     /* free operands */
     IF (run_stack(sp - 1) > 0)
     THEN string_area(run_stack(sp - 1)) = -string_area(run_stack(sp - 1));
     IF (run_stack(sp) > 0)
     THEN string_area(run_stack(sp)) = -string_area(run_stack(sp));
     rs(assign_rs(sp - 1)) = i;
     sp = sp - 1;
     ic = ic + 1;
     RETURN;

op(28): /* sge (string relation) - the truth value of the string relation
          >= is placed on top of the stack */
     IF (string (run_stack(sp - 1)) >= string (run_stack(sp)))
     THEN i = 1;
     ELSE i = 0;

     /* free operands */
     IF (run_stack(sp - 1) > 0)
     THEN string_area(run_stack(sp - 1)) = -string_area(run_stack(sp - 1));
     IF (run_stack(sp) > 0)
     THEN string_area(run_stack(sp)) = -string_area(run_stack(sp));
     rs(assign_rs(sp - 1)) = i;
     sp = sp - 1;
     ic = ic + 1;
     RETURN;

op(29): /* sgt (string relation) - the truth value of the string relation
          > is placed on top of the stack */
     IF (string (run_stack(sp - 1)) > string (run_stack(sp)))
     THEN i = 1;
     ELSE i = 0;

     /* free operands */
     IF (run_stack(sp - 1) > 0)
     THEN string_area(run_stack(sp - 1)) = -string_area(run_stack(sp - 1));
     IF (run_stack(sp) > 0)
     THEN string_area(run_stack(sp)) = -string_area(run_stack(sp));
     rs(assign_rs(sp - 1)) = i;
     sp = sp - 1;
     ic = ic + 1;
     RETURN;
```

Fig. 3-6   Source code for the interpreter (cont'd.)

```
op(30): /* sle (string relation) - the truth value of the string relation
          <= is placed on top of the stack */
       IF (string (run_stack(sp - 1)) <= string (run_stack(sp)))
       THEN i = 1;
       ELSE i = 0;

       /* free operands */
       IF (run_stack(sp - 1) > 0)
       THEN string_area(run_stack(sp - 1)) = -string_area(run_stack(sp - 1));
       IF (run_stack(sp) > 0)
       THEN string_area(run_stack(sp)) = -string_area(run_stack(sp));
       rs(assign_rs(sp - 1)) = i;
       sp = sp - 1;
       ic = ic + 1;
       RETURN;

op(31): /* slt (string relation) - the truth value of the string relation
          < is placed on top of the stack */
       IF (string (run_stack(sp - 1)) < string (run_stack(sp)))
       THEN i = 1;
       ELSE i = 0;

       /* free operands */
       IF (run_stack(sp - 1) > 0)
       THEN string_area(run_stack(sp - 1)) = -string_area(run_stack(sp - 1));
       IF (run_stack(sp) > 0)
       THEN string_area(run_stack(sp)) = -string_area(run_stack(sp));
       rs(assign_rs(sp - 1)) = i;
       sp = sp - 1;
       ic = ic + 1;
       RETURN;

op(32): /* sne (string relation) - the truth value of the string relation
          ¬= is placed on top of the stack */
       IF (string (run_stack(sp - 1)) ¬= string (run_stack(sp)))
       THEN i = 1;
       ELSE i = 0;

       /* free operands */
       IF (run_stack(sp - 1) > 0)
       THEN string_area(run_stack(sp - 1)) = -string_area(run_stack(sp - 1));
       IF (run_stack(sp) > 0)
       THEN string_area(run_stack(sp)) = -string_area(run_stack(sp));
       rs(assign_rs(sp - 1)) = i;
       sp = sp - 1;
       ic = ic + 1;
       RETURN;
```

Fig. 3-6   Source code for the interpreter (cont'd.)

```
op(33): /* store - the variable is assigned the value */
        t = find (code(ic + 1));
        IF (scope = 'l')
        THEN rs(assign_rs(t)) = run_stack(sp);
        ELSE global(globall(t)) = run_stack(sp);
        sp = sp - 1;
        ic = ic + 2;
        RETURN;

op(34): /* storei (store indirect) - the variable is assigned the value */
        t = find (code(ic + 1));
        IF (run_stack(t) > 0)
        THEN rs(assign_rs(run_stack(t))) = run_stack(sp);
        ELSE global(globall(-run_stack(t))) = run_stack(sp);
        sp = sp - 1;
        ic = ic + 1;
        RETURN;

op(35): /* subtract - the difference is placed on dtop of the stack */
        rs(assign_rs(sp - 1)) = run_stack(sp - 1) - run_stack(sp);
        sp = sp - 1;
        ic = ic + 1;
        RETURN;

op(36): /* substring - a string descriptor of the substring (from the
           cursor position to the end of the string) is placed on top
           of the stack. */
        IF (run_stack(sp) < 1)
        THEN chars = string (run_stack(sp - 1));
        ELSE IF (run_stack(sp) > LENGTH (string (run_stack(sp - 1))))
                THEN chars = '';
                ELSE chars = SUBSTR (string (run_stack(sp - 1)), run_stack(sp));
        IF (run_stack(sp - 1) > 0)
        THEN string_area(run_stack(sp - 1)) = -string_area(run_stack(sp - 1));
        rs(assign_rs(sp - 1)) = descriptor (chars);
        sp = sp - 1;
        ic = ic + 1;
        RETURN;

op(37): /* substring1 (substring given the length argument) - a string
           descriptor of the substring (from the cursor position and
           with the given length) is placed on top of the stack */
        IF (run_stack(sp - 1) > LENGTH (string (run_stack(sp - 2))))
        THEN chars = '';
        ELSE DO;
                n = run_stack(sp - 1) + run_stack(sp) - 1;
                IF (run_stack(sp - 1) < 1)
                THEN IF (n <= LENGTH (string (run_stack(sp - 2))))
```

Fig. 3-6 Source code for the interpreter (cont'd.)

```
                THEN chars = SUBSTR (string (run_stack(sp - 2)), 1, n);
                ELSE chars = string (run_stack(sp - 2));
            ELSE IF (n <= LENGTH (string (run_stack(sp - 2))))
                THEN chars = SUBSTR (string (run_stack(sp - 2)),
                            run_stack(sp - 1), run_stack(sp));
                ELSE chars = SUBSTR (string (run_stack(sp - 2)),
                            run_stack(sp - 1));
    END;
    IF (run_stack(sp - 2) > 0)
    THEN string_area(run_stack(sp - 2)) = -string_area(run_stack(sp - 2));
    rs(assign_rs(sp - 2)) = descriptor (chars);
    sp = sp - 2;
    ic = ic + 1;
    RETURN;


OP(38):        /* template - a template for the array is built */
    t = find (code(ic + 1));
    ctr = 0;
    p = 1;
    DO i = 1 TO code(ic + 2);
            size = run_stack(sp - 2 * (code(ic + 2) - i))
                - run_stack(sp - 2 * (code(ic + 2) - i) - 1) + 1;
        IF (i = 1)
        THEN ctr = ctr - run_stack(sp - 2 * (code(ic + 2) - i) - 1);
        ELSE ctr = ctr - run_stack(sp - 2 * (code(ic + 2) - i) - 1) * p;
        p = p * size;
        rs(assign_rs(t + 3 * (i - 1) + 2)) = p;
        rs(assign_rs(t + 3 * (i - 1) + 3)) =
                run_stack(sp - 2 * (code(ic + 2) - i) - 1);
        rs(assign_rs(t + 3 * (i - 1) + 4)) =
                run_stack(sp - 2 * (code(ic + 2) - i));
    END;
    rs(assign_rs(t)) = ctr;
    rs(assign_rs(t + 1)) = code(ic + 2);
    sp = sp - 2 * code(ic + 2);
    ic = ic + 3;
    RETURN;

op(39): /* return - control is returned to the calling procedure */
    ic = run_stack(abp + 1);
    n = abp - 1;
    abp = run_stack(abp);
    sp = n;
    RETURN;

op(40): /* returnval (return value) - return from a procedure
        with a value */
    ic = run_stack(abp + 1);
```

Fig. 3-6 Source code for the interpreter (cont'd.)

```
        n = run_stack(sp);
        sp = abp;
        abp = run_stack(abp);
        rs(assign_rs(sp)) = n;
        RETURN;

op(41): /* saveabp (save activation base pointer) - the activation base
            pointer is placed on top of the stack */
        sp = sp + 1;
        rs(assign_rs(sp)) = abp;
        ic = ic + 1;
        RETURN;

op(42): /* incrsp - the stack pointer is incremented to allocate space
            for local variables  */
        IF (code(ic + 1) < 0)
        THEN DO;
                CALL error ('stack pointer incremented by ' ||
                    'negative amount', 1);
                RETURN;
        END;
        DO i = sp + 1 TO code (ic + 1) + sp;
                rs(i) = 0;
        END;
        sp = sp + code(ic + 1);
        ic = ic + 2;
        RETURN;

op(43):  /* and - the logical conjunction is placed on top of the stack */
        IF (run_stack(sp) = 0 | run_stack(sp - 1) = 0)
        THEN rs(assign_rs(sp - 1)) = 0;
        ELSE rs(assign_rs(sp - 1)) = 1;
        sp = sp - 1;
        ic = ic + 1;
        RETURN;

op(44): /* not - the logical compliment is placed on top of the stack */
        IF (run_stack(sp) = 0)
        THEN rs(assign_rs(sp)) = 1;
        ELSE rs(assign_rs(sp)) = 0;
        ic = ic + 1;
        RETURN;

op(45): /* or - the logical disjunction is placed on top of the stack */
        IF (run_stack(sp - 1) = 1 | run_stack(sp) = 1)
        THEN rs(assign_rs(sp - 1)) = 1;
        ELSE rs(assign_rs(sp - 1)) = 0;
        sp = sp - 1;
```

Fig. 3-6   Source code for the interpreter (cont'd.)

```
            ic = ic + 1;
            RETURN;

op(46): /* branch - the instruction counter is reset */
            ic = code(ic + 1);
            RETURN;

op(47): /* branchf - the instruction counter is reset on a false
            condition */
            IF (run_stack(sp) = 0)
            THEN ic = code(ic + 1);
            ELSE ic = ic + 2;
            sp = sp - 1;
            RETURN;

op(48): /* pop - the value on top of the stack is popped as a response to
            a compilation error */
            sp = sp - 1;
            ic = ic + 1;
            RETURN;

op(49): /* replace - a substring of the host string (from the cursor
            position to the end of the string) is replaced by the
            replacement string */
            str = '';
            IF (run_stack(sp - 2) > 0)
            THEN IF (run_stack(run_stack(sp - 2)) = 0)
                    THEN str = string (run_stack(run_stack(sp - 2)));
                    ELSE;
            ELSE IF (run_stack(sp - 2) < 0)
                    THEN IF (global(globall(-run_stack(sp - 2))) = 0)
                            THEN str = string (run_stack(sp - 2));
            IF (run_stack(sp - 1) <= 1 | LENGTH (str) = 0)
            THEN t = descriptor (string (run_stack(sp)));
            ELSE t = descriptor (SUBSTR (str, 1, run_stack(sp - 1) - 1) ||
                    string(run_stack(sp)));
            IF (run_stack(sp) > 0)
            THEN string_area(run_stack(sp)) = -string_area(run_stack(sp));
            IF (run_stack(sp - 2) > 0)
            THEN string_area(run_stack(run_stack(sp - 2))) =
                    -string_area(run_stack(run_stack(sp - 2)));
            ELSE IF (run_stack(sp - 2) < 0)
                    THEN IF (global(globall(-run_stack(sp - 2))) < 0)
                            THEN string_area(-global(globall(-run_stack(sp - 2)))) =
                                    -string_area(-global(globall(-run_stack(sp - 2))));
            IF (run_stack(sp - 2) > 0)
            THEN rs(assign_rs(run_stack(sp - 2))) = t;
            ELSE global(globall(-run_stack(sp - 2))) = -t;
```

Fig. 3-6 Source code for the interpreter (cont'd.)

```
        sp = sp - 3;
        ic = ic + 1;
        RETURN;

op(50): /* replace1 (replace given the length argument) - a substring of
        the host string (from the cursor position to the end of the string)
        is replaced by the replacement string */
        str = '';
        IF (run_stack(sp - 3) > 0)
        THEN IF (run_stack(run_stack(sp - 3)) ¬= 0)
                THEN str = string (run_stack(run_stack(sp - 3)));
                ELSE;
        ELSE IF (global(globall(-run_stack(sp - 3))) ¬= 0)
                THEN str = string (run_stack(sp - 3));
        IF (run_stack(sp - 2) <= 1)
        THEN chars = '';
        ELSE IF (run_stack(sp - 2) > LENGTH (str))
                THEN chars = str;
                ELSE chars = SUBSTR (str, 1, run_stack(sp - 2) - 1);
        chars = chars || string (run_stack(sp));
        IF (run_stack(sp - 1) + run_stack(sp - 2) < 1)
        THEN chars = chars || str;
        ELSE IF (run_stack(sp - 1) + run_stack(sp - 2) <= LENGTH (str))
                THEN chars = chars ||
                        SUBSTR (str, run_stack(sp - 1) + run_stack(sp - 2));
        IF (run_stack(sp) > 0)
        THEN string_area(run_stack(sp)) = -string_area(run_stack(sp));
        IF (run_stack(sp - 3) > 0)
        THEN string_area(run_stack(run_stack(sp - 3))) =
                -string_area(run_stack(run_stack(sp - 3)));
        ELSE IF (run_stack(sp - 3) < 0)
                THEN IF (global(globall(-run_stack(sp - 3))) < 0)
                        THEN string_area(-global(globall(-run_stack(sp - 3)))) =
                                -string_area(-global(globall(-run_stack(sp - 3))));

        /* save the descriptor pointer */
        IF (run_stack(sp - 3) > 0)
        THEN rs(assign_rs(run_stack(sp - 3))) = descriptor (chars);
        ELSE global(globall(-run_stack(sp - 3))) = -descriptor (chars);
        sp = sp - 4;
        ic = ic + 1;
        RETURN;

op(51): /* stop - the program is terminated */
        abend = '1'B;
        RETURN;
```

Fig. 3-6   Source code for the interpreter (cont'd.)

```
op(52): /* storea (store absolute) - the variable is assigned the value */
        IF (run_stack(sp - 1) > 0)
        THEN rs(assign_rs(run_stack(sp - 1))) = run_stack(sp);
        ELSE global(globall(-run_stack(sp - 1))) = run_stack(sp);
        sp = sp - 2;
        ic = ic + 1;
        RETURN;


op(53): /* readint (read integer) - a value is read into the integer
            variable */
        ON FIXEDOVERFLOW BEGIN;
                CALL error ('overflow, input number too large', 2);
                flag = '1'B;
                DO WHILE (flag & LENGTH (input_stream) > 0);
                        next_char = SUBSTR (input_stream, 1, 1);
                        IF (next_char >= '0' | next_char <= '9')
                        THEN DO;
                                GET EDIT (input_stream) (A(80));
                                flag = '0'B;
                        END;
                        ELSE input_stream = SUBSTR (input_stream, 2);
                END;
                IF (flag)
                THEN GET EDIT (input_stream) (A(80));
        END;

        /* scan input stream until data type found */
        CALL scan_over;
        IF (eof | real_eof)
        THEN DO;
                CALL error ('attempt to read past end of file', 1);
                RETURN;
        END;

        /* integer data type found? */
        IF (SUBSTR (input_stream, 1, 1) ¬= '-' &
                        (SUBSTR (input_stream, 1, 1) < '0' |
                        SUBSTR (input_stream, 1, 1) > '9'))
        THEN DO;
                CALL error ('invalid data type in input, integer expected', 2);
                RETURN;
        END;
        IF (SUBSTR (input_stream, 1, 1) = '-')
        THEN DO;
                neg = '1'B;
                input_stream = SUBSTR (input_stream, 2);
        END;
        ELSE neg = '0'B;
```

Fig. 3-6 Source code for the interpreter (cont'd.)

```
        number = 0;
        flag = '1'B;
        DO WHILE (flag & SUBSTR (input_stream, 1, 1) >= '0' &
                    SUBSTR (input_stream, 1, 1) <= '9');
              GET STRING (SUBSTR (input_stream, 1, 1)) EDIT (digit) (F(1));
              number = number * 10 + digit;
              IF (LENGTH (input_stream) = 1)
              THEN DO;
                    flag = '0'B;
                    input_stream = '';
              END;
              ELSE input_stream = SUBSTR (input_stream, 2);
        END;
        IF (neg)
        THEN number = - number;
        IF (run_stack(sp) > 0)
        THEN rs(assign_rs(run_stack(sp))) = number;
        ELSE global(globall(-run_stack(sp))) = number;
        sp = sp - 1;
        ic = ic + 1;
        RETURN;

op(54): /* readstr (read string) - a value is read into the string
        variable  */
        CALL scan_over;
        IF (eof | real_eof)
        THEN DO;
              CALL error ('attempt to read past end of file', 1);
              RETURN;
        END;

        /* check if string is next input type */
        IF (SUBSTR (input_stream, 1, 1) ¬= ' ')
        THEN DO;
              CALL error ('invalid data type in input, literal expected', 1);
              RETURN;
        END;

        /* read string */
        chars = '';
        IF (LENGTH (input_stream) > 1)
        THEN input_stream = SUBSTR (input_stream, 2);
        ELSE input_stream = '';
        not_done = '1'B;
        DO WHILE (LENGTH (input_stream) > 0 & not_done);
              flag = '1'B;
              DO WHILE (LENGTH (input_stream) > 0 & flag);
                    IF (SUBSTR (input_stream, 1, 1) = ' ')
```

Fig. 3-6   Source code for the interpreter (cont'd.)

```
                THEN flag = '0'B;
                ELSE DO;
                        chars = chars || SUBSTR (input_stream, 1, 1);
                        IF (LENGTH (input_stream) > 1)
                        THEN input_stream = SUBSTR (input_stream, 2);
                        ELSE input_stream = '';
                END;
          END;
          IF (LENGTH (input_stream) > 0)
          THEN DO;
                  IF (LENGTH (input_stream) > 1)
                  THEN input_stream = SUBSTR (input_stream, 2);
                  ELSE input_stream = '';
                  IF (LENGTH (input_stream) > 0)
                  THEN IF (SUBSTR (input_stream, 1, 1) = ' ')
                          THEN DO;
                                  chars = chars || ' ';
                                  IF (LENGTH (input_stream) > 1)
                                  THEN input_stream = SUBSTR (input_stream, 2);
                                  ELSE input_stream = '';
                          END;
                          ELSE not_done = '0'B;
                  ELSE not_done = '0'B;
          END;
      END;
      IF (not_done)
      THEN CALL error ('attempt to read literal past end of line', 2);
      IF (run_stack(sp) > 0)
      THEN rs(assign_rs(run_stack(sp))) = descriptor (chars);
      ELSE global(globall(-run_stack(sp))) = -descriptor (chars);
      sp = sp - 1;
      ic = ic + 1;
      RETURN;

op(55): /* write - the write pointer is set to the address of the first
         value to be written  */
      sp = sp - code(ic + 1);
      wp = sp + 1;
      ic = ic + 2;
      RETURN;

op(56): /* writeint (write integer) - the integer is written */
      IF (code(ic + 1) < 0)
      THEN CALL error ('negative field width', 2);
      IF (code(ic + 1) <= 0)

      /* must directly access stack as wp > sp (from operation write)  */
      THEN PUT EDIT (rs (wp)) (F(6));
```

Fig. 3-6   Source code for the interpreter (cont'd.)

```
        ELSE IF ((rs (wp) > 0 &
                 TRUNC (LOG10 (ABS(rs(wp)) * 1.0)) + 1 <= code (ic + 1)) |
                 (rs (wp) < 0 &
                 TRUNC (LOG10 (ABS (rs(wp)) * 1.0)) + 2 <= code (ic + 1)))
            THEN PUT EDIT (rs (wp)) (F(code(ic + 1)));
            ELSE IF (rs (wp) > 0)
                    THEN PUT EDIT (rs (wp))
                            (F(TRUNC (LOG10 (rs (wp) * 1.0)) + 1));
                    ELSE IF (rs (wp) < 0)
                            THEN PUT EDIT (rs (wp))
                                    (F(TRUNC (LOG10 (rs (wp) * -1.0)) + 2));
                            ELSE PUT EDIT (rs (wp)) (F(code(ic + 1)));
        wp = wp + 1;
        ic = ic + 2;
        RETURN;

op(57): /* writelog (write logical) - the Boolean value is written */
        IF (rs (wp) = 0)
        THEN PUT EDIT ('TRUE') (A);
        ELSE PUT EDIT ('FALSE') (A);
        wp = wp + 1;
        ic = ic + 1;
        RETURN;

op(58): /* writestr (write string) - the string is written */
        IF (code(ic + 1) < 0)
        THEN CALL error ('negative field width', 2);
        chars = string (rs (wp));
        IF (code(ic + 1) <= 0 | LENGTH (chars) > code(ic + 1))
        THEN PUT EDIT (chars) (A);
        ELSE PUT EDIT (chars) (A(code(ic + 1)));
        wp = wp + 1;
        ic = ic + 2;
        RETURN;

op(59): /* space - the output device advances x spaces */
        IF (code(ic + 1) < 1)
        THEN CALL error ('spacing by a nonpositive amount', 2);
        ELSE PUT EDIT ('') (X(code(ic + 1)), A);
        ic = ic + 2;
        RETURN;

op(60): /* tab - the output device advances to column x */
        IF (code(ic + 1) < 1)
        THEN CALL error ('tab to a nonpositive column', 2);
        ELSE PUT EDIT ('') (COL(code(ic + 1)), A);
        ic = ic + 2;
        RETURN;
```

Fig. 3-6   Source code for the interpreter (cont'd.)

```
op(61): /* end_of_file - puts 1 on the stack if the end of input has
        been reached. */
    IF (real_eof & ¯eof)
    THEN CALL scan_over;
    sp = sp + 1;
    IF (eof | real_eof)
    THEN rs(assign_rs(sp)) = 1;
    ELSE rs(assign_rs(sp)) = 0;
    ic = ic + 1;
    RETURN;

op(62): /* loads (load string) - the descriptor of a new copy of the
        string is placed on the stack */
    sp = sp + 1;
    t = find (code(ic + 1));
    IF (scope = 'g')
    THEN IF (global(globall(t)) ¯= 0)
            THEN rs(assign_rs(sp)) = descriptor (string (-t));
            ELSE rs(assign_rs(sp)) = descriptor ('');     /* empty string */
    ELSE IF (run_stack(t) ¯= 0)
            THEN rs(assign_rs(sp)) = descriptor (string (run_stack(t)));
            ELSE rs(assign_rs(sp)) = descriptor ('');
    ic = ic + 2;
    RETURN;

op(63): /* loadsi (load string indirect) - the descriptor of the new
        string is placed on the stack */
    sp = sp + 1;
    t = find (code(ic + 1));
    IF (run_stack(t) > 0)
    THEN IF (run_stack(run_stack(t)) ¯= 0)
            THEN rs(assign_rs(sp)) = descriptor (string (run_stack(run_stack(t))));
            ELSE rs(assign_rs(sp)) = descriptor ('');
    ELSE IF (run_stack(t) < 0)
            THEN IF (global(globall(-run_stack(t))) ¯= 0)
                    THEN rs(assign_rs(sp)) = descriptor (string (run_stack(t)));
                    ELSE rs(assign_rs(sp)) = descriptor ('');
            ELSE rs(assign_rs(sp)) = descriptor ('');
    ic = ic + 2;
    RETURN;

op(64): /* loadsa (load string absolute) - the descriptor of the new
        string is placed on the stack */
    IF (run_stack(sp) > 0)
    THEN IF (run_stack(run_stack(sp)) ¯= 0)
            THEN rs(assign_rs(sp)) =
                    descriptor (string (run_stack(run_stack(sp))));
            ELSE rs(assign_rs(sp)) = descriptor ('');
```

Fig. 3-6 Source code for the interpreter (cont'd.)

```
        ELSE IF (run_stack(sp) < 0)
            THEN IF (globall(globall(-run_stack(sp))) = 0)
                    THEN rs(assign_rs(sp)) = descriptor (string (run_stack(sp)));
                    ELSE rs(assign_rs(sp)) = descriptor ('');
            ELSE rs(assign_rs(sp)) = descriptor ('');
        ic = ic + 1;
        RETURN;


op(65): /* length - the length of the string is placed on top of
            the stack.  */

        /* out of bounds? */
        IF (run_stack(sp) >= 0)
        THEN IF (run_stack(sp) >= str_ptr | run_stack(sp) = 0)
                THEN DO;
                        CALL error ('out of string storage area', 1);
                        RETURN;
                END;
                ELSE;
        ELSE IF (ABS (run_stack(sp)) >= globalptr)
                THEN DO;
                        CALL error ('out of global storage area', 1);
                        RETURN;
                END;

        /* get length */
        IF (run_stack(sp) > 0)
        THEN t = string_area(run_stack(sp));
        ELSE IF (globall(globall(-run_stack(sp))) > 0)
                THEN t = global(globall(global(globall(-run_stack(sp)))));
                ELSE t = string_area(-global(globall(-run_stack(sp))));

        /* free operand */
        IF (run_stack(sp) > 0)
        THEN string_area(run_stack(sp)) = - string_area(run_stack(sp));

        rs(assign_rs(sp)) = t;
        ic = ic + 1;
        RETURN;

        /****************************************************/
        /*                                                  */
        /*              run_stack                           */
        /*                                                  */
        /****************************************************/

        /* this procedure checks the index to the run-time stack to make
        sure it is valid before it returns the value at that location.  */
```

Fig. 3-6 Source code for the interpreter (cont'd.)

```
run_stack: PROCEDURE (index) RETURNS (FIXED BIN (15));
     DECLARE
            index FIXED BIN (15);          /* index into array */
     IF (abend)
     THEN RETURN (1);
     IF (index < 1 | index > sp)
     THEN DO;
            CALL error ('out of run-time stack area', 1);
            RETURN (1);
     END;
     RETURN (rs(index));
END run_stack;

/************************************************/
/*                                              */
/*            assign_rs                         */
/*                                              */
/************************************************/

     /* this procedure checks that the index is valid and returns a valid
     index value before an assignment is made to the run-time stack. */

assign_rs: PROCEDURE (index) RETURNS (FIXED BIN (15));
     DECLARE
            index FIXED BIN (15);          /* index into run-time stack */

     IF (abend)
     THEN RETURN (0);
     IF (index < 1 | index > sp)
     THEN DO;
            CALL error ('out of run-time stack area', 1);
            RETURN (0);
     END;
     RETURN (index);
END assign_rs;

/************************************************/
/*                                              */
/*            globall                           */
/*                                              */
/************************************************/
     /* this procedure checks that the index into the global storage
     area is valid. */

globall: PROCEDURE (index) RETURNS (FIXED BIN (15));
DECLARE
     index FIXED BIN (15);                 /* index into global array    */
     IF (abend)
```

Fig. 3-6 Source code for the interpreter (cont'd.)

```
        THEN RETURN (0);
        IF (index < 1 | index >= globalptr)
        THEN DO;
                CALL error ('out of global storage area', 1);
                RETURN (0);
        END;
        RETURN (index);
END globall;
```

```
/ * * * * * * * * * * * * * * * * * * * * * * * * * * * * * * * * * * * * * * * * * * * * * * * * /
/ *                                                                      * /
/ *                         find                                         * /
/ *                                                                      * /
/ * * * * * * * * * * * * * * * * * * * * * * * * * * * * * * * * * * * * * * * * * * * * * * * * * /
```

/* this procedure returns the location of a variable in the run-time
stack from its absolute address. */

```
find: PROCEDURE (order_number) RETURNS (FIXED BIN (15));
      DECLARE
              order_number FIXED BIN (15);         /* absolute address */
      IF (order_number < 0)
      THEN DO;
              scope = 'l';
              RETURN (abp - order_number - 1);
      END;
      ELSE DO;
              scope = 'g';
              RETURN (order_number);
      END;
END find;
```

```
/ * * * * * * * * * * * * * * * * * * * * * * * * * * * * * * * * * * * * * * * * * * * * * * * * /
/ *                                                                      * /
/ *                        string                                        * /
/ *                                                                      * /
/ * * * * * * * * * * * * * * * * * * * * * * * * * * * * * * * * * * * * * * * * * * * * * * * * * /
```

/* this procedure returns the string stored at the location designated
by its parameter in the string storage area. */

```
string: PROCEDURE (descriptor) RETURNS (CHAR (256) VAR);
        DECLARE
                descriptor FIXED BIN (15),    /* string descriptor        */
                find_string ENTRY ((*) FIXED BIN (15), FIXED BIN (15))
                        RETURNS (CHAR (256) VAR);
```

Fig. 3-6 Source code for the interpreter (cont'd.)

```
/* out of bounds? */
IF (descriptor >= 0)
THEN IF (descriptor >= descr_ptr | descriptor = 0)
        THEN DO;
                CALL error ('out of string storage area', 1);
                RETURN ('');
        END;
        ELSE;
ELSE IF (ABS (descriptor) >= globalptr)
        THEN DO;
                CALL error ('out of global storage area', 1);
                RETURN ('');
        END;

IF (descriptor > 0)
THEN RETURN (find_string (string_area, descriptor));
ELSE IF (global(globall(-descriptor)) > 0)
        THEN RETURN (find_string (global, global(globall(-descriptor))));
        ELSE RETURN (find_string (string_area, -global(globall(-descriptor))));


/***********************************************************/
/*                                                         */
/*                 find_string                             */
/*                                                         */
/***********************************************************/
```

/* this procedure returns the string from the area and its beginning
position in the array passed to it. */

```
find_string: PROCEDURE (string_area, descriptor) RETURNS (CHAR (256) VAR);
DECLARE
            string_area (*) FIXED BIN (15), /* string storage area */
            descriptor FIXED BIN (15),    /* pointer to descriptor    */
            location FIXED BIN (31),       /* location in string   */
            len FIXED BIN (15),            /* length of string         */
            i FIXED BIN (15),              /* temporary string var     */
            str CHAR (256) VAR;            /* string to return         */

/* compute the string */
str = '';
location = string_area (descriptor + 1) * 32767
        + string_area (descriptor + 2);
len = string_area (descriptor);
IF (len < 0)
THEN len = -len;
IF (len = 0)
THEN RETURN ('');
```

Fig. 3-6 Source code for the interpreter (cont'd.)

```
           DO i = location TO location + (len / 2 - 1);
                   UNSPEC (str) = UNSPEC (str) || UNSPEC (string_area (i));
           END;
           IF (MOD (len, 2) = 0)
           THEN UNSPEC (str) = UNSPEC (str) || SUBSTR (UNSPEC (string_area
                   (location + len / 2)), 1, 8);
           RETURN (str);
     END find_string;

     END string;
```

```
           /***********************************************************/
           /*                                                         */
           /*                descriptor                               */
           /*                                                         */
           /***********************************************************/
```

```
     /* this procedure returns the string descriptor for the string
     passed as its parameter once the string is saved in the string
     storage area. */
```

```
descriptor: PROCEDURE (string) RETURNS (FIXED BIN (15));
     DECLARE
             (i, j) FIXED BIN (15),          /* counted loop variable */
             flag BIT (1),                   /* Boolean flag */
             string CHAR (*) VAR,            /* string to be saved */
             garbage_collect ENTRY;

     /* scan for the first empty descriptor location */
     i = 1;
     flag = '1'B;
     DO WHILE (i < descr_ptr & flag);
             IF (string_area(i + 2) < 0)
             THEN flag = '0'B;
             ELSE i = i + 4;
     END;
     IF (flag)
     THEN DO;
             i = descr_ptr;
             descr_ptr = descr_ptr + 4;
     END;

     /* overflow in storage area */
     IF (descr_ptr >= str_ptr - (LENGTH (string) / 2 - 1)
                   - MOD (LENGTH (string), 2))
     THEN CALL garbage_collect;
     IF (descr_ptr >= str_ptr - (LENGTH (string) / 2 - 1)
                   - MOD (LENGTH (string), 2))
```

Fig. 3-6   Source code for the interpreter (cont'd.)

```
THEN DO;
        CALL error ('local string storage area overflow', 1);
        RETURN (0);
END;

string_area(i) = LENGTH (string);
string_area(i + 1) = 0;
string_area(i + 2) = str_ptr - (LENGTH (string) / 2 - 1)
        - MOD (LENGTH (string), 2);
string_area(i + 3) = 0;
IF (prev_descr ¬= 0)
THEN string_area (prev_descr + 3) = i;
prev_descr = i;

/* store the string */
str_ptr = str_ptr - LENGTH (string) / 2 - MOD (LENGTH (string), 2);
DO j = 1 TO LENGTH (string) - 1 BY 2;
        UNSPEC (string_area(str_ptr + j / 2 + 1)) =
                UNSPEC (SUBSTR (string, j, 2));
END;
IF (MOD (LENGTH (string), 2) ¬= 0)
THEN UNSPEC (string_area(str_ptr + j / 2 + 1)) =
                UNSPEC (SUBSTR (string, LENGTH (string), 1) || ' ');
RETURN (i);

        /****************************************************/
        /*                                                  */
        /*              garbage_collect                     */
        /*                                                  */
        /****************************************************/

/* this procedure performs garbage collection on the local string
   area, recovering now unused space that once stored strings. */

garbage_collect: PROCEDURE;
    DECLARE
            (i, j) FIXED BIN (15),          /* counted loop variables  */
            previous FIXED BIN (15),        /* previous descriptortor  */
            flag BIT (1);                   /* logical flag            */

    /* scan for first descriptor */
    prev_descr = 0;
    i = 1;
    previous = 0;
    DO WHILE (ABS(string_area(i)) / 2 + MOD (ABS (string_area(i)), 2) +
            string_area(i + 1) * 32767 + string_area(i + 2) < strsize &
            i < descr_ptr - 4);
            i = i + 4;
    END;
```

Fig. 3-6 Source code for the interpreter (cont'd.)

```
/* scan looking for first free location */
flag = '1'B;
DO WHILE (flag & string_area(i + 3) > 0);
       IF (string_area(i) < 0)
       THEN flag = '0'B;
       ELSE DO;
              i = string_area(i + 3);
              previous, prev_descr = i;
       END;
END;

/* no free locations */
IF (flag)
THEN RETURN;

/* move strings to recover space */
str_ptr = ABS (string_area(i)) / 2 + MOD (ABS (string_area(i)), 2) - 1
       + string_area(i + 1) * 32767 + string_area(i + 2);
DO WHILE (i ¬= 0);
       IF (string_area (i) < 0)
       THEN /* free location, pass over */
              string_area(i + 2) = -1;
       ELSE DO;
              prev_descr = i;
              IF (previous ¬= 0)
              THEN string_area(previous + 3) = i;
              previous = i;

              /* copy the string */
              DO j = string_area(i + 1) * 32767 + string_area(i + 2) +
                     string_area(i) / 2 + MOD (string_area(i), 2) - 1
                     TO string_area(i + 1) * 32767 + string_area(i + 2) BY -
                     string_area(str_ptr) = string_area(j);
                     str_ptr = str_ptr - 1;
              END;
              string_area(i + 1) = (str_ptr + 1) / 32767;
              string_area(i + 2) = MOD (str_ptr + 1, 32767);
       END;
       j = i;
       i = string_area(i + 3);
       string_area(j + 3) = 0;
END;
RETURN;
END garbage_collect;

END descriptor;
```

Fig. 3-6   Source code for the interpreter (cont'd.)

```
/****************************************************/
/*                                                  */
/*              scan_over                           */
/*                                                  */
/****************************************************/

/* this procedure scans over the input stream until it finds the
next valid data type (i.e., integer, literal, Boolean) */

scan_over: PROCEDURE;
      DECLARE
              flag BIT (1),                /* Boolean flag */
              warning BIT (1);             /* skipped over nonblank chars. */

      flag = '1'B;
      warning = '0'B;

      /* check for end of file */
      IF (LENGTH (input_stream) = 0)
      THEN GET EDIT (input_stream) (A(80));
      IF (LENGTH (input_stream) = 80)
      THEN IF (SUBSTR (input_stream, 1, 7) = '?OPTION' |
                  SUBSTR (input_stream, 1, 8) = '?PROGRAM')
            THEN DO;
                    eof = '1'B;
                    line_buf = input_stream;
            END;

      DO WHILE (eof & flag);
            IF (SUBSTR (input_stream, 1, 1) = '-' |
                  (SUBSTR (input_stream, 1, 1) >= '0' &
                  SUBSTR (input_stream, 1, 1) <= '9') |
                  SUBSTR (input_stream, 1, 1) = ' ')
            THEN IF (LENGTH (input_stream) > 1)
                  THEN IF (SUBSTR (input_stream, 1, 1) = '-' &
                        SUBSTR (input_stream, 2, 1) <= '9' &
                        SUBSTR (input_stream, 2, 1) >= '0')
                        THEN flag = '0'B;
                        ELSE IF (SUBSTR (input_stream, 1, 1) = '-')
                                THEN flag = '0'B;
                                ELSE warning = '1'B;
                  ELSE IF (SUBSTR (input_stream, 1, 1) >= '0' &
                              SUBSTR (input_stream, 1, 1) <= '9')
                  THEN flag = '0'B;
                  ELSE;
```

Fig. 3-6   Source code for the interpreter (cont'd.)

```
                    ELSE IF (LENGTH (input_stream) >= 4)
                        THEN IF (SUBSTR (input_stream, 1, 4) = 'TRUE')
                            THEN flag = '0'B;
                            ELSE IF (LENGTH (input_stream) >= 5)
                                THEN IF (SUBSTR (input_stream, 1, 5) =
                                    'FALSE')
                                    THEN flag = '0'B;
                IF (flag & SUBSTR (input_stream, 1, 1) ¬= ' ')
                THEN warning = '1'B;
                IF (LENGTH (input_stream) > 1 & flag)
                THEN input_stream = SUBSTR (input_stream, 2);
                ELSE IF (flag)
                    THEN DO;
                        GET EDIT (input_stream) (A(80));
                        IF (¬eof & ¬real_eof)
                        THEN IF (SUBSTR (input_stream, 1, 7) = '?OPTION' |
                                SUBSTR (input_stream, 1, 8) =
                                    '?PROGRAM')
                            THEN DO;
                                eof = '1'B;
                                line_buf = input_stream;
                            END;
                    END;
            END;
        IF (warning)
        THEN CALL error ('ignored characters in input', 2);
END scan_over;
```

```
        /************************************************/
        /*                                              */
        /*                  error                       */
        /*                                              */
        /************************************************/
```

/* this procedure prints the error message passed to it and sets
the abend flag if necessary. */

```
error: PROCEDURE (line, flag);
        DECLARE
            line CHAR (*) VAR,          /* error message */
            flag FIXED BIN (15);        /* set abend flag? */

        PUT SKIP (2) EDIT ('*** error - ', line, ' ***') (A, A, A);
        IF (line_number ¬= 0)
        THEN PUT SKIP EDIT ('*** error occurs near line', line_number) (A, F(5));
        IF (flag = 1)
        THEN abend = '1'B;
END error;
```

Fig. 3-6 Source code for the interpreter (cont'd.)

END next_instruction;

```
/ * * * * * * * * * * * * * * * * * * * * * * * * * * * * * * * * * * * * * * * * * * * * * * * * * * * /
/ *                                                                          * /
/ *                              dump                                        * /
/ *                                                                          * /
/ * * * * * * * * * * * * * * * * * * * * * * * * * * * * * * * * * * * * * * * * * * * * * * * * * * * /
```

/ * this procedure prints the run-time stack and the code stack
at run-time, permitting the compiler to be debugged. The parameter
is a dummy paramter. */

```
dump: PROCEDURE;
      DECLARE
            (i, j) FIXED BIN (15),          /* counted loop variables    */
            chars CHAR (2);                 /* temporary string variable */

      PUT SKIP(3) EDIT ('*** run-time stack ***') (A);
      DO i = 1 TO sp;
            PUT SKIP EDIT (i, ':', rs(i)) (F(3), A, F(6));
      END;
      PUT SKIP EDIT ('instruction counter is ', ic) (A, F(4));
      PUT SKIP (3) EDIT ('line number: ', line_number) (A, F(4));
      PUT SKIP (2) EDIT ('write pointer (wp): ', wp) (A, F(4));
END dump;

END execution_phase;
```

Fig. 3-6   Source code for the interpreter (cont'd.)

3-2.5   Sample Programs

This subsection gives two example GAUSS programs that are executed using the GAUSS interpreter. Included with each program are a source listing, the intermediate code generated (in a mnemonic form), and a brief explanation of the program and intermediate code.

3-2.5.1   Factorial Program

The *factorial* program inputs a series of integers and, for each value, prints its factorial. Illegal values are rejected by the program. The program calls the procedure *factorial*. This procedure returns the factorial of the number passed as its argument after recursively calling itself. The input data used to execute the program is 2, –1, and 6. The *factorial* program and its associated input is given in Fig. 3-7. The code generated by the GAUSS compiler for the program is given immediately following the source program.

Several things can be observed by examining the code area dump. The first three intermediate instructions, beginning at locations 1, 2, and 4, respectively, create the activation record for the main level procedure. After making the jump to location 10, data space for the local variables is allocated. When the main-level procedure has finished executing, the procedure returns to location 7, the location immediately following the jump instruction. This is a stop instruction.

Locations 8 and 9 are always present in the code area for every machine-code program. A function call is made to location 8 whenever the *end-of-file* function is called in a GAUSS program. The "end-of-file" instruction at location 8 determines whether the input stream has been entirely read, and the next instruction, "return value," returns the logical value computed by the "end-of-file" instruction.

Locations 10 to 71 comprise the code for the main-level procedure. Location 10 allocates space for the local variable. The instruction "line number" is given at the start of the intermediate code for every executable statement in the GAUSS program. One is found in location 12, and it indicates that the following code corresponds to the statement beginning at line 8 in the GAUSS program. Locations 56 to 61 start preparing a new activation record for a call to the factorial function. First the old activation base pointer is saved. Then the instruction at location 57 saves the return address. The next instruction pushes the address of the function call's argument. Finally, the "jump" instruction jumps to the code for

```
 1:  ?OPTION CODE_DEBUG
 2:  $$ THIS PROGRAM READS INTEGERS AND
 3:  $$ PRINTS FOR EACH THEIR FACTORIAL VALUE
 4:
 5:  INTEGER PROC FACTORIAL (INTEGER PARM) FORWARD;
 6:  PROC MAIN
 7:      INTEGER I;
 8:      LOOP
 9:      WHILE NOT END_OF_FILE;
10:          READ I;
11:          IF I < 0
12:          THEN
13:                  WRITE "ILLEGAL VALUE READ IN:", I USING
14:                      "S, X2, I, N";
15:          ELSE
16:                  WRITE FACTORIAL (I) USING "I10, N";
17:          ENDIF;
18:      ENDLOOP;
19:  ENDPROC;
20:  $$ 'FACTORIAL' RETURNS THE VALUE OF ITS ARGUMENT FACTORIAL.
21:  INTEGER PROC FACTORIAL (INTEGER I)
22:      INTEGER I_MINUS_ONE;
23:      IF I > 1
24:      THEN
25:          I_MINUS_ONE := I - 1;
26:          RETURN I * FACTORIAL (I_MINUS_ONE);
27:      ELSE
28:          RETURN 1;
29:      ENDIF;
30:  ENDPROC;
31:  ?DATA
```

Fig. 3-7   Source and generated code for factorial program

CODE AREA IS:
```
 1  SAVE ACT BASE PTR
 2  PUSH                    7
 4  JUMP                   10                   0
 7  STOP
 8  END OF FILE
 9  RETURN VALUE
10  INCR STACK PTR          1
12  LINE NUMBER             8
14  SAVE ACT BASE PTR
15  PUSH                   20
17  JUMP                    8                   0
20  NOT
21  BRANCH ON FALSE             71
23  LINE NUMBER            10
25  ABSOLUTE           -3
27  READ INTEGER
28  LINE NUMBER            11
30  LOAD                  -3
32  PUSH                   0
34  INT <
35  BRANCH ON FALSE             54
37  LINE NUMBER            12
39  PUSH            -1
41  LOAD                  -3
43  START WRITE            2
45  WRITE STRING           0
47  SPACE                  2
49  WRITE INTEGER          0
51  NEWLINE
52  BRANCH                69
54  LINE NUMBER           15
56  SAVE ACT BASE PTR
57  PUSH            64
59  ABSOLUTE          -3
61  JUMP            72              1
64  START WRITE           1
66  WRITE INTEGER           10
68  NEWLINE
69  BRANCH          14
71  RETURN
72  INCR STACK PTR          1
74  LINE NUMBER           23
76  LOAD INDIRECT         -3
78  PUSH            1
80  INT >
81  BRANCH ON FALSE            108
83  LINE NUMBER           24
85  LOAD INDIRECT         -3
87  PUSH            1
89  SUBTRACT
90  STORE           -4
92  LINE NUMBER           26
94  LOAD INDIRECT         -3
96  SAVE ACT BASE PTR
97  PUSH           104
99  ABSOLUTE          -4
```

Fig. 3-7   Source and generated code for factorial program (cont'd.)

```
101  JUMP            72              1
104  MULTIPLY
105  RETURN VALUE
106  BRANCH               113
108  LINE NUMBER               27
110  PUSH            1
112  RETURN VALUE
113  STOP
```

```
OUTPUT -->
     2
ILLEGAL VALUE READ IN:              -1
     120
```

Fig. 3-7   Source and generated code for factorial program (cont'd.)

the function. The "jump" instruction resets the instruction counter and the activation base pointer.

The instructions in the code area between locations 72 and 112, inclusive, consist of the intermediate code for the function. Locations 105 and 112 each return a value to the calling procedure. Locations 96 to 103 contain the code that, if executed, makes a recursive call.

3-2.5.2   Simple Sort Program

The simple sort program output given in Fig. 3-8 reads a series of words, each having a corresponding phrase or word. The words are then sorted and printed with their corresponding phrase in alphabetical order. This program was given in Sec. 1-12, and the reader is referred to that section for a more complete description of the program. The input for the program consists of the following three people and their sexes:

"BOB"   "MALE"
"VIVIAN"   "FEMALE"
"LYLE"   "MALE"

The structure of the code area for the *sort* program is similar to the structure of the code area for the *factorial* program as described in the previous subsection. Locations 10 to 27 comprise the code for the main level procedure, including the call to the procedure *sort*.

Locations 28 to 282 contain the code for the procedure *sort*. Notice that locations 28 to 49 allocate storage for the local variables. The instructions "push," "load indirect," "template," and "allocate" are given twice, once to allocate storage for the array *name* and once for the array *page*. The increment stack pointer instruction found at location 28 allocates storage for the local string integer and string constant variables.

Indirect referencing is required to retrieve the value of the procedure's parameter *n*. For example, the value of *n* is pushed onto the run-time stack by the instruction at location 60 using indirect referencing. Thus, it can be compared against the value of *i*. This statement is found in lines 46 and 47 of the GAUSS program.

3-3 RUN-TIME ERRORS

As an intermediate code program is being executed, conditions sometimes arise in which execution cannot continue or, in the best possible case, must be rectified. When such conditions are detected, a run-time error has occurred. When an error condition occurs, the GAUSS interpreter reports the error, and if the error condition cannot be rectified, the interpreter terminates execution. There are three major causes for run-time errors. Program or logic errors such as division by zero or reading past the end of input is one cause of errors. The remedy for this type of error involves fixing the logic of the GAUSS program. A second cause of errors occurs when there is no more free space in the local area or string area and more memory is being requested. In this case, the size of the local area or the string area must be increased and the GAUSS compiler has to be recompiled. The third cause of errors is invalid code generated by the compiler. In this case, an illegal or unknown code is to be executed, or accesses to unallocated memory may be tried.

Once an error is detected, an error message is printed. The line number instruction succeeding the error message indicates the line in the source listing near which the error occurs. Because a GAUSS statement may occur in more than one line of the source listing, the line number printed gives the line in which the GAUSS statement began. If the error is unrecoverable, execution terminates immediately after one or more error messages are printed. If the interpreter can recover from the error, execution resumes once the error message is printed.

```
 1:  ?OPTION CODE_DEBUG
 2:  $$ THIS PROGRAM READS IN A SERIES OF WORDS, EACH OF WHICH
 3:  $$ HAS AN ASSOCIATED PAGE NUMBER. THE WORDS ARE THEN
 4:  $$ SORTED SO THAT THEY CAN BE PRINTED IN ALPHABETICAL
 5:  $$ ORDER, EACH WITH A LIST OF PAGE NUMBERS ASSOCIATED WITH IT.
 6:  $$ EACH WORD IS PRINTED ONLY ONCE, BUT ALL PAGE NUMBERS
 7:  $$ ASSOCIATED WITH EACH OCCURRENCE OF THE WORD WILL BE PRINTED.
 8:  $$ DUPLICATE PAGE NUMBERS IN THE INPUT WILL APPEAR DUPLICATED
 9:  $$ IN THE OUTPUT AS WELL.
10:
11:  PROC SORT (INTEGER N)
12:     FORWARD;
13:
14:  PROC MAIN
15:     INTEGER N;
16:
17:     READ N; $$ THE NUMBER OF WORDS IS KNOWN BEFOREHAND.
18:     SORT     (N);
19:  ENDPROC;
20:
21:  $$ THIS 'SORT' ROUTINE DOES ALL THE WORK, IN THAT IT READS, SORTS
22:  $$ AND PRINTS THE WORDS.
```

Fig. 3-8 Source and generated code for sort program

```
23:   $$ A SIMPLE SELECTION SORT IS USED, AND NAMES ARE PRINTED AS
24:   $$ THEY ARE SORTED.
25:
26:   PROC SORT (INTEGER N)
27:       ARRAY (N) OF STRING NAME;
28:       ARRAY (N) OF STRING PAGE;
29:       STRING FIRST, PAGELIST;
30:       INTEGER I, J;
31:       STRING CONST LARGE = "ZZ", VERY_LARGE = "ZZZ";
32:
33:       I := 1;
34:       LOOP
35:       WHILE I <= N;
36:               READ NAME (I), PAGE (I);
37:               I := I + 1;
38:       ENDLOOP;
39:
40:       $$ NOW DO THE SORT AND PRINT:
41:
42:       LOOP
43:               FIRST := LARGE;
44:               I := 1;
45:               J := 0;
46:               LOOP
47:               WHILE I <= N;
48:                       IF NAME (I) < FIRST
49:                       THEN
50:                               IF J <> 0
51:                               THEN
52:                                       NAME (J) := FIRST;
53:                                       PAGE (J) := PAGELIST;
54:                               ENDIF;
55:
56:                               J := I;
57:                               FIRST := NAME (I);
58:                               NAME (I) := VERY_LARGE;
59:                               PAGELIST := PAGE (I);
60:                       ELSE
61:                               IF NAME (I) = FIRST
62:                               THEN
63:                                       NAME (I) := VERY_LARGE;
64:                                       PAGELIST := PAGELIST & "," & PAGE (I);
65:                               ENDIF;
66:                       ENDIF;
67:                       I := I + 1;
68:       ENDLOOP;
69:
70:       WHILE FIRST <> LARGE;
71:
72:               WRITE FIRST, PAGELIST USING "S20,X3,S40,N";
73:       ENDLOOP;
74:   ENDPROC;
75:   ?DATA

CODE AREA IS:
  1   SAVE ACT BASE PTR
  2   PUSH                    7
```

Fig. 3-8   Source and generated code for sort program (cont'd.)

4	JUMP	10	0
7	STOP		
8	END OF FILE		
9	RETURN VALUE		
10	INCR STACK PTR	1	
12	LINE NUMBER	17	
14	ABSOLUTE	−3	
16	READ INTEGER		
17	LINE NUMBER	18	
19	SAVE ACT BASE PTR		
20	PUSH	27	
22	ABSOLUTE	−3	
24	JUMP	28	1
27	RETURN		
28	INCR STACK PTR	18	
30	PUSH	1	
32	LOAD INDIRECT	−3	
34	TEMPLATE	−4	1
37	ALLOCATE	−9	−4
40	PUSH	1	
42	LOAD INDIRECT	−3	
44	TEMPLATE	−11	1
47	ALLOCATE	−16	−11
50	LINE NUMBER	33	
52	PUSH	1	
54	STORE	−20	
56	LINE NUMBER	34	
58	LOAD	−20	
60	LOAD INDIRECT	−3	
62	INT <=		
63	BRANCH ON FALSE	88	
65	LINE NUMBER	36	
67	LOAD	−20	
69	DEREFERENCE	−9	
71	READ STRING		
72	LOAD	−20	
74	DEREFERENCE	−16	
76	READ STRING		
77	LINE NUMBER	37	
79	LOAD	−20	
81	PUSH	1	
83	ADD		
84	STORE	−20	
86	BRANCH	58	
88	LINE NUMBER	42	
90	LINE NUMBER	43	
92	ABSOLUTE	−18	
94	PUSH	1	
96	PUSH	−1	
98	REPLACE UNTIL END		
99	LINE NUMBER	44	
101	PUSH	1	
103	STORE	−20	
105	LINE NUMBER	45	
107	PUSH	0	
109	STORE	−21	
111	LINE NUMBER	46	

Fig. 3-8   Source and generated code for sort program (cont'd.)

```
113  LOAD                    -20
115  LOAD INDIRECT                      -3
117  INT <=
118  BRANCH ON FALSE                    258
120  LINE NUMBER              48
122  LOAD                    -20
124  DEREFERENCE              -9
126  LOAD STRING ABSOLUTE
127  LOAD STRING             -18
129  STRING <
130  BRANCH ON FALSE                    206
132  LINE NUMBER              49
134  LOAD                    -21
136  PUSH                    0
138  INT <>
139  BRANCH ON FALSE                    163
141  LINE NUMBER              51
143  LOAD                    -21
145  DEREFERENCE             -9
147  PUSH          1
149  LOAD STRING                        -18
151  REPLACE UNTIL END
152  LINE NUMBER                        53
154  LOAD                    -21
156  DEREFERENCE            -16
158  PUSH          1
160  LOAD STRING                        -19
162  REPLACE UNTIL END
163  LINE NUMBER                        56
165  LOAD                    -20
167  STORE         -21
169  LINE NUMBER             57
171  ABSOLUTE          -18
173  PUSH                    1
175  LOAD                    -20
177  DEREFERENCE             -9
179  LOAD STRING ABSOLUTE
180  REPLACE UNTIL END
181  LINE NUMBER             58
183  LOAD                    -20
185  DEREFERENCE                -9
187  PUSH                    1
189  PUSH          -6
191  REPLACE UNTIL END
192  LINE NUMBER                        59
194  ABSOLUTE                  -19
196  PUSH                    1
198  LOAD                    -20
200  DEREFERENCE                -16
202  LOAD STRING ABSOLUTE
203  REPLACE UNTIL END
204  BRANCH            247
206  LINE NUMBER             60
208  LOAD                    -20
210  DEREFERENCE             -9
212  LOAD STRING ABSOLUTE
213  LOAD STRING             -18
215  STRING =
```

Fig. 3-8   Source and generated code for sort program (cont'd.)

```
216   BRANCH ON FALSE              247
218   LINE NUMBER            62
220   LOAD              -20
222   DEREFERENCE              -9
224   PUSH              1
226   PUSH              -6
228   REPLACE UNTIL END
229   LINE NUMBER                  64
231   ABSOLUTE          -19
233   PUSH              1
235   LOAD STRING                  -19
237   PUSH              -12
239   CONCATENATE
240   LOAD              -20
242   DEREFERENCE                  -16
244   LOAD STRING ABSOLUTE
245   CONCATENATE
246   REPLACE UNTIL END
247   LINE NUMBER                  67
249   LOAD                  -20
251   PUSH                  1
253   ADD
254   STORE             -20
256   BRANCH          113
258   LOAD STRING           -18
260   PUSH          -1
262   STRING <>
263   BRANCH ON FALSE              282
265   LINE NUMBER                  72
267   LOAD STRING                  -18
269   LOAD STRING                  -19
271   START WRITE                  2
273   WRITE STRING                 20
275   SPACE         3
277   WRITE STRING             40
279   NEWLINE
280   BRANCH          90
282   RETURN
```

```
OUTPUT -->
BOB                       MALE
LYLE                      MALE
VIVIAN                    FEMALE
```

Fig. 3-8   Source and generated code for sort program (cont'd.)

The following list gives the meanings of the error messages. After the error message is given, execution terminates.

OUT OF CODE AREA: The instruction counter gives an address of an instruction that is not in the code area.

OUT OF STRING AREA: A string descriptor does not point to a string within the string area.

OUT OF GLOBAL AREA: An access to an invalid global location is attempted.

OUT OF RUN-TIME STACK AREA: An access outside of the local area is attempted.

ILLEGAL INSTRUCTION: An unknown intermediate GAUSS instruction is found.

ACTIVATION BASE POINTER OUT OF STACK AREA: An illegal or invalid value for the *abp* is detected.

STACK POINTER INCREMENTED BY NEGATIVE AMOUNT: An attempt to allocate a negative amount of space to the local area is made. This is not an underflow condition, as the request is asking for a negative number of locations to be allocated.

RUN-TIME STACK AREA OVER(UNDER)FLOW: No more space can be allocated (freed) to the local area as all the free space is consumed (or there is insufficient allocated space to be freed).

STRING AREA OVERFLOW: No more space can be allocated to the string area.

INTEGER OVER(UNDER)FLOW: A numeric operation results in a number that is too large (that is, > 32767) or too small (that is, < -32768).

ATTEMPT TO DIVIDE BY ZERO: Division by zero is attempted.

DIMENSION FOR ARRAY IS OUT OF BOUNDS: A dimension of an array element subscript is too large or too small for the declared dimensions.

ATTEMPT TO READ PAST END OF FILE: A read is requested after the input stream has been entirely read.

INVALID DATA TYPE IN INPUT, INTEGER EXPECTED: A data type other than an integer is found in the input stream when an integer value is to be read.

INVALID DATA TYPE IN INPUT, LITERAL EXPECTED: A data type other than a literal is found in the input stream when a string literal is to be read.

INVALID DATA TYPE IN INPUT, BOOLEAN CONSTANT EXPECTED: A data type other than a Boolean constant is found in the input stream when a logical value is to be read.

The following run-time errors are not severe and do not terminate execution.

OVERFLOW, INPUT NUMBER TOO LARGE: This error occurs when a number being read is too large or too small. The value 32767 or –32767 is used.

NEGATIVE FIELD WIDTH: The printer is to include a negative number of spaces before the next item is to be written. The field width is ignored.

SPACING BY A NONPOSITIVE AMOUNT: The output device is to insert 0 or less spaces. The spacing format item is ignored.

TAB TO A NONPOSITIVE COLUMN: The output device is to advance to column 0 or to a negative column. The tab format item is ignored.

IGNORED CHARACTERS IN INPUT: In attempting to read the next input data type, characters not corresponding to any valid data type were found in the input stream. The characters are ignored. This error can occur if a string is not delimited by quotes or if the logical values "true" or "false" have been misspelled. Note that blanks can separate data items and do not cause this error.

DESCRIPTION OF THE OBJECT-MACHINE LANGUAGE

1 NOTATION

Let sp represent the stack pointer.
Let op represent an operand of an instruction.
Let ic represent the instruction counter.
Let x be an order number of an identifier.
Then $|x|$ represents the absolute address of the identifier.
The absolute address of a global identifier is known at compile time; the absolute address of a local variable is known at run time.
Therefore

$$|x| = \begin{cases} \text{abp} - x & \text{if } x < 0 \\ x & \text{if } x > 0 \end{cases}$$

where abp is the activation base pointer of the executing procedure.
Let z be an absolute address.
Then $[z]$ represents the contents of absolute address z in the run-time stack, and $/z/$ represents the contents of the absolute address z in the global stack.
Let s be a string.

Then r = descriptor(s) is the string descriptor for the string s, and s = string(r) is the string described by descriptor r. (If d is positive, the string is stored in the local string area. If d is negative and the pointer in the global string area is positive, then the string is stored in the global string area. Otherwise, it is stored in the local string area.)

2   INSTRUCTIONS

name:	absolute
operand:	order number of an identifier
action:	sp = sp + 1
	[sp] = |op|
meaning:	The absolute address of the identifier is placed on top of the stack.

name:	add
stack:	[sp] is an integer.
	[sp − 1] is an integer.
action:	[sp − 1] = [sp − 1] + [sp]
	sp = sp − 1
meaning:	The sum is placed on top of the stack.

name:	allocate
operand1:	x, the order number of an array identifier
operand2:	y, the order number of a template
stack:	|y| is the absolute address of the template t.
	[t] is the relative constant part of the address RC.
	[t + 1] is the dimension of the array n.
	[t + 2] is the size of the array's template S.
action:	[|x|] = t (save absolute address of template)
	[|x| + 1] = RC + sp + 1 (save absolute constant part)
	sp = sp + 3 * (S − 1) + 2 + [|x|] (increment stack pointer)
meaning:	Space is allocated for a dynamic array.

Consider the example declaration:

    array (10:12,4) of integer z;

Fig. 1 shows the stack before the allocate instruction.
Fig. 2 shows the stack after the allocate instruction.

name:	and
stack:	[sp] is Boolean.
	[sp − 1] is Boolean.
action:	[sp − 1] = [sp − 1] & [sp]
	sp = sp − 1
meaning:	The logical conjunction is placed on top of the stack.

name:	branch
operand:	instruction address
action:	ic = op
meaning:	The instruction counter is reset.

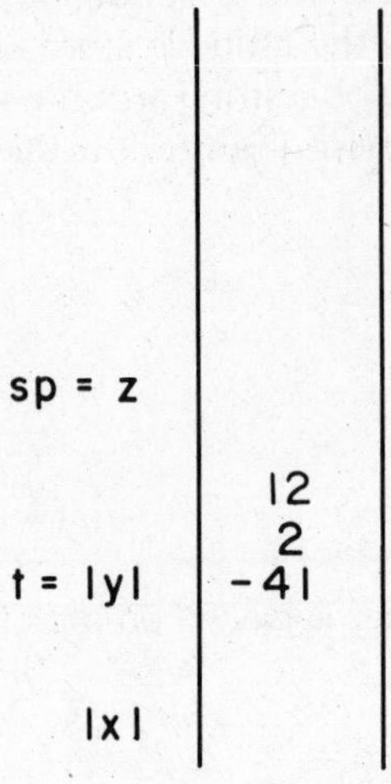

Fig 1.   Before 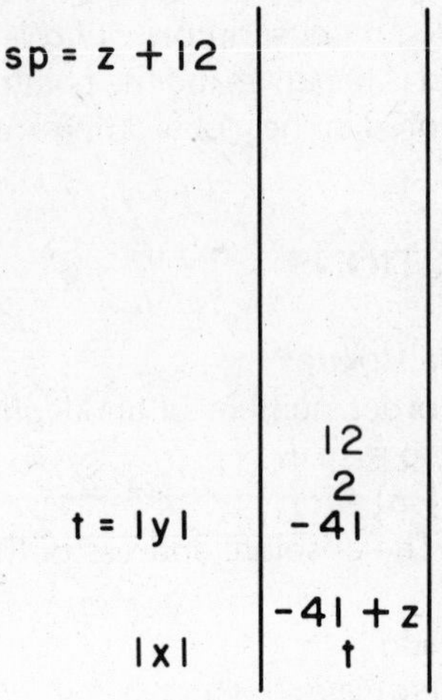   Fig. 2   After

name: branchf (branch on false)
operand: instruction address
stack: [sp] is Boolean.
action: if [sp] = 0, then ic = op.
             sp = sp − 1
meaning: The instruction counter is reset on a false condition.

name: concat
stack: [sp] is a string descriptor.
             [sp − 1] is a string descriptor.
action: [sp − 1] = descriptor(string([sp − 1]) o string ([sp]))
             sp = sp − 1
meaning: A descriptor for the concatenated strings is placed on top of the
             stack. (Note that the original string descriptors point to temporary
             variables and will be marked as free. Therefore, the descriptor and
             the string space it points to will be available for garbage collection.)

name: deref (dereference array element)
operand: x, the order number of an array identifier
stack: [|x|] is the absolute address of the template t.
             [|x| + 1] is the absolute constant part of the array AC.
             [t + 1] is the dimension of the array n.
             [t + 3(i−1) + 2] is the size of dimensions i to n, P(i).
             [t + 3(i−1) + 3] is the lower bound of dimension i, L(i).
             [t + 3(i−1) + 4] is the upper bound of dimension i, U(i)
             [sp − (n−i)] is the ith subscript, V(i).
action: sp = sp − (n−1)

$$[sp] = AC + \sum_{i=1}^{n} V(i)\, P(i-1)$$

meaning:	The absolute address of the array element is placed on top of the stack. (See also template instruction)
error:	if $V(i) < L(i)$ or $V(i) > U(i)$, then the subscript is out of range.

name:	derefi (dereference array element indirectly)
operand:	y, the order number of an array parameter
stack:	$[\,[\,|y|\,]\,]$ is the absolute address of the template t.
	$[\,[\,|y|\,]+1\,]$ is the absolute constant part of the array AC.
	$[t+1]$ is the dimension of the array n.
	$[t+3(i-1)+2]$ is the size of dimensions i to n, $P(i)$.
	$[t+3(i-1)+3]$ is the lower bound of dimension i, $L(i)$.
	$[t+3(i-1)+4]$ is the upper bound of dimension i, $U(i)$.
	$[sp-(n-i)]$ is the ith subscript, $V(i)$.
action:	$sp = sp - (n-1)$

$$[sp] = AC + \sum_{i=1}^{n} V(i)\, P(i-1)$$

meaning:	The absolute address of the array element is placed on top of the stack. (See also template instruction.)
error:	If $V(i) < L(i)$ or $V(i) > U(i)$, then the subscript is out of range.

name:	divide
stack:	$[sp]$ is an integer.
	$[sp-1]$ is an integer.
action:	$[sp-1] = [sp-1]\,/\,[sp]$
	$sp = sp - 1$
meaning:	The quotient is placed on top of the stack.
error:	If there is an underflow, then low-order bits are lost.

name:	dump
meaning:	Dump contents of appropriate memory locations.

names:	ieq, ige, igt, ile, ilt, ine (integer relations)
stack:	$[sp]$ is an integer.
	$[sp-1]$ is an integer.
action:	Let R be the integer relation
	if $[sp-1]\,R\,[sp]$,
	then $[sp-1] = 1$
	else $[sp-1] = 0$
	$sp = sp - 1$
meaning:	The truth value of the integer relation is placed on top of the stack.

name:	incrsp (increment stack pointer)
operand:	positive integer
action:	$sp = sp + op$
meaning:	The stack pointer is incremented to allocate space for local variables.

name: end_of_file
action: sp = sp + 1
            if the end of the input stream has been reached,
            then [sp] = 1
            else [sp] = 0
meaning: Pushes true onto the stack if the end of input has been reached and
            false otherwise.

name: index
stack: [sp] is the string descriptor of the configuration.
            [sp − 1] is the string descriptor of the host string.
action: [sp − 1] = index(string([sp − 1]), string([sp]))
            sp = sp − 1
meaning: The index of the configuration in the host string is placed on top of
            the stack. (Note that the string descriptor is that of a temporary
            variable and will be marked as free. Therefore, the descriptor and the
            string space it points to will be available for garbage collection.)

name: jump
operand1:   z, the address of first instruction in procedure
operand2:   n, the number of arguments in procedure
stack: [sp − (n−i)] is the ith argument.
            [sp − n] is return address.
            [sp − (n+1)] is old activation base pointer.
action: abp = sp − n − 1
            ic = z
meaning: Control is transfered to another procedure: the activation base
            pointer and the instruction counter are reset. (See also return
            instruction.)

name: length
stack: [sp] is the string descriptor.
action: [sp] = length(string([sp]))
meaning: The length of the string is placed on top of the stack. (Note that the
            string descriptor is that of a temporary variable and will be marked as
            free. Therefore, the descriptor and the string space it points to will be
            available for garbage collection.)

name: line
operand: line number
action: lnc = op
meaning: The line number is saved in the line number counter, lnc.

name: load
operand: op, the order number of a simple identifier
action: sp = sp + 1
            if op < 0
            then [sp] = [|op|]
            else [sp] = / |op| /
meaning: The value of the variable is placed on the stack.

name:	loada (load absolute)
stack:	[sp] is absolute address of variable.
action:	if [sp] > 0
	then [sp] = [[sp]]
	else [sp] = / −[sp] /
meaning:	The value of the variable is placed on the stack.

name:	loadi (load indirect)
operand:	op, the order number of a simple parameter
action:	sp = sp + 1
	if [|op|] < 0
	then [sp] = [[|op|]]
	else [sp] = / −[|op|] /
meaning:	The value of the variable is placed on the stack.

name:	loads (load string)
operand:	op, the order number of a string descriptor
action:	sp = sp + 1
	if op < 0
	then [sp] = descriptor(string([|op|])) (local)
	else [sp] = descriptor(string([−|op|])) (global)
meaning:	The descriptor of a new copy of the string is placed on the stack.

name:	loadsa (load string absolute)
stack:	[sp] is the absolute address of the string descriptor.
action:	if [sp] > 0
	then [sp] = descriptor(string([[sp]])) (local)
	else [sp] = descriptor(string([sp])) (global)
meaning:	The descriptor of a new copy of the string is placed on the stack.

name:	loadsi (load string indirect)
operand:	op, the order number of a string descriptor parameter
action:	sp = sp + 1
	if [|op|] > 0
	then [sp] = descriptor(string([[|op|]])) (local)
	else [sp] = descriptor(string([|op|])) (global)
meaning:	The descriptor of a new copy of the string is placed on the stack.

name:	multiply
stack:	[sp] is an integer.
	[sp − 1] is an integer.
action:	[sp − 1] = [sp − 1] * [sp]
	sp = sp − 1
meaning:	The product is placed on top of the stack.
error:	If there is overflow, then the high-order bits are lost.

name:	negate
stack:	[sp] is an integer.
action:	[sp] = −[sp]
meaning:	The arithmetic negation is placed on top of the stack.

name: newline
meaning: The output device advances to a new line.

name: not
stack: [sp] is a Boolean.
action: [sp] = ~ [sp]
meaning: The logical complement is placed on top of the stack.

name: or
stack: [sp] is a Boolean.
            [sp – 1] is a Boolean.
action: [sp – 1] = [sp – 1] V [sp]
            sp = sp – 1
meaning: The logical disjunction is placed on top of the stack.

name: pop
action: sp = sp – 1
meaning: The value on top of the stack is popped as a response to a compilation error.

name: push
operand: value
action: sp = sp + 1
            [sp] = op
meaning: The value is placed on top of the stack.

name: readint
stack: [sp] is absolute address of an integer variable.
action: if next input is an integer
            then if [sp] > 0
                 then [[sp]] = value of integer
                 else / –[sp] / = value of integer
                 sp = sp – 1
            else error
meaning: A value is read into the integer variable.

name: readlog
stack: [sp] is absolute address of a Boolean variable.
action: if next input is Boolean
            then if [sp] > 0
                 then [[sp]] = value of Boolean (0 or 1)
                 else / –[sp] / = value of Boolean
                 sp = sp – 1
            else error
meaning: A value is read into the Boolean variable.

name: readstr
stack: [sp] is absolute address of a string variable.
action: if next input is string
            then if [sp] > 0

then [[sp]] = descriptor (string)
else / –[sp] / = –descriptor (string)
sp = sp – 1
else error

meaning: A value is read into the string variable. (Note that the string descriptor is that of a temporary variable and will be marked as free. Therefore, the descriptor and the string space it points to will be available for garbage collection.)

name: rem (remainder on division)
stack: [sp] is an integer.
[sp – 1] is an integer.
action: [sp – 1] = [sp – 1] % [sp]
sp = sp – 1
meaning: The remainder of the division is placed on top of the stack.

name: replace
stack: [sp] is string descriptor of replacement string.
[sp – 1] is the cursor position.
[sp – 2] is the absolute address of the host string.
action: if [[sp – 2]] > 0
then [[sp – 2]] =
descriptor(substring(string([[sp – 2]]),1,
[sp – 1] – 1) o string([sp]))
else / –[sp – 2] / =
–descriptor(substring(string([[sp – 2]]),1,
[sp – 1] – 1) o string([sp]))
sp = sp – 3
meaning: A substring of the host string (from the cursor position to the end of the string) is replaced by the replacement string. (Note that the descriptor used for the host string will be marked as free. Therefore, the descriptor and the string space it points to will be available for garbage collection.)

name: replacel (replace given the length argument)
stack: [sp] is the string descriptor of the replacement string.
[sp – 1] is the length of the substring.
[sp – 2] is the cursor position.
[sp – 3] is the absolute address of the host string.
action: if [sp – 3] > 0
then [[sp – 3]] =
descriptor(substring(string([[sp – 3]]),1,
[sp – 2] – 1) o string([sp])
o substring(string([[sp – 3]]),[sp – 1] + [sp – 2]))
else / –[sp – 3] / =
–descriptor(substring(string([[sp – 3]]),1,
[sp – 2] – 1) o string([sp])
o substring(string([[sp – 3]]),[sp – 1] + [sp – 2]))
sp = sp – 4

meaning: A substring of the host string (from the cursor position and with the given length) is replaced by the replacement string. (Note that the descriptor used for the host string will be marked as free. Therefore, the descriptor and the string space it points to will be available for garbage collection.)

name: return
action: ic = [abp + 1]   (reset instruction counter)
             sp = abp – 1   (reset stack pointer)
             abp = [abp]   (reset activation base pointer)
meaning: Control is returned to the calling procedure. (See also jump instruction.)

name: returnval (return value)
stack: [sp] is a value.
action: ic = [abp + 1]   (reset instruction counter)
             temp = [sp]   (save return value)
             sp = abp   (reset stack pointer)
             abp = [abp]   (reset activation base pointer)
             [sp] = temp   (place value on top of stack)
meaning: Return from a procedure with a value. (See also jump instruction.)

name: saveabp (save activation base pointer)
action: sp = sp + 1
             [sp] = abp
meaning: The activation base pointer is placed on top of the stack

names: seq, sge, sgt, sle, slt, sne (string relations)
stack: [sp] is a string descriptor.
             [sp – 1] is a string descriptor.
action: Let R be the string relation
             If string([sp – 1]) R string([sp])
             then [sp – 1] = 1
             else [sp – 1] = 0
             sp = sp – 1
meaning: The truth value of the string relation is placed on top of the stack. (Note that the string descriptors point to temporary variables and will be marked as free. Therefore, the descriptor and the string space it points to will be available for garbage collection.)

name: space
operand: x, a positive integer
meaning: The output device advances x spaces.

name: stop
meaning: The program is terminated.

name: store
operand: Order number of a simple identifier.
stack: [sp] is a value.

action: if op < 0
              then [|op|] = [sp]
              else / |op| / = [sp]
              sp = sp – 1
meaning: The variable is assigned the value.

name: storea (store absolute)
stack: [sp] is a value.
              [sp – 1] is absolute address of a variable.
action: if [sp – 1] > 0
              then [[sp – 1]] = [sp]
              else / –[sp – 1] / = [sp]
              sp = sp – 2
meaning: The variable is assigned the value.

name: storei (store indirect)
operand: Order number of simple parameter.
stack: [sp] is a value.
action: if [|op|] > 0
              then [[|op|]] = [sp]
              else / –[|op|] / = [sp]
              sp = sp – 1
meaning: The variable is assigned the value.

name: subtract
stack: [sp] is an integer.
              [sp – 1] is an integer.
action: [sp – 1] = [sp – 1] – [sp]
              sp = sp – 1
meaning: The difference is placed on top of the stack.

name: substring
stack: [sp] is the cursor position.
              [sp – 1] is the string descriptor.
action: [sp – 1] = descriptor(substring(string([sp – 1]), [sp]))
              sp = sp – 1
meaning: A string descriptor of the substring (from the cursor position to the
              end of the string) is placed on top of the stack. (Note that the string
              descriptor is that of a temporary variable and will be marked as free.
              Therefore, the descriptor and the string space it points to will be
              available for garbage collection.)

name: substringl (substring given the length argument)
stack: [sp] is the length of the substring.
              [sp – 1] is the cursor position.
              [sp – 2] is the string descriptor.
action: [sp – 2] = descriptor(substring(string([sp–2]),
                            [sp–1],[sp]))
              sp = sp – 2
meaning: A string descriptor of the substring (from the cursor position and

with the given length) is placed on top of the stack. (Note that the string descriptor is that of a temporary variable and will be marked as free. Therefore, the descriptor and the string space it points to will be available for garbage collection.)

name: tab
operand: x, a positive integer
meaning: The output device advances to column x

name: template
operand1: x, the relative address of the template.
operand2: n, the dimension of the array.
stack: $[sp - 2(n{-}i)]$ is the upper bound of the ith subscript, $U(i)$.
              $[sp - 2(n{-}i) - 1]$ is the lower bound of the ith subscript, $L(i)$.
action: Let $S(i) = U(i) - L(i) + 1$, the size of dimension i
              Let $P(0) = 1$

$$\text{Let } P(i) = \prod_{j=1}^{i} S(j)$$

$$\text{Let RC} = - \sum_{i=1}^{n} L(i) P(i{-}1), \text{ the relative constant part}$$

Let $t = |x|$, the absolute address of the template
$[t] = RC$
$[t + 1] = n$
$[t + 3(i{-}1) + 2] = P(i)$
$[t + 3(i{-}1) + 3] = L(i)$
$[t + 3(i{-}1) + 4] = U(i)$
$sp = sp - 2n$

meaning: A template for the array is built. (See also deref instruction.)

Consider the example declaration:

     array (10:12,4) of integer z;

Fig. 3 shows the stack before the template instruction.
Fig. 4 shows the stack after the template instruction.

name: write
operand: n, the number of arguments
stack: $[sp - (n{-}i)]$ is the ith argument.
action: $sp = sp - n$
              $wp = sp + 1$
meaning: The write pointer is set to the address of the first value to be written.

name: writeint
operand: x, a nonnegative integer.

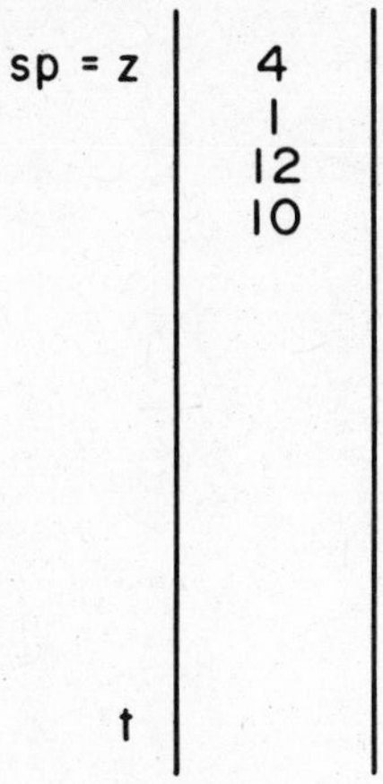

Fig. 3 Before 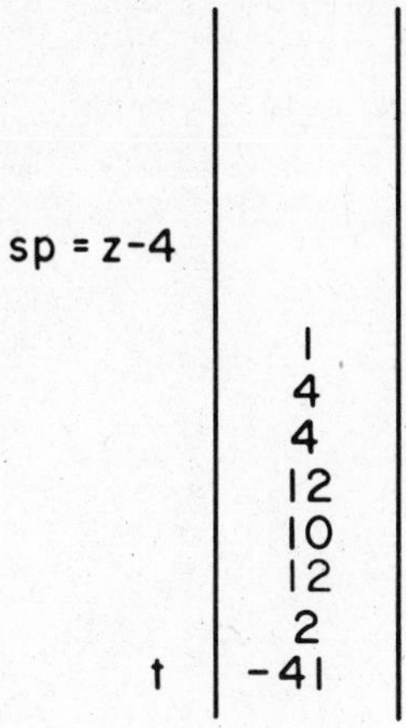   Fig. 4 After

stack: [wp] = integer value
action: if $x = 0$
            then output integer value
            else output integer value in a field of length x
            wp = wp + 1
meaning: The integer is written.

name: writelog
stack: [wp] is Boolean value.
action: If Boolean value is 1
            then output "TRUE"
            else output "FALSE"
            wp = wp + 1
meaning: The Boolean is written.

name: writestr
operand: x, a nonnegative integer.
stack: [wp] is a string descriptor.
action: If $x = 0$
            then output string ([wp])
            else output string ([wp]) in a field of length x
            wp = wp + 1
meaning: The string is written. (Note that the string descriptor is that of a temporary variable and will be marked as free. Therefore, the descriptor and the string space it points to will be available for garbage collection.)

INDEX